**Learn to Fight from Victory,
Not for Victory!**

THE ULTIMATE GUIDE TO
SPIRITUAL WARFARE

PEDRO OKORO

(Award winning Author of *Crushing the Devil*)

Also by Pedro Okoro:

Crushing The Devil: Your Guide to Spiritual Warfare and Victory in Christ

Desmascarando As Artimanhas do Inimigo

Your Best Life Ever: 7 Keys to Maximising Your Potential and Enjoying Your Ordinary, Everyday Life

The best way to connect with Pedro Okoro is via his blog:
www.pedrookoro.com

You may also contact him:
On Twitter: **@PedroOkoro**
On Facebook: **Facebook.com/PedroOkoro7**

ENDORSEMENTS

Pedro Okoro has a gift for making complex subjects readily understandable. This book is a considerable achievement, not only for its clarity but also for its comprehensiveness.

Dr Hugh Osgood
Founder and President of Churches in Communities International
Co-Chair of The UK Charismatic and Pentecostal Leaders' Conference

A fascinating book with an enlightened look into the supernatural world of spiritual warfare and its consequences in our lives. In *The Ultimate Guide to Spiritual Warfare* Pedro Okoro peels off each layer of the enemy's combat plan to destroy our path to freedom. He does this meticulously, until the reader is in full and complete understanding of: who the enemy is, when the enemy will attack, where he will attack, how the enemy attacks and the weapons that he uses. With this knowledge Pastor Okoro then gives us the weapons needed to combat effectively our most wicked enemy, the devil, along with his adversaries.

You don't believe or are sceptical? Well, I challenge you. I personally came to it with many questions myself. In the pages of this page-turning book you'll find many fascinating real life stories where lives were changed, influenced and even destroyed because of the power the enemy exerted in their lives and very often in the lives of their ancestors. The Bible speaks of generational curses...they are real. There is no sugar coating in this book. From birth to death we have one great enemy, but Pastor Pedro Okoro teaches us that from birth to death we can fight from Victory not for Victory!

This book has captivated me because it has gone deeper than any other book I've ever read on this topic. Today, I'm using it as a companion book to the Bible Study I'm currently working on and I know that undoubtedly it will transform my life.

Elsie J. Ruiz
Founder, Shepherd's Way International, Inc.
Cumming, GA, USA.

The church is in a war, but many Christians either don't know it, don't fully understand its nature and tactics or are reluctant to engage. They are being destroyed or at least seriously damaged for lack of knowledge. Every day I see the enemy running rampant in the lives of believers, and the tragedy is that this does not need to happen!

That is why we need books like this. I would say "western" Christians need them even more. Biblically-based, practical books, based on personal experience, which take us through the problem and provide us with step by step instructions on how to deal with every work and plan of the enemy. I resonated with so many things in this book that parallel almost word for word what I have been thinking, praying, discussing, teaching and ministering.

If I had to pick out one aspect of the teaching here that is particularly helpful, it is the material on the nature and consequences of satanic altars and covenants and the curses that go with them. The case studies that the book outlines hammer home the principles very effectively, and very disturbingly. I defy readers not to recognize some recurring patterns in their lives and families in these accounts. This book can help you to diagnose and treat the very root!

Pastor Pedro has written in a very accessible and readable style. His passionate desire to help fellow believers war from a place of strength and victory in Christ comes through clearly on every page. I for one will be encouraging members of this ministry to read this book.

Pastor Lorenzo Heighway
Open Heaven Ministries
Nottingham, United Kingdom

The Ultimate Guide to Spiritual Warfare is a spiritually fantastic book. It is well researched, with practical and applicable insights. The book will set a lot of believers and non-believers free. The presentation is so clear and simple that any believer will surely benefit from it. Definitely led by the Spirit!

Atty Constantino Banjo Navarro III
Lawyer, and Creator of Biblegal
The Philippines.

> *"Oh, oh, oh . . .*
> *How gold is treated like dirt,*
> *the finest gold thrown out with the garbage,*
> *Priceless jewels scattered all over,*
> *jewels loose in the gutters.*
> *And the people of Zion, once prized,*
> *far surpassing their weight in gold,*
> *Are now treated like cheap pottery,*
> *like everyday pots and bowls mass-produced by a potter."*
>
> —Lamentations 4:1–2, *The Message*

• • •

> *"Christ redeemed us from the curse of the law by becoming a curse for us, for it is written: 'Cursed is everyone who is hung on a pole.' He redeemed us in order that the blessing given to Abraham might come to the Gentiles through Christ Jesus, so that by faith we might receive the promise of the Spirit."*
>
> —Galatians 3:13–14, New International Version

To
Ola, Jess, and Mychaela
You give me reasons to go on.

THE ULTIMATE GUIDE TO SPIRITUAL WARFARE

© 2015 Pedro Okoro

All rights reserved. No part of this publication may be reproduced, stored in a retrieval system, or transmitted in any form or by any means—electronic, mechanical, photocopy, recording, or any other—except for brief quotations in printed reviews, without the prior written permission of the publisher.

Some of the anecdotal illustrations in this book are public knowledge. Others are composites of real situations, in which case the names and locales have been changed to provide anonymity.

Unless otherwise indicated, all Scripture quotations are taken from THE HOLY BIBLE, NEW INTERNATIONAL VERSION®, NIV® Copyright © 1973, 1978, 1984, 2011 by Biblica, Inc.™ Used by permission. All rights reserved worldwide.

Scripture quotations marked "AMP" are taken from the Amplified® Bible, Copyright © 1954, 1958, 1962, 1964, 1965, 1987 by The Lockman Foundation. Used by permission. (www.Lockman.org)

Scripture quotations marked "ASV" are taken from the American Standard Version of the Bible. Public domain.

Scripture quotations marked "CEV" are taken from the Contemporary English Version. Copyright © 1995 by American Bible Society. Used by permission.

Scripture quotations marked "ESV" are taken from The ESV® Bible (The Holy Bible, English Standard Version®) copyright © 2001 by Crossway Bibles, a publishing ministry of Good News Publishers. The ESV® text has been reproduced in cooperation with and by permission of Good News Publishers. All rights reserved. Used by permission.

Scripture quotations marked "GW" are taken from GOD'S WORD®, © 1995 God's Word to the Nations. Used by permission of Baker Publishing Group.

Scripture quotations marked "ISV" are taken from the Holy Bible: International Standard Version®. Copyright © 1996–2008 by The ISV Foundation. ALL RIGHTS RESERVED INTERNATIONALLY. Used by permission.

Scripture quotations marked "KJV" are taken from the King James Version of the Bible. Public domain.

Scripture quotations marked "MSG" are taken from *THE MESSAGE*. Copyright © by Eugene H. Peterson 1993, 1994, 1995, 1996, 2000, 2001, 2002. Used by permission of NavPress Publishing Group.

Scripture quotations marked "NASB" are taken from the New American Standard Bible®, Copyright © 1960, 1962, 1963, 1968, 1971, 1972, 1973, 1975, 1977, 1995 by The Lockman Foundation. Used by permission. (www.Lockman.org)

Scripture quotations marked "NCV" are taken from the New Century Version®. Copyright © 2005 by Thomas Nelson, Inc. Used by permission. All rights reserved.

Scripture quotations marked "NKJV" are taken from the New King James Version®. Copyright © 1982 by Thomas Nelson, Inc. Used by permission. All rights reserved.

Scripture quotations marked "NLT" are taken from the Holy Bible, New Living Translation, copyright © 1996, 2004, 2007. Used by permission of Tyndale House Publishers, Inc., Wheaton, IL 60189 USA. All rights reserved.

Published by
Pedro Sajini Publishing
London, United Kingdom
www.pedrookoro.com/publishing

ISBN 13: 9780993303005
ISBN 10: 0993303005

Printed in the United Kingdom

Cover design by David Litwin, Pure Fusion Media (www.purefusionmedia.com)

ACKNOWLEDGMENTS

I am indebted to Miss Bianca Hendicott and Minister Kike Adebiyi for their corrections, helpful suggestions, and the great work they did on the first draft.

I am grateful to Dr Hugh Osgood, Founder and President, Churches in Communities International; Senior Minister of Cornerstone Christian Centre, Bromley; Co-Chair of the UK Charismatic and Pentecostal Leaders' Conference, and Moderator of the Free Churches Group, for taking time out of his very busy schedule to write the foreword.

My special thanks to my editor, Rachel Starr Thomson, for making the final product what it is today. Rachel, I couldn't have done this without your amazing ability to bring out the best in a manuscript. You're so good at what you do, it is surreal! Thank you so much for being my Destiny Helper on this journey. You're simply awesome!

Despite the wonderful work by my editor, any errors remain my responsibility.

It is in the nature of this book that over the years certain wise remarks and observations may have been picked up or even pilfered from friends, acquaintances, ministry colleagues, and mentors, and I hope that a collective thank you—or apology—will suffice.

CONTENTS

Foreword by Dr. Hugh Osgood   xv
Preface: What Happened to You?   xvii

Chapter 1:   Your Authority as a Believer   1
Chapter 2:   Winning the Battle in Your Mind   8
Chapter 3:   A Spiritual Warfare Primer   15
Chapter 4:   Understanding Deliverance   32
Chapter 5:   Like Father, Like Son?   39
Chapter 6:   Family Laws and Evil Patterns   52
Chapter 7:   Understanding the Altar   68
Chapter 8:   The Power of the Spoken Word   84
Chapter 9:   The Sins That Enslave Us   97
Chapter 10:   Rolling Away the Reproach   106
Chapter 11:   But I'm Born Again!   117
Chapter 12:   Breaking the Curse and Activating the Blessing   130
Chapter 13:   Surely There Is an End!   147
Chapter 14:   Maintaining Your Freedom   155

Afterword: Fight from Victory, Not for Victory!   171
Appendix: 101 Ways to Crush the Devil   177
End Notes   187

FOREWORD

Pedro Okoro has a gift for making complex subjects readily understandable. This book is a considerable achievement, not only for its clarity but also for its comprehensiveness. It touches on a wide-range of spiritual warfare issues; some that tend to be known only to those of us who travel extensively, and of which we seldom speak lest they sound too far-fetched to those who have never been troubled by them. We are all too aware of how the devil would love us to assist him in his scare-mongering role. The amazing thing is that Pedro is able to deal with these issues case-by-case in such a well-illustrated and matter-of-fact way that any fear-generating pretensions the devil may have are always well and truly thwarted.

Given the comprehensive nature of the book (the title, 'The Ultimate Guide to Spiritual Warfare', is well deserved), it is not surprising that the writer has taken steps to ensure that the reader is not spiritually overwhelmed, and here the appendix is as important as the main text. There are almost certainly too many case studies in this book for any one person to lay claim to them all, so this is probably not the book for the deliverance addict who ricochets from one demonic diagnosis to another without ever being set free – unless, of course, that deliverance addict wants to be finally liberated from his or her addiction. And liberation is exactly what is on the writer's heart from cover to cover.

The Apostle Paul wrote to the Galatians, 'Stand fast therefore in the liberty by which Christ has made us free, and do not be entangled with a yoke of bondage'. Any book that examines the potential yokes of bondage as fully as this one does, needs a strong undergirding emphasis on the liberty that is ours through Christ's sacrifice. This book repeatedly confirms that it is this freedom that Christ has bought us through His work on the cross that is spiritual warfare's cornerstone and capstone. I commend it for this as well as for its comprehensiveness and clarity.

May each page give you cause to assert your freedom in Christ with ever increasing enthusiasm and certainty, even as you pray for those who might still have much to claim or apply from such an accessible resource.

Dr Hugh Osgood
Founder and President of Churches in Communities International
Co-Chair of the Uk Charismatic and Pentecostal Leaders' Conference
London 2015

Preface:

WHAT HAPPENED TO YOU?

"How the gold has lost its luster, the fine gold become dull!
The sacred gems are scattered at every street corner. How the precious children of Zion, once worth their weight in gold, are now considered as pots of clay, the work of a potter's hands!"

Lamentations 4:1-2

Before you can understand anything else about your life, you need to understand this: You were not mass-produced like a Toyota.[1] You are an original. Not a copy! You were handcrafted and handmade by God, who took his time to create you, making you "wonderfully complex."[2] You're unique. You're special. You're one of a kind. There is no one else quite like you, dead or alive, in the whole world. Nor will there ever be.

As human beings, we are distinct. Even twins, triplets, quadruplets, quintuplets, sextuplets, octuplets, and nonuplets, though they have similar DNA, have distinctly different personality traits.

See how the psalmist describes you:

What is man that You take thought of him,
And the son of man that You care for him?
Yet You have made him a little lower than God,
And You crown him with glory and majesty![3]

You have incredible potential. At your birth, you were loaded with everything you need to make an impact on the world. You were prewired to make the world a better place. Regardless of the circumstances of your birth, there is greatness locked up inside you!

In the same way, at the time of your new birth, when you receive Jesus into your heart and become born again, God deposits within you the divine seed and gives you everything you need to live as a child of God.[4] Before you can understand anything else about your new life, you need to understand this. When you become saved, you're given the capacity to live victoriously in this world. At the new birth, you receive the ability to enjoy your ordinary, everyday life. Jesus put it this way: "The thief comes only to steal and kill and destroy; I have come that they may have life, and have it to the full."[5]

In God's plan, you were formed as fine, pure gold. You were destined for greatness, designed to enrich the world around you. You were ordained to make the world better than it was at your birth—you are blessed to be a blessing. God blesses you so you can bless not only those you come in contact with, but also your seed after you. He wants you to bequeath this blessing to your children and their children to a thousand generations.[6]

If you're like most people, however, it seems your reality is very different. Instead of unleashing your potential and enriching the world like fine gold, you appear to have become tarnished. You are struggling through life and living way below your potential.

The majority of Christians are just like that: they have no idea who they are, and they have no inkling whatsoever of the extraordinary potential that is locked up inside them.

> Look how the gold has become tarnished!
> The fine gold has changed!
> The sacred stones are scattered at every street corner.
> Zion's precious children, who are worth their weight in fine gold,
> Are now treated like clay pots, like those made by a potter's hands.[7]

What happened to your *real* life? The one you were created to live. The one you used to dream about. The one you probably *still* dream about.

Take a moment to think back and reflect on the things you were going to do—the person you longed to be—the promise of a healthy, wealthy, joyful life, full to overflowing with wonderful things. If you're like most people, you're not living that life right now. If that's the case, how did you become tarnished? What happened to you?

It wasn't always like this. When you started out in life, you had direction, you had energy, you had purpose, and you had momentum. You started out like a powerful jetliner ready for take-off. The runway stretched out before you: straight, clear, open, and inviting. Air traffic control gave you the all clear. You were moving along at a good pace, your whole future ahead of you. Then all of a sudden, you suffered an unexpected loss of power. Now you're unable to take off. You're stuck on the runway, your dreams a distant memory.

So what happened? How did you, *worth your weight in gold*, lose your glitter and become tainted and dull? Is it possible that the enemy has become involved?

Every child of God is *automatically* involved in spiritual warfare. It is a battle between the forces of God and the forces of the enemy. And Satan, who is also known as the devil, is the enemy. He hates God with a passion. And because you were created in God's image, he hates you too! He was an angelic being who lost his place in heaven because of rebellion and pride. He was thrown out of heaven with all who sided with him, about a third of the angels.[8] These billions of angels are now his demonic and evil spirits.

The devil's primary purpose is to steal, kill and destroy. If you let him, he will steal your seed (your potential) and thereby prevent you from becoming anything in life. If you give him room, he will kill your dreams, ideas, and vision. He will destroy your life. But the good news is Jesus came to undo everything the devil has done so you can have life in all its fullness. This conflict is the essence of spiritual warfare. As we shall see later, spiritual warfare is real and happens all the time, whether you know it or not.

So back to my question: What has happened to you? Has a dark shadow from your past tampered with your destiny? Specifically, could it be that you are affected in anyway by evil family patterns, generational curses, or ancestral covenants? Or perhaps you've invited a curse into your life through your own personal choices and lifestyle. And these curses, whether self-inflicted or generational, have become an unseen force that always seems to locate you and cause you to stumble *just* when you're about to experience your big break. It happens again—and again, and again! You've come to accept this as your lot, the story of your life.

Somebody says, "Wait a minute. What are curses, evil family patterns, and ancestral covenants?" These concepts are looked at in more detail later in the book. For now, we can describe a curse as an affliction that is the result of defilement. It can either be self-inflicted or generational in nature, i.e., the result of something that may have taken place many generations ago. For example, if a parent opens him or herself up to satanic contamination through involvement in the occult, the effects of that defilement can be passed on to you. The Bible puts it this way: "Our ancestors sinned, but they have died—and we are suffering the punishment they deserved!"[9]

Not only is the uncleanliness of such curses handed down, but demons move right in and take advantage of this opening, often at a very young age in a person's life, and establish a stronghold. The child then goes through life struggling with the same problems the parents had. These can include sexual immorality, violence, gambling, gluttony, occultism, and more. Much of the warfare we experience in life gets its start right here.

When a generational curse takes root, it gives birth to evil family patterns. These are horrible patterns of behaviour that run in families and are passed from generation to generation. If your parents struggled with issues like alcoholism, criminal behaviour, child abuse, low self-esteem, depression, eating disorders, etc., and you find yourself battling with the same issues or see siblings with the same problems, it is quite possible that you are suffering from the effects of a generational curse. Many times when two or three generations of a family die from alcoholism, it's a generational curse at work. A Bacchus or Dionysus spirit (named for the Greek and Roman god of wine and madness) may have taken advantage through a defilement passed down.

On the other hand, an ancestral covenant is a legally binding agreement between a human being and a satanic being, usually for short-term benefit but with a promise included that both the covenanter and future generations of the covenanter's family will behave in a certain way. This covenant becomes a law that is passed down from generation to generation. For instance, the covenant may stipulate that everybody in the family will go through multiple divorces, or that none of the men will marry, or that certain diseases will be prevalent, or that nobody is permitted to eat certain foods, or that every first son will be an alcoholic. If you're not a Christian, or if you're a first- or even second-generation Christian, your ancestors may have done something that is having a negative effect on you. These curses, evil patterns, and covenants run through the bloodline. They affect you because of the link to your past, just like certain diseases are common among families. A generational curse or covenant cannot affect you if there is no causal link or connection with the originator of the curse or covenant, because a curse without a cause does not alight.[10]

Does all of this sound way "out there" to you? Think about it this way: In the United Kingdom, as in many other countries, everybody is required to have a family doctor (usually referred to as a general practitioner or GP) within close proximity of where they live. I registered with my current GP sometime in 2003 when my family moved to a different neighbourhood. As part of the registration process, I completed a medical questionnaire. I was asked many questions including whether or not there is a history of certain diseases in my family.

Many health problems can run in families. The most common ones include:

- Alzheimer's disease/dementia
- arthritis
- asthma
- blood clots
- cancer
- depression
- diabetes
- heart disease
- high cholesterol
- high blood pressure
- pregnancy losses and birth defects
- stroke

To these you may add social problems, which also tend to run in families: alcoholism, drug abuse, barrenness, child abuse, domestic violence, divorce, and more. The reason these diseases and social problems run in families is the blood connection. *And distance doesn't make any difference.* If your family roots are in Madagascar and you now live in Toronto, Canada, you will still be susceptible to diseases common to your family members, notwithstanding the fact that you are over fourteen thousand kilometres away!

If you can get your head around that, why is it so difficult to understand that curses and covenants also run through the bloodline? The reality is we are sometimes affected by things other people have done. If we want to get back to the life God created for us, if we want to get back on track, we need to first confront these evil patterns, curses, and covenants. We do this by tracing the problems to their source and taking the appropriate action required to release us from their grip.

Many people in these situations can't see a way back from *here* to *there*. But God can. He makes a way where there's none; that's why he sent Jesus!

The idea of spiritual warfare might scare you. It shouldn't! As far as God is concerned, warfare is a good thing. God takes pride in spiritual warfare because it is the number-one sure-fire way of ensuring the devil is made into Jesus's footstool.[11] God takes enormous satisfaction in seeing you victorious in your everyday life. He is delighted when you plunder the kingdom of darkness through evangelism and effective follow-up. He wants you to take territories for him. He wants you to advance his kingdom in this world. Jesus said, "Occupy until I come."[12] Through spiritual warfare, you are able to effectively occupy until the Lord returns.

Spiritual warfare also allows you to display God's manifold wisdom to the devil.[13] You do this by depending totally upon the Holy Spirit to lead and guide you. You do not depend on your experience or expertise; instead, you completely rely on the leading and guidance of the Holy Spirit, acknowledging him in all your ways.

I have written this book to examine some of these difficult issues, and more importantly, to show us how to get back to God's original plan for us—his best for you and me, what he created us to be. There are, of course, no easy solutions or answers. The waters of spiritual warfare are sometimes murky. However, Scripture and experience give us powerful principles and truths that *can* make a difference in our lives—that can even set us free and cause our gold to glitter once more, as we fight *from* victory, not *for* victory!

I pray this book provides illumination and insight and helps you to *regain* the victory in spiritual warfare, one truth at a time!

Chapter 1:

YOUR AUTHORITY AS A BELIEVER

> "I have given you authority to trample on snakes and scorpions and to overcome all the power of the enemy; nothing will harm you."
>
> **Luke 10:19**

At a time when slavery was legal in the United States, a gentleman came across a slave market in the corner of a crowded street.[1] The man paused to observe. As he watched from the edge of the crowd, he saw slave after slave led onto a platform, their hands and legs shackled as if they were animals.

One by one they were auctioned off, jeered by the watching crowd. He watched as some purchasers inspected the "goods," grabbing disrespectfully at the women, examining the muscular arms of the men. The gentleman studied the group of slaves waiting nearby. He stopped when he saw a young girl standing near the back. Her eyes were filled with fear. He hesitated for a moment and then disappeared briefly.

When he returned, the auctioneer was about to start the bidding for the young girl. As the bidding opened, the gentleman shouted a bid that was twice the amount of any other selling price offered that day. There was silence for an instant. Then the gavel fell as the auctioneer announced, "Sold to the gentleman over in the corner."

The gentleman stepped forward, making his way through the crowd. He waited at the bottom of the steps as the young girl was led down to her new owner. The chain with which she was bound was handed to him. He accepted it without a word.

The young girl stared at the ground for a moment—but suddenly, she looked up and spat in his face.

Silently, the gentleman reached for a handkerchief and wiped the spittle from his face. He smiled gently at the girl and said, "Follow me." She did so reluctantly.

He took her to a nearby area where the deal would be legally closed. The gentleman paid the purchase price and signed the necessary documents. When the transaction was complete, he turned to the young girl and presented the documents to her.

She was being manumitted—set free.

She couldn't believe what was happening. Was this a dream? Her eyes narrowed, she asked him, "What are you doing?"

"Here, take these papers," he said, looking into her tear-filled eyes. "They are your manumission papers. I bought you to set you free. As long as you have these papers in your possession, nobody can ever make you a slave again."

The girl looked into his face in shock and disbelief. Could this be real? She took the papers from him and stared blankly at him. There was silence for what seemed like an eternity. Then she broke the silence.

"You bought me to set me free?" she asked, still not quite sure what was happening to her.

She repeated the phrase over and over.

"You bought me to set me free?"

As she spoke the words, the implications of what had just happened began to dawn on her.

"You bought me to set me free?"

Was it possible that a complete stranger had just granted her freedom, that she could never again be bought or sold as a slave?

As she began to grasp the significance of the documents she now held in her hands, she fell to her knees and wept at the gentleman's feet. Through her tears of joy and gratitude, she said, "You bought me to set me free? I will serve you forever!"

YOU ARE REDEEMED

Jesus did something similar to what this gentleman did. You and I were once bound in slavery to sin. We sinned because it was in our nature to sin. We didn't have any choice. We were enslaved by the devil. However, Jesus shed his blood to set us free. He *redeemed* us. He redeemed you! The Bible puts it this way:

> In him we have redemption through his blood, the forgiveness of sins, in accordance with the riches of God's grace.[2]

You cannot fathom and fully grasp your authority as a believer without an understanding of redemption. In redeeming us through the blood of Jesus, God did many things for us. We can glean three of them from the three different Greek words translated "redeem" in the New Testament. Here they are:

Agorazo.[3] This means to purchase in the marketplace. Jesus paid the ransom and made you free from the bondage of sin. The Bible says, "You were bought at a price. Therefore honor God with your bodies."[4]

Exagorazo.[5] This word means to purchase out of the market, to buy up for one's own use. He took you out of the slave market so that you can never be traded again. The Bible describes what Jesus did for you as follows: "Christ redeemed us from the curse of the law by becoming a curse for us, for it is written: 'Cursed is everyone who is hung on a pole.'"[6]

Lutroo.[7] This means to redeem, liberate by payment of ransom. Jesus has made you completely and truly free from all sin, past, present and future. The Bible puts it this way, "He gave his life to free us from every kind of sin, to cleanse us, and to make us his very own people, totally committed to doing good deeds."[8]

YOU ARE SEATED ABOVE THE DEVIL

Not only that, but through redemption God seats you in the heavenly places with Jesus, far above principalities and powers of darkness.[9] You can exercise your authority as a believer because you are seated with Jesus in the heavenly places. And because in the heavenly places you are above principalities and the powers of darkness, you can exercise authority over them.

It gets even better! Through redemption you become a joint–heir with Christ. God places all the resources of heaven at your disposal. They are yours to enjoy!

YOU ARE JUSTIFIED AND GLORIFIED

And there's more. Let me show you an absolute gem of a Scripture, one that is little talked about. It says, "And those he predestined, he also called; those he called, he also justified; those he justified, he also glorified. What, then, shall we say in response to these things? If God is for us, who can be against us?"[10]

If you are a believer in Christ, then you were predestined in eternity *yet called in time.* Obviously, everyone has this invitation. All are called but, unfortunately, only a few respond.[11]

Because you responded to the call and received Jesus, God justifies you. You can stand before God as if you have never committed any sin, ever. As confirmation of this, God gives you a right standing with himself by clothing you with his righteousness. You have access to God's presence through the blood of Jesus.[12]

And that's not all. God has left the best till last. Having been justified, God *glorifies* you! The Bible actually uses the past tense here: "Those he justified, he also glorified."[10] You are not glorified in the flesh *yet,* but as far as God is concerned, in the spiritual, you're glorified! *Hence if God is for you, no one can be against you.* Not even the devil!

HOW DO YOU EXERCISE YOUR AUTHORITY AS A BELIEVER?

Once when Smith Wigglesworth[13] was waiting at a bus stop somewhere in England, he observed a woman who came out of an apartment with a small dog following her. We don't know the woman's name or the name of her dog. But let's just call her Sally and her dog Skittles.

Sally was having trouble getting Skittles to go back home. First she tried sweet-talking him. She said, "Honey, you're going to have to go back home." Skittles didn't pay any attention to her. He just wagged his tail and rubbed up against her affectionately.

"Now, dear," Sally said, "you can't come with me." The little dog wagged his tail, rubbed up against her again, and ignored her.

About that time, the bus arrived. Out of desperation, Sally stamped her foot and yelled at Skittles, "Go home at once!" The dog immediately took off toward the apartment with his tail between his legs.

Wigglesworth said he hollered out loud without even thinking, "That's the way you've got to do with the devil!"[14]

As a child of God, you have the authority to trample, crush, and walk over all the power of the enemy. Your authority is not just over some of the enemy's powers: you can exercise influence over every sphere of his operations and over every single one of his powers. You have complete and total authority over Satan, the devil, the enemy of your soul.

WHAT IS AUTHORITY?

What is authority? The word translated "authority" in the New Testament is the Greek word *exŏusia*.[15] It means the power to do as one pleases. It includes physical and mental power, authority, and the power of government; that is, the power of someone whose will and command must be obeyed and submitted to. It is "the power or right to give orders, make decisions, and enforce obedience."[16]

As a born-again child of God, you have absolute authority over the devil through Jesus Christ. The authority God has given you over Satan, the enemy, is comprehensive. It is ample, wide-ranging, thorough, far-reaching, sweeping, and all-embracing. It is not *just* authority over Satan, but also authority over all of Satan's cohorts, assistants, and associates, as well as over all his powers. The devil will do everything he can to keep you from coming into the knowledge that you have authority over him. It shouldn't therefore come as a surprise that there's a lot of wrong teaching in this area.

JESUS IS THE SOURCE OF YOUR AUTHORITY

God is the source of every good thing. God is your source. Everything you have is a resource provided by God! Nowhere is this truer than in spiritual warfare. Through his death and resurrection, Jesus conquered the devil. Not only that, Jesus disarmed him and obtained a name that is mightier than every other name. Jesus is enthroned at the Father's right hand, and Satan will never have authority over him.

Jesus's resurrection is not just a fact of history. It is a present reality today. Your authority as a believer comes from Jesus's triumph over the enemy. It is only available to those who have a personal relationship with Jesus—those who are born again through faith in Jesus!

In other words, your authority is a delegated authority. It is allocated by Jesus to you. It emanates from your relationship with Jesus. Therefore, you can only exercise your authority in Christ, using his name. By using Jesus's name, I don't mean merely prefacing what you want to say by "in the name of Jesus." That would be an incantation. No. You use his name by first recognising who you are in Jesus, then standing in your place of delegated authority and exercising the rights that have been given to you by him, in the same way that an ambassador can act in the name of the country that he represents. If you're not a believer in Christ, you don't have this authority, even if you mention the name of Jesus.

A group of Jews learned this lesson the hard way. The seven sons of Sceva, a leading priest, travelled from town to town casting out evil spirits. They tried to use the name of the Lord Jesus in their incantation, saying, "I command you in the name of Jesus, whom Paul preaches, to come out!" But one time when they tried it, the evil spirit replied, "I know Jesus, and I know Paul, but who are you?" Then the man with the evil spirit leaped on them, overpowered them, and attacked them with such violence that they fled from the house naked and battered.[17]

However, if you're in Christ, you can address the enemy in the name of Jesus, and he will obey. Resist him and he will run away.[18] Remember Sally and Skittles? When Sally put her foot down, Skittles obeyed and ran back home.

For instance, you can say:

"You demon, I command you to come out in Jesus's name."

"You spirit of infirmity, I rebuke you in the name of the Lord Jesus Christ."

"You foul spirit of fear, I bind you in the name of Jesus."

"Poverty, I release myself from your grip in Jesus's name."

"You foul spirit, I command you to stop your activities in the name of Jesus."

HOW FAR CAN YOU GO IN EXERCISING AUTHORITY?

The only limitation on your authority is the Word of God. You cannot act contrary to the Bible in exercising authority. If you do, heaven will not back you because the Word of God is forever settled in heaven,[19] and the Scriptures cannot be broken.[20] So know the Word!

There are a few principles that will help you line up with the Word of God when it comes to spiritual warfare and your authority.

First off, you've got to realise that you don't have authority over your fellow human beings. There are two reasons for this. One, God gives every one of his creations a free will. Trying to exercise authority over them and make them do what they don't want to do is manipulation. It is a form of witchcraft. Two, spiritual warfare is actually a *spiritual* battle. The Bible says the fight is not against "flesh and blood."[21] It is the devil who is the enemy. Therefore, you have authority over the devil, not your next-door neighbour. You can exercise authority over the spirit behind a person, but you can't exercise authority over the person.

Second, you can only exercise authority within your sphere of authority—i.e., your life, family, and anything else you have responsibility for. You can command the devil to completely vacate your city or country immediately and expect that he will do so—but if somebody else in your city or country asks him in, he's going to come *back* in. As we will see later in the book, this can happen through many forms of satanic contamination.

Third, if anybody who is not within your area of responsibility is demon possessed, you will need their permission to drive out the devil from their lives. If they don't want to be free, there's nothing you can do. Even where they give you permission, and you lead them into freedom, they can open the door to the devil and go back into bondage. We will look at this in more detail when we consider deliverance in chapter 4.

With this understanding, I will now show you where the main battles of life are fought and how to remain victorious. Are you ready? Let's jump right in!

Chapter 2:

WINNING THE BATTLE IN YOUR MIND

"For as he thinks within himself, so he is."

Proverbs 23:7, NASB

"The best fighter in the world. Nobody can beat me."

"The best fighter in the world. Nobody can beat me."

"The best fighter in the world. Nobody can beat me."

Constantine "Cus" D'Amato, the legendary boxing trainer, made his young trainee say those words to himself all day, over and over again, from the age of thirteen. This was years before he became a professional boxer. With time, the trainee began to believe that he was the best boxer in the world. He began to believe that nobody could defeat him in a boxing ring.

He combined the affirmations with an insane amount of hard work. Every day he would run about three miles, spend hours training and honing his skills in the gym, and spend more hours watching videos of former boxing greats. He read every book on boxing that D'Amato had in his vast library. He had a voracious appetite for anything boxing, and he sponged up everything D'Amato taught him.

Mike Tyson may not be your cup of tea. But the fact is, years later Tyson became the undisputed heavyweight champion of the world. He became one of the all-time boxing greats. To date, he holds the record as the youngest boxer to win the World Boxing Council, World Boxing Association, and International Boxing Federation heavyweight titles at twenty years, four months, and twenty-two days old. He has also been inducted into the International Boxing Hall of Fame.

What did D'Amato know that most people don't? This: the mind is incredibly powerful. Your thoughts matter. They invariably determine your choices, which in turn shape who you are. And if it was true for Tyson, it is true for you. The Bible puts it this way: "As [a person] thinks within himself, so he is." In other words, your mind is so powerful it flows into your thoughts, words, and ultimately your actions.

THE BATTLEFIELD OF THE MIND

The mind is like a computer with a highly sophisticated processor. It processes thousands of thoughts every day. All kinds of thoughts go through your mind. A vast majority of the thoughts your mind processes are ideas, negative and positive. Others are temptations. Your mind has the ability to sift through and filter these thoughts.

God gave your mind this awesome ability because it is the chief battleground of life. Your mind is where the battles of life are fought. It is where warfare is won or lost. As a human being, you go wherever your mind goes! TV Evangelist Joyce Meyers says, "I believe that where the mind goes, the man follows. Jesus said in Luke 6:45…out of the abundance of the heart his mouth speaks. And in Proverbs 23:7 the Bible says…as he thinks in his heart, so is he…In both of these scriptures, the word heart refers to the mind. In other words, our thoughts are the forerunners of both our words and actions. Whatever you and I allow into our inner life will eventually be seen in our outer life. So in order to deal with wrong behavior, we need to deal with wrong thinking."[1]

PROTECT YOUR MIND

Where the mind goes, the man follows! The Bible puts it this way: "Above all else, guard your heart, for everything you do flows from it."[2] The word *heart* in Proverbs 4:23 is of course not the physical heart underneath your chest, which pumps blood around your body. Instead, it is derived from the Hebrew word *leb* and can be defined as *mind, inner man, will,* and *heart*.[3]

Your inner man is your spirit being, sometimes called the spirit-man. This is the real you, the part of you that connects with God. Your mind is your intellect, your ability to think and reason. It is the seat of your emotions and the place where your reasoning takes place. Your will is your volition, the ability to make a choice. You exercise your will in your mind. Your heart is another word for your soul, and it is a combination of your mind and will.

These four words are essentially one and the same and so can be used interchangeably. So for instance, you can say, "Guard your mind, for everything you do flows from it." "Guard your will, for everything you do flows from it. Or even "Guard your inner man, for everything you do flows from it."

Because everything you do flows from your mind, the mind is of strategic importance. Wherever your mind goes, you will follow. The devil knows the importance of your mind. That's why your mind is under constant and relentless attack from the devil, as we shall see shortly. King Solomon, who wrote the words we've been looking at, doesn't say, "When you get round to it, guard your mind." No! He says, "above all else": in other words, *make it your number-one priority* to guard and protect your mind.

How do you guard your mind? By being very careful what you allow into it!

UNDERSTANDING THE DEVIL'S STRATEGIES

Picture the devil coming to you as a monstrous, one-eyed, fork-wielding villain dressed in a red cape and pointy horns. What would you do? Let me see…smile at him and give him a bear hug, or take to your heels in fright? If you're like me, you'd run for dear life! And the devil is aware of this. He is very smart! So he's constantly reinventing himself to make his ideas more appealing.

Temptation

There is a reason the devil doesn't come dressed in a red cape and pointy horns. As they say, the devil wears Prada…or Versace, Burberry, Chanel, or Dior. He comes as your dreams come true. He comes through your thinking, dropping ideas into your mind. Let's be clear: God gives you thoughts. So does the devil! God's thoughts are what you call an inspiration, while the thoughts the devil drops into your mind are temptation. And make no mistake about it: the goal of temptation is to make you fail and fall. Through temptation, the devil seeks to make you sin and give him a foothold into your life. That's why God won't tempt you. He might test you, but he will never tempt you.

The devil is a spirit being, and he understands you better than you can imagine. He knows your strengths and weaknesses and adapts his evil schemes to your circumstances to make it easier for you to fall for his temptations. He will tempt you at your weakest. If you have anger issues, but would never steal, no matter how poor you were, most of your temptations will come in the area of anger. You will find all kinds of people and situations provoking you and making your blood boil. With each situation, your head will be filled with a million and one ways to react and get even. You will probably never be tempted to steal, because the devil knows you won't fall for it. Why would he waste his energy?

After Jesus had fasted forty days and forty nights, he was very hungry. And what did the devil tempt him with? Fornication? Of course not! That wouldn't have worked. So what did the devil do? He told Jesus that if he was indeed the Son of God, he should turn stones into bread.[4]

The Bible describes it this way: "Temptation comes from our own desires, which entice us and drag us away."[5] The devil is very good at dropping evil and alluring thoughts into the mind. You must understand, however, that although God doesn't tempt you himself, he will never allow the devil to tempt you beyond your capacity.[6] That's why all the devil can do is make suggestions and leave you to say either yes or no. If you can say no while the temptation is still in your mind, then you've won that particular battle. However, if you say yes to his suggestion in your mind, you will fall when the situation is played out in real life.

The Five Senses

When dropping his ideas into your mind, the devil uses the five senses. He can tempt you through what you see, what you hear, what you taste, what you touch, and what you smell. Science teaches that we use our senses to gather and respond to information about our environment, which aids in our survival. And each sense provides different information which is combined, processed and interpreted by your brain.

Something similar happens in the realm of the spirit. Each of the five senses has direct access to your mind, making it easy for the devil to tempt you through what you see, hear, touch, taste, or smell. Let's look at the example of David,[7] the Old Testament king who was an ancestor of Jesus. On a beautiful spring evening when he should have been in battle, he was enjoying the views from the penthouse suite of his palace when he saw her: Bathsheba, a very beautiful young lady who was having a shower.

The devil, knowing David was a womaniser who would go for anything in a skirt, dropped a thought into his mind: "Wow, what a sight! Imagine what it would feel like to have this beautiful woman! Why not take a closer look? Look at the curves. She's like none of your wives—she's young, alluringly beautiful. Imagine…" David said yes in his mind before Bathsheba was ever in his house, and at that moment, he fell. It all began with what David saw.

Next, the devil tempted David using what he heard. After David slept with her, Bathsheba became pregnant. When he heard this, the devil dropped an idea into David's mind. "Why not make her husband sleep with her so he'll think he's the father of the child?" So he recalled Bathsheba's husband, Uriah, from the battlefield. But Uriah wouldn't go home to his wife. And then came another idea from the devil: "Why not take him out? Get somebody to kill Uriah, and Bathsheba is all yours!" Unfortunately, David said yes to the devil and had Uriah killed, making God really angry with him.[8] The consequences of that grievous sin affected David's family for generations.

THE DEVIL HAS OTHER METHODS TOO

For the sake of balance, it is important to point out that the devil doesn't always work by going straight to your mind. There are times when he uses people to bring temptation your way. This can be a friendly suggestion, a subtle idea from a relative, pressure from a work colleague, an instruction from your boss, or even a life-or-death option from a criminal. In such cases, what is said to you is the actual temptation itself. An example is when a father tells a child who has recently become a Christian to choose between Jesus and disinheritance, or where a terrorist tells a Christian to recant his faith and become a Muslim or be killed.

A good example is what happened to Joseph in Potiphar's house. Mrs Potiphar, the wife of his COO, told him, "Come to bed with me."[9] Joseph wasn't dealing with a thought here. He heard the woman proposition him. And he said no!

PULL DOWN THE STRONGHOLDS

The devil uses strongholds as a tool of control and manipulation. A stronghold is basically a demonic fortress in the mind that controls the lives of people. It is an incorrect thinking pattern that has taken root and become a strong belief or opinion. It is usually based on falsehood. Strongholds can also come into being through deception, brainwashing, wrong teaching, or a traumatic experience.

What do you do to strongholds? You pull them down! The Bible tells us, "We demolish arguments and every pretension that sets itself up against the knowledge of God, and we take captive every thought to make it obedient to Christ."[10] You pull down strongholds by renewing your mind.

RENEW YOUR MIND

Your mind is like a sponge. It soaks up everything you see, hear, touch, smell, and taste! And it retains them, all stored away in the deep recesses of your subconscious mind. You never forget them unless you consciously delete them! That's why God expects you to renew your mind with his Word. The Bible says, "Do not conform to the pattern of this world, *but be transformed by the renewing of your mind*. Then you will be able to test and approve what God's will is—his good, pleasing, and perfect will"[11] (emphasis mine).

Mind renewal is the process by which you:

- Tear down mental strongholds
- Delete anything that's harmful to your spiritual well-being from your mental memory and replace it with what the Word of God says.

As you study, meditate upon, and apply the Word of God to your everyday situations, the Word dismantles all the junk you've picked up over the years. With the Word, which is the sword of the Spirit,[12] you are able to tear down any demonic strongholds in the mind. This leads to transformation as God makes you more and more Christ-like!

In the next chapter, we will look at the broader picture of spiritual warfare and debunk some myths about the devil.

Chapter 3:

A SPIRITUAL WARFARE PRIMER

> "A final word: Be strong in the Lord and in his mighty power. Put on all of God's armor so that you will be able to stand firm against all strategies of the devil. For we are not fighting against flesh-and-blood enemies, but against evil rulers and authorities of the unseen world, against mighty powers in this dark world, and against evil spirits in the heavenly places."
>
> **Ephesians 6:10-12, NLT**

"I don't think you should teach on spiritual warfare," Peter told Hilda firmly. Hilda was the associate pastor in the church. "Concentrate on Jesus, not the devil."

"Pastor, I do concentrate on Jesus and his victory," Hilda responded, trying to show the utmost respect to her lead pastor. "Jesus taught that we have authority over the evil one. Until I began to use Christ's authority in spiritual warfare, I had four children going to hell. I've learned to bind the enemy's work in my family members' lives. Today, all my children and grandchildren serve the Lord. I've seen the results of spiritual warfare, and I want to help others."[1]

Spiritual warfare is a fierce battle between the forces of God and the forces of evil. It's good versus evil; light versus darkness. It's the kingdom of God versus the system of this world, where the devil reigns as god. It's the battle for your soul. It is going on all the time.

As we said earlier, the devil hates God with a passion. And because you are made in God's image, he hates you too. He also hates you because he is jealous and envious of you because you've taken his place as a worshipper. He used to offer God praise and worship, which you now offer to God.

Spiritual warfare is real.

Billy Graham explained the reality of spiritual warfare in his book *Angels*:

> We live in a perpetual battlefield...The wars among the nations on earth are mere popgun affairs compared to the fierceness of battle in the spiritual unseen world. This invisible spiritual conflict is waged around us incessantly and unremittingly. Where the Lord works, Satan's forces hinder; where angel beings carry out divine directives, the devils rage. All this comes about because the powers of darkness press their counterattack to recapture the ground held for the glory of God...
>
> Since the fall of Lucifer, that angel of light and son of the morning, there has been no respite in the bitter Battle of the Ages. Night and day Lucifer, the master craftsman of the devices of darkness, labors to thwart God's plan of the ages. We can find inscribed on every page of human history the consequences of the evil brought to fruition by the powers of darkness with the devil in charge. Satan never yields an inch, nor does he ever pause in his opposition to the plan of God to redeem the "cosmos" from his control."[2]

DEBUNKING THE MYTHS ABOUT THE DEVIL

> There are two equal and opposite errors into which our race can fall about the devils. One is to disbelieve in their existence. The other is to believe, and to feel an excessive and unhealthy interest in them. They themselves are equally pleased by both errors and hail a materialist or a magician with the same delight.[3]

The waters of spiritual warfare are extremely muddy and murky. This is my attempt to shed the light of God's Word on some of the falsehood being peddled around.

Satan Is Real

There are two extremes to avoid in spiritual warfare. One is to believe that the devil is a myth. As we saw in the preface, Satan, who is also known as the devil, was an angelic being who lost his place in heaven because of rebellion and pride. He was thrown out of heaven with the angels who sided with him, about a third of all the angels. Unfortunately, there are Christians who actually believe the devil doesn't exist. Ironically, that's a lie of the devil! You cannot accept the Bible as the infallible Word of God without coming to the conclusion that the devil is real. Scripture makes it very clear that he exists. The devil showed up among the angels who presented themselves to God just before Job's afflictions,[4] he tempted Jesus,[5] and he hindered Paul,[6] just to mention a few of his appearances in the Bible. Make no mistake, the devil isn't a figure of speech. He is real!

The word translated "devil" in Matthew's account of the temptation of Jesus is the Greek word *diabolos*.[7] It is the root of the modern English words *diabolical* and *devil*. Diabolos is often used as a noun and means a traducer, a false accuser, and a slanderer.

Not only is he real, the devil is the supreme embodiment of evil. He is not a fun-loving, beer-swigging guy who just wants you to have a good time. If he could, he would devour you!

The second extreme is to see the devil behind every calamity. The problem with this is that it stops you from taking responsibility for your own actions. There are demon hunters who feel an unnecessary interest in the devil. They spend all their waking moments chasing the devil and his demons. This is unhealthy. Spend your time more productively. The devil is a defeated foe. Stop trying to defeat a defeated enemy. Instead, simply rest in what Jesus did for you, and fight from victory!

Sometimes, the devil must think "Why is he blaming me for that accident? He slept at the wheel and had a crash. That had nothing to do with me!"

Satan Is Not All-Powerful

Only God is all-powerful. God is omnipotent. The devil isn't. Think about it. If the devil was all-powerful, he would have stopped you from receiving Christ! He would stop you from going to church. He would prevent you from praying. He would stop you from reading the Bible.

Satan relies on two things to be able to hurt you: your ignorance and your cooperation. Because you have such **great authority** in Christ, his greatest weapon against you as a Christian is ignorance. The Bible says, "My people are destroyed from lack of knowledge."[8] It is God's people who are destroyed, not the unbelievers. Sometimes the enemy adds a bit of deception into the mix. The combination of ignorance and deception can be lethal. Many Christians are deceived into feeling guilt-ridden and worthless because they don't see themselves the way God sees them. Some feel unloved and not good enough to be accepted by God. They've been deceived into seeing God as a distant and cruel taskmaster instead of a loving Father who longs to have a loving relationship with them!

It's time to smell the coffee and wake up, both to the reality of the enemy and to the reality of your own position in Christ.

Secondly, the devil can't make you do what you don't want to do. He relies on your cooperation. That's why he is a liar, a cheat, and the master of deceit. He needs that to get to you. He can't control you. All he does is drop ideas into your mind, which (as we saw in chapter 2) is the chief battlefield of life. That's all he can do. Sugar-coat sin to make it look attractive and then suggest you try it. Sow seeds of doubt in your mind. That's the way he tempted Eve. And he works the same way today. If you can say no to the devil, he can't force you. He can persuade you, but he can't make you. The devil who can compel you to do what you don't want to do has not yet been born.

The exception to this principle is those who are possessed by a demon. We consider demonic possession and oppression in chapter 4, "Understanding Deliverance."

Satan Is Not Omnipresent

Only God is present everywhere at the same time. The devil has a complex and highly organised network of demon spirits and is able to communicate within this network faster than the speed of light. Because of this, he sometimes appears omnipresent, but he is not.

In the context of spiritual warfare, this truth is liberating. It means the devil has a significant limitation: he is limited by space. Therefore, you can place an embargo on information transfer between demonic spirits as a tactic of spiritual warfare. For instance, you can say, "I seal up this atmosphere with the blood of Jesus and decree that what's happening here in this place [room, hall, programme etc] will not be seen elsewhere within the kingdom of darkness."

The Devil Is Not a Roaring Lion

The Bible says, "Be alert and of sober mind. Your enemy the devil prowls around like a roaring lion looking for someone to devour."[9] Some people have used this verse of Scripture to suggest that the devil is a lion, able to devour us. But is he? What is the Bible teaching here? Satan is not a lion, and he can't devour you if you're a believer.

Peter says the devil prowls around *like* a roaring lion. He behaves like a roaring lion. He does this to instil fear in the minds of his targets. The very next verse says, "Resist him, standing firm in the faith."[10] You don't resist a lion. You run away from it! However, the Bible exhorts us to *resist* the devil because he is only a pretender. He is *not* a lion. If you resist him, he will run away from you!

Satan Doesn't Have All Knowledge

The devil has only limited knowledge. Although he knows some things, he is not all-knowing. The devil does have psychic powers, which he uses to empower fortune-tellers to predict future events, but only God is all-knowing.

The devil can tell some of (not all of) your thoughts. How do we know this? Because mind readers often can read your mind and tell you what you're thinking, and they don't do that by the power of God! For this to happen, however, you have to give them access to your mind by going to see them or submitting to their control. By contrast, God is able to tell everything that's on your mind all the time.

If the devil was all-knowing, he wouldn't have crucified Jesus! He did not know that Jesus was born to die. He had no idea that by killing Jesus, he was helping Jesus fulfil his purpose for coming into the world. The Bible describes it this way:

> We do, however, speak a message of wisdom among the mature, but not the wisdom of this age or of the rulers of this age, who are coming to nothing. No, we declare God's wisdom, a mystery that has been hidden and that God destined for our glory before time began. None of the rulers of this age understood it, for if they had, they would not have crucified the Lord of glory.[11]

The devil is, of course, the ruler of this age. Be empowered by this information. The devil has limited knowledge.

UNDERSTANDING THE ARMOUR OF GOD

> Put on all of God's armor so that you will be able to stand firm against all strategies of the devil.[12]

In Ephesians 6, the apostle Paul introduces the armour of God. The armour isn't a set of tips to help us get by. It is the ultimate protection kit, and we need it because we are already in spiritual warfare. It's what you might call God's impregnable defence mechanism against the attacks of the devil. No surprise then that Paul tells us to put on the *full* armour!

> Finally, be strong in the Lord and in his mighty power. Put on the full armor of God, so that you can take your stand against the devil's schemes. For our struggle is not against flesh and blood, but against the rulers, against the authorities, against the powers of this dark world and against the spiritual forces of evil in the heavenly realms. Therefore put on the full armor of God, so that when the day of evil comes, you may be able to stand your ground, and after you have done everything, to stand. Stand firm then, with the belt of truth buckled around your waist, with the breastplate of righteousness in place, and with your feet fitted with the readiness that comes from the gospel of peace. In addition to all this, take up the shield of faith, with which you can extinguish all the flaming arrows of the evil one. Take the helmet of salvation and the sword of the Spirit, which is the word of God. And pray in the Spirit on all occasions with all kinds of prayers and requests. With this in mind, be alert and always keep on praying for all the Lord's people.[13]

As a Christian, you've got to understand that you're in spiritual warfare. Anybody who tells you otherwise is being deceitful. In spiritual warfare you fight an unseen enemy, who is devious and wicked. To stand any chance, you must put on the full armour of God—not some of it, but all of it!

The armour is made up of seven pieces. This is not surprising because seven is God's number. It is the perfect number. When you put on the full armour:

- You stand in grace and rest in the accomplished work of Jesus on the cross at Calvary. You stand perfect in the righteousness of Christ.
- You have access to the same armoury and arsenal that Jesus had when he walked the earth about two thousand years ago.
- You are equipped to overcome all the evil schemes and fiery darts of the devil.
- You fight *from* victory, not *for* victory, in a battle whose outcome has already been determined.
- The devil doesn't see your weaknesses. He can't see them because they are covered up by the armour. When he looks at you he sees Jesus Christ, crucified, raised from the grave, and glorified.

The devil hates you because you're a child of God. And he will attack you. But when you've got on the full armour, he can't harm you. He will come one way and disappear seven ways!

So what are the seven pieces of the armour of God?

The Belt of Truth

This is the first piece of armour mentioned by Paul. Not the breastplate of righteousness, not prayer, not the shield of faith, but a belt. Why? And what has truth got to do with a belt?

A Roman soldier's belt played a crucial role in his effectiveness. It held together all the other pieces of the armour and provided a place to store his sword. Jesus said, "Sanctify them by Your truth. Your word is truth."[14] The Word of God is truth. Without the Word of God holding everything in your life in place, you will not be ready for the fight. The rest of the armour will lack effectiveness if you are not strong in the truth. You must gird yourself with the Word. Let it dwell richly in you. Let it become part of your everyday routine.

The Breastplate of Righteousness

This is one of the most powerful pieces of the armour of God. It is a defensive weapon. A breastplate is a piece of armour worn over the upper body to protect the vital organs around the chest. As a child of God, you are righteous. The Bible says, "God made him who had no sin to be sin for us, so that in him we might become the righteousness of God."[15] If you're saved, then automatically, you are in right standing with God. That's who you are. Not because of what you've done. It is simply by grace. It is your position in Christ.

On the other hand, if you deliberately *choose* to engage in sin (in other words, to walk in unrighteousness), you need to repent to restore fellowship with God. If you choose to do this in an ongoing, continuous manner, then I would question whether you're saved in the first place, because a person born of God does not deliberately commit sin.[16] He may sin because of a mistake or through negligence or ignorance, but not deliberately and with continued intention. If you know the breastplate is not covering you because you are continually and deliberately engaged in unrighteousness, you need to repent, believe, and let the righteousness of Jesus Christ come into your life and act as your covering.

The Helmet of Salvation

I believe this is the most powerful piece of the armour. Your salvation is the very foundation of spiritual warfare. You are risen with Christ, seated with Christ, sharing in the righteousness and authority of Christ, and given new life in Christ! The helmet is another defensive weapon. In olden times, soldiers wore helmets as part of their armour to protect their heads from attack in battle. The helmet of salvation speaks of your redemption and the new birth as a child of God. If you don't know Jesus as your personal Saviour and Lord, you're not saved. And if you're not saved, you are missing a vital part of the armour. To be saved, you need to acknowledge that you are sinner and invite Jesus into your heart as your Saviour and Lord.

The Shield of Faith

The shield is primarily a defensive weapon, and in spiritual warfare, it is used to stop the flaming arrows of the enemy. These fiery darts come in different guises and include arrows of fear, doubt, false accusation, evil desire, guilt, lust, jealousy, hate, evil speaking, and all kinds of temptation. By holding up the shield of faith, you extinguish the flaming spiritual arrows sent against you by the devil.

Faith is your trust in God as Saviour and Deliverer. Your faith is that vital weapon that can be manoeuvred toward each and every attack, no matter its size or the direction it is coming from. Faith grows as you study the Word of God.

The Sword of the Spirit: The Word of God

There are only two offensive weapons in the armour. This is one of them. In spiritual warfare, the Word of God acts as a sword, not when you leave the Bible on your bookshelf or place it under your pillow, but when you speak the Word in faith. The Word of God, spoken in faith, is very powerful and "sharper than the sharpest two-edged sword."[17] You make use of this weapon when you speak God's Word to the enemy concerning your situation, just like Jesus did in Matthew 4. He constantly referred to the Scriptures when he was tempted by the devil. And he prefaced his counterattacks by saying "it is written."

The Word of God is so powerful and different from the words spoken by mere mortals because:

- It is flawless, like silver purified in a crucible, like gold refined seven times.[18]
- It is eternal and forever settled in heaven.[19]
- God watches over it to ensure it is fulfilled.[20]

Footgear

As a soldier of Christ, you need to wear protective gear for your feet as you march valiantly to battle. It is not enough to wear just any old sandals! Your footwear must be appropriate in terms of size and comfort; if not, you will not be able to walk and run when necessary. The good news of the gospel is your footwear. We must share our faith with the unsaved. This is an important part of the armour! The Bible says, "How beautiful are the feet of those who preach the good news of salvation!"[21]

The New Living Translation says, "For shoes, put on the peace that comes from the Good News so that you will be fully prepared."[22] Jesus gives those who are saved the peace that defies understanding. With this peace, you won't trip up when the enemy tries to condemn you or accuse you falsely.

Praying in the Holy Spirit

This is the other offensive weapon in your arsenal. Praying in the Spirit is a powerful means of attacking the enemy in spiritual warfare. So how does one pray in the Spirit? To pray in the Spirit is to pray with the help and assistance of the Holy Spirit. Although you can pray in the Spirit without praying in tongues, you cannot pray in tongues without praying in the Spirit. Therefore, to my mind, the easiest way to pray in the Spirit is by praying in tongues. However, if the Lord is leading you to pray with your understanding, start by asking the Holy Spirit to help you pray. Then seek to pray God's will as revealed in the Bible. It can be helpful to pray the Scriptures directly.

SPIRITUAL WARFARE MADE EASY

> He trains my hands for battle; my arms can bend a bow of bronze.[23]

Effectiveness in spiritual warfare begins with knowing who you are in Christ. If you know that, waging warfare against the enemy should be as easy as ABC!

You see, you are born of God. The greatest force in the universe is behind you and on your side. God the Holy Spirit dwells in you. You are God's ambassador here on earth. You are more than a conqueror. You are a joint-heir with Jesus. You are seated in the heavenly places with Christ Jesus. *You are destined to reign and rule* in this world!

Here then, is the A–Z of spiritual warfare.

A: Adoration

God inhabits the praises of his people. Spiritual warfare begins and ends with praise. Develop an attitude of gratitude. This requires a life of thanks*living*. Make thanksgiving your lifestyle. Give him praise in all things. And give him praise for all things.

As long as we remain in this fallen world, there will always be something we are waiting for God to do for us. At the same time, there is so much to be thankful for every day of our lives. So instead of moaning and complaining about what you don't have, take a moment to reflect on God's goodness. And give praise for what God has done for you, what he is doing for you, and what he will do for you!

B: Belief

Believe what God says about you. Everything he says about you is relevant for warfare. For instance, he says you're righteous. See yourself as righteous. He says you're blessed. Take him at his word. He says you're more than a conqueror. See yourself as victorious. He says you have authority over all the power of the devil. Step out in faith and exercise your authority. God will back you.

C: Christ-likeness

Become Christ-like. Seek transformation into the image of Christ. Grow in grace and the knowledge of him. Seek to become more and more Christ-like through prayer and the study of the Word of God. The more Christ-like you are, the more God will reveal himself to you. The more he reveals himself to you, the more insight you will have in the things of God, including spiritual warfare.

D: Depend on God

Be completely reliant on God. Depend on him. He's the one who defeated Satan and delegated his authority to you. He is your source. Recognise that without God, you're nothing. Without God, you cannot engage in spiritual warfare. The devil will devour you! But in God, you have complete authority over the devil and the kingdom of darkness.

E: Engage

Engage the enemy. Did you notice that none of the seven pieces of the armour of God covers your back? Your back is bare. That means God's got your back. Literally! It also means there's no turning back. You have to constantly be on the front foot. Be on the attack. Engage the enemy in warfare.

F: Fear Not

God is with you. So you don't need to be afraid. Greater is the Holy Spirit who dwells within you than the devil in the world. The words "Fear not" and "do not be afraid" (depending on your translation) appear 366 times in the Bible![24] That's one for each day, with an extra "Fear not" for every leap year. Fear is a spirit that can cripple you. That's why the words "Fear not" are a command. So be bold, be strong, for the Lord your God is with you!

G: Grace

Realise that all of **G**od's **r**iches have become yours **at C**hrist's **e**xpense. It doesn't matter whether you think you deserve it or not. All the treasures and resources of heaven are at your disposal. Every single one of them! All paid for by Jesus. All credited to your account. You don't have to work for it. You don't have to do a thing. You can't lose it. It can't be taken from you.

Grace shows that the Christian race is God's race. Grace—G's race. God's race! It's his race. He's doing all the running. He does all the hard work. You're simply a passenger. All God asks is that you be a willing passenger!

Simply see yourself the way God sees you and receive his provision. *Understand* this, and spiritual warfare becomes that much easier!

H: Honour Your Parents

The admonition to honour your parents comes with a promise. The Bible says honour your parents "So that it may go well with you and that you may enjoy long life on the earth."[25] This is one verse of Scripture that is really self-explanatory. If you obey this Scripture, then it will be well with you, no matter what the devil throws at you. So what are you waiting for? Just do what it says!

I: Intercede

Be an intercessor. To intercede is to place yourself in someone else's position and cry out to God on their behalf. You can also intercede for a city or nation. To intercede is to do warfare!

One of the most powerful illustrations of intercessory prayer is found in a gentleman known as Epaphras. Paul said Epaphras was "always wrestling in prayer" for the Colossians, that they may "stand firm in all the will of God, mature and fully assured."[26] The King James Version says he was "always labouring fervently" for them in prayers, while the God's Word Translation says he "always prays intensely" for them.

And here is the crucial bit: though Scripture indicates that he was in prison along with Paul, Epaphras wasn't praying to be released from prison. Instead, he wrestled with God in prayer that the Colossians would be perfect and complete in all the will of God! What an awesome example!

J: Joy

We are not talking about happiness here, but the joy that is a fruit of the Holy Spirit. You need a lot of supernatural strength for spiritual warfare. The Bible says the joy of the Lord is your strength.[27] The Bible also says in God's presence is fullness of joy.[28] So how do you obtain joy? Well, spend time with God. Learn to wait on him. Spend time in his presence, and you will find that his joy will fill your life.

K: Kingdom

Prioritise God's kingdom. In teaching his disciples to pray, Jesus taught us a valuable lesson. He asked them to tell the Father, "Your kingdom come, your will be done, on earth as it is in heaven."[29] Be kingdom-minded. You can never go wrong there! Through spiritual warfare, you enforce Jesus's victory over the devil. By so doing, you're seeking to establish God's kingdom here on earth.

L: Learn

Be a learning machine. Commit to lifelong learning. Read the Bible. Study the Bible. Meditate on the Bible. Seek God wholeheartedly. Read godly books. Read widely. Be willing to be taught. But above all, have a teachable heart! There's strategy in spiritual warfare. If you're teachable, the Lord will open your eyes.

M: The Micah Challenge

Adopt the Micah challenge. Micah 6:8 says, "O people, the Lord has already told you what is good, and this is what he requires: to do what is right, to love mercy, and to walk humbly with your God."[30] This is one way to crush the devil! Keep the less privileged in your thoughts. Show mercy.

N: Nurture

Nurture your relationship with God. Love God with everything you've got. Seek God wholeheartedly. Seek to know God. Give attention to the Word of God. Love it. Desire it. Spend time on it. Renew your mind with the Word.

Learn to trust God for small things, and watch your faith grow.

O: Open

Be open to God. Open up your heart to the leading, direction, and guidance of the Holy Spirit. God speaks all the time. He wants to guide you. Learn how the Holy Spirit speaks to you. Seek his direction. Acknowledge him in everything you do. Depend on his leading. This is crucial because the devil is an unseen enemy.

P: Pray Without Ceasing

Prayer is one of the seven pieces of the armour of God. But we aren't talking about just any kind of prayer. We are talking about praying in the Holy Spirit, which is a weapon of warfare. It is always wonderful to pray. However, praying in the Spirit without ceasing is a key to unlocking the treasures of darkness. It requires a constant awareness of the presence of God.

Q: Queen Esther

Be like Queen Esther: seek to do God's will at all times and in all circumstances.[31] You must seek out God's purpose for your life. Ask yourself, "Why am I here?" "What on earth am I doing here?" You're not where you currently are by accident. There are no coincidences with God, only *God-incidents*! Like Esther, if it comes to it, be willing to die for your faith. You will be a terror to the kingdom of darkness.

R: Resist the Devil

Resist the devil. You do this by standing your ground against him and opposing him in the name of Jesus. You need to do this fairly regularly because, as a Christian, you're in a battlefield. You're constantly in warfare. When you resist him, he runs away from you. He doesn't have a choice. As we saw in chapter 2, "Winning the Battle in Your Mind," the devil attacks the mind. This can happen through low self-esteem, feelings of insecurity, self-loathing, sinful thoughts, and the inability to forgive yourself even when God has forgiven you.

However, there's a condition to successfully resisting the devil. The Bible says, "Submit yourselves, then, to God. Resist the devil, and he will flee from you."[32] The key is to first submit and yield to God. Remember that your authority as a believer is delegated from the Lord. You cannot resist the devil if you're not submitted to God. If you try, he won't run from you. But if you are submitted to God, the devil will not be able to stand against you.

S: Shine

You are the light of the world. Don't hide your light. Let it shine. Arise and shine, for your light has come.[33] Your dawn has broken! The whole of creation is waiting for your manifestation as a child of God.[34] Don't hold back. This is your moment. This is your time. Display God's manifold wisdom as you subdue the enemy and make him Jesus's footstool.[35]

T: Trust and Obey

Put your trust in God, not in any system. Not in your riches. Not in your experience. In trusting God, you may have to burn your bridges such that if God doesn't come through, you're doomed. Learn to trust God completely. Trust him to do what he says he will do.

Not only that, be obedient. Do what he tells you to do. Be a doer of the Word of God, not a hearer only.[36] Ask the Lord to help you to be willing and obedient.

U: U-Turn

You may be surprised at what I have to say here: you can't make a U-turn! Remember we said at *E: Engage* that the armour of God doesn't cover your back. Your back is bare. Jesus said, "No one who puts a hand to the plow and looks back is fit for service in the kingdom of God."[37] That's why you've got to count the cost before deciding to follow Jesus.

That said, you *can* make a U-turn if you fall into sin or error. Here the U-turn takes you back to God!

V: Veil

In Jesus's day, the interior of the temple was divided into two holy places. The part nearest the entrance was the sanctuary or Holy Place. The second area was known as the Holy of Holies or the Most Holy Place.

Only the high priest could enter into the Holy of Holies. And he could only do this once a year, with the blood of an animal sacrifice for atonement. The Most Holy Place was separated from the Holy Place by an enormous curtain, or veil.

At the precise moment when Jesus died, that enormous veil was torn in two from top to bottom.[38] This signified that Jesus Christ has become our high priest, who gives us direct access to God by his blood. You have access to the throne of grace.[39] Make use of it. You will need it!

W: Wait on God

Ask the Lord to teach you to wait on him and learn quickly. Your walk with God is not a sprint. It is a marathon. To avoid burnout, you must know how and *when* to wait on God. Remove yourself from everything and everybody, and spend time alone with God. You will renew your strength. Those who wait on God not only renew their strength, they soar effortlessly like eagles.

X: X-Rayed

Be open and transparent. Be visible inside and out. Don't live a double life. You're a child of God, not a double agent! Ensure the devil has nothing hidden in your closet. Get rid of anything that belongs to the devil.

The devil had no claim on Jesus. That's why Jesus could say, "The ruler of the world is coming, and he has nothing in me."[40] We need to live in the same way.

Y: Yearn

Yearn for God. Seek to empty yourself. Die to self. You have to understand that God wants you to enjoy your ordinary, everyday life. Jesus said he came that you might have life in all its fullness.[41] Dying to self doesn't mean you should be gloomy and miserable. To die to self is to discipline yourself such that you are controlled by the Holy Spirit and not by the desires of your flesh!

When you die to self, you become empty, and the fullness of Christ is revealed in you. You decrease so that Christ may increase in you. When this happens, you become a weapon of mass destruction in God's hands! Paul said, "I have been crucified with Christ and I no longer live, but Christ lives in me. The life I now live in the body, I live by faith in the Son of God, who loved me and gave himself for me."[42]

Z: Zoë

Recognise that God's life, the eternal life expressed in the Greek word *zoë*, is in you! At the new birth, God imparted a part of his divine nature into you. You carry the divine in your earthen vessel. You're a walking wonder. God's life flows through you.

The Bible puts it this way:

> No one born (begotten) of God [deliberately, knowingly, and habitually] practices sin, for God's nature abides in him [His principle of life, the divine sperm, remains permanently within him]; and he cannot practice sinning because he is born (begotten) of God.[43]

In your daily pursuits, always remember that you're a carrier of God's very life.

THE KEY TO VICTORY

The one sure-fire key to victory as a Christian in this fallen world is to be filled with the Holy Spirit—that is, to be completely submitted to and empowered by him.[44] The armour of God, the A–Z of spiritual warfare—ultimately, all of these things are about being continually filled with the Spirit of God.

Having looked broadly at spiritual warfare, it's time for us to consider an often misunderstood aspect of spiritual warfare. Deliverance is a major part of spiritual warfare. Because of its vital importance, the devil has really muddied the waters of this important topic. The next chapter is an attempt to shed the light of God's Word on deliverance. Are you ready to see what the Bible teaches about it? I can't wait for you to join me there.

Chapter 4:

UNDERSTANDING DELIVERANCE

> "... how God anointed Jesus of Nazareth with the Holy Spirit and power, and how he went around doing good and healing all who were under the power of the devil, because God was with him."
>
> **Acts 10:38**

Once when I was leading a deliverance conference in a city in Midwestern America, a lady called Janet came to the healing line. She was a lovely lady who was part of the praise team. I asked her what she wanted prayers for. All of a sudden, she changed and became very aggressive. Then she began to speak with a husky male voice.

"You don't belong to this body," I told the demon. "You will have to come out." In response, she lunged toward me and had to be restrained by two men.

"I don't want to speak to you," I told the demon. "I want to speak to Janet." She acted aggressively for a little while longer and then became calm.

"Janet," I said, "would you want to be rid of this demonic spirit?"

"Yes please," she answered in her normal female voice. I then led her to reaffirm her commitment to Jesus, to break any evil ties, and to ask the demon to stop tormenting her.

At that point, I declared deliverance over her: "Right now, you foul spirit, in the name of Jesus, I command you to come out and never return to Janet's body." As the demon left her, Paul, a young man who was in the service, started screaming and jumping up and down, trying to take off his jacket. He said there was fire all over him. At that precise moment, the host pastor's wife had a revelation: she saw the demon leave Janet and enter the young man. I prayed over Paul and commanded the demon to come out. I gave specific instruction for the demon to go to the waterless places to await judgement. I also declared that there would be no reinforcement for him. After that, Paul stopped screaming.

The following day, Paul reported to me that he'd slept through the night like a baby for the first time in years.

The subject of demons, demon possession, and deliverance has always seemed kind of remote and far-fetched to sophisticated twenty-first-century Americans and Europeans. Christians have always accepted the fact of demons and their activity in New Testament times. However, most now wrongly relegate demonic activity to missionary experiences in pagan lands. At the same time, a lot of wrong teaching has cropped up around this whole topic.

CAN A CHRISTIAN BE DEMON POSSESSED?

Janet and Paul were both Christians, so the experience I just shared raises some important questions. Would you say Janet and Paul were demon possessed or demon oppressed? Can a person who has been redeemed by the precious blood of Jesus be demon possessed? And what is the difference between demonic possession and demonic oppression?

When you become a Christian, your body becomes the temple of the Holy Spirit. I suppose the question of demonic possession for a believer becomes, "Can the Holy Spirit share the same home with a demon?"

I believe there is a real distinction between possession and oppression, although it can be subtle. A demoniac—someone who is possessed—has all his or her faculties controlled by the devil. On the other hand, those who are under demonic oppression can exercise their free will and tell the devil to stop oppressing them.

The Reverend Kenneth Hagin, the late influential Pentecostal pastor, had this to say about the question:

> Many years ago I was holding a meeting here in Oklahoma, and as I was ministering to the sick in the healing line, I had an inward intuition—I knew by the inward witness—that somebody in the line

had a demon in him. That doesn't mean he was demon possessed—that's a different thing entirely. To be possessed is to be taken over entirely—spirit, soul, and body. You can have a demon in your body without being possessed by a demon. I kept looking around. When a certain man stood within four persons of me, I knew the demon was in him. I never said anything out loud.

Before the man stepped in front of me I thought to myself, I'm going to cast that thing out of him. I didn't say anything out loud; I just thought it. When he stepped up in place, before I could say anything, he spoke up. The demon spoke through him, whining in a high-pitched, nasal voice, "You can't cast me out! You can't cast me out! You can't cast me out!"

I said, "Yes I can, in the Name of Jesus."

He said, "No you can't. This man wants me to stay. And if he wants me to stay, I can." I said, "You're right," and passed him by.

Several days later I saw that man on the street, stopped him, and engaged him in conversation. He wasn't crazy; he had all his mental faculties. As I talked to him, I found out what kind of a spirit he had. It was a religious spirit. People need to know there are such spirits. They make people act very religious. Actually, this fellow had three evil spirits in him. The others were deceiving and lying spirits. He believed in a mixture of some Bible along with eastern religions. He leaned more toward the eastern religions. I talked to him about this.

I said, "Those beliefs are not scriptural. They're not according to the New Testament."

He replied, "Bible or no Bible, I like it this way, and I'm going to stay with it." I said, "Anytime you want to get rid of those devils, come to see me. But as long as you want it that way, that's the way it's going to be." He said, "Well, that's the way I want it."

You've got to walk off and leave people when they want it that way. If people want to live in sin, they can. If they want to be free, they can be free. But as long as they don't want to be free, neither Jesus nor anybody else can set them free...

Back in the 1950s a church member came in my healing line, and I realized the man had a demon in his body. This man had been in nearly every well-known evangelist's healing line, but he hadn't gotten healed, because that spirit that was oppressing him had to be dealt with. This wasn't a case for healing.

In praying for him, I explained to the people, "This man's body is oppressed by a demon. He is not possessed by a demon. I'll use this illustration: Suppose you live in a house built nearly one hundred years ago, and somebody tells you, 'That house has got termites in it.' That doesn't mean you've got termites in you!

"Your body is the house you live in. If you know how, you can keep the termites out of your natural house—and the demons out of your physical house. They won't be there if you use the right precautions."[1]

Every human being has three parts. You are a spirit. You have a soul, and you live in a body. In the example of Janet and Paul, the demon was oppressing their "house," the body, not possessing the spirit and mind. Although demons can afflict the mind and body (i.e. oppression) they cannot take over the spirit, which is the part of us the Holy Spirit refuses to share.

The other thing Pastor Hagin mentioned, which I have alluded to elsewhere, is the fact that if people don't want to be free, there's nothing you can do to set them free. It comes down to the principle of the free will mentioned in chapter 1. You have a choice. God honours your choice, and he will not force you to go against your free will.

WHAT IS DELIVERANCE?

Within the context of spiritual warfare, deliverance is freedom from any satanic bondage. This can be demonic possession or demonic oppression. It is important to understand that, as a believer, you already have eternal victory over the devil and his demons. As we saw at the end of chapter 3, the key to victory in the Christian life is to be filled (i.e. controlled and empowered) with the Holy Spirit.[2] If every believer was filled with the Holy Spirit, then deliverance would only be relevant to unbelievers!

In the chapters to come, we'll be looking at many ways the devil oppresses Christians and explore ways we can close the door to demons, live filled with the Spirit, and experience deliverance from oppression in our own lives.

THE TWO ASPECTS OF DELIVERANCE

Deliverance ministry is a vital part of spiritual warfare. There are two main aspects to the ministry of deliverance. One is casting out demons, and the other is setting free those who are under demonic oppression.

Both aspects of deliverance were evident in the earthly ministry of Jesus.

The Gerasene Demoniac

This demon-possessed man met with Jesus, who drove out a legion of demons from him. The story is narrated beautifully by Robert L. Deffinbaugh for Bible.org as follows:

> At the conclusion of this day of teaching by parables, the Lord had instructed his disciples to cross over the Sea of Galilee to the other side. This is when the storm arose which threatened to destroy the ship (Mark 4:35-41). Sometime after the Lord Jesus miraculously calmed the storm, the ship landed, perhaps late in the evening, on the other side of the lake in the country of the Gerasenes. If, indeed, it was late at night, the scene must have been an eerie one, with the nerves of the disciples already worn thin by the terrifying experience of the storm.
>
> Immediately, as this weary group disembarked from the ship, they were met by what appeared to be a madman. Our children would probably understand best if I said that his appearance must have been somewhat like that of the television creation, The Incredible Hulk. Although his symptoms would have appeared to be those of an insane man, the Gospel writers inform us that he was demon possessed.
>
> Although the manifestations of demonization vary widely, this man evidenced several of the classic symptoms.
>
> (1) *Severe personality change*. The "before" and "after" descriptions of the demoniac reveal that he was a totally different person under demonic influence. It is something like the behaviour and personality change in a man who is totally intoxicated. More than this, however, is the fact that the man's own identity and individuality were swallowed up by the demons with him. When Jesus asked his name the man answered, "Legion, for we are many" (Mark 5:9). Those who have witnessed demon possession tell us that each demon has its

own distinct personality and that the individual possessed begins to manifest the distinct personality of the demon by which he is possessed. If it is a feminine spirit, the voice will be a feminine one, if masculine then very manly.

(2) *Anti-social behaviour.* The conduct of this pathetic individual was obviously anti-social. That is why he was living in the solitude of the tombs, away from civilisation.

(3) *Spiritual insight.* The demoniac further evidenced demon activity by the depth of his spiritual insight. Instantly he recognised the Lord Jesus to be the Son of God (verse 7). There was a source of spiritual insight beyond human capabilities here. In addition, Matthew includes the comment, "Have You come here to torment us before the time?" (Matthew 8:29). This reveals to us that demons have an intuitive knowledge of their impending doom.

(4) *Super-human strength.* Also, frequently associated with demon possession was a super-human strength (cf. Acts 19:16). The demoniac was uncontrollable by any of the normal means of human confinement. No matter what men attempted to bind him with, he broke loose. No one was strong enough to subdue him (verses 3,4).

(5) *Torment.* The price tag of possession was high, for those who fell victim to the demons agonised in constant torment. Such was the case with this man (cf. verse 5). His animal-like shrieks must have sent chills up the spines of any who were nearby.

(6) *Tendency towards self-destruction.* Another indication of demonic control is the fact that this man was continually doing harm to himself by gashing himself with stones (verse 5). Other demoniacs described in Scripture were bent on self-destruction as well (cf. Mark 9:17-29). The destructive desires of the demons were dramatically carried out in the drowning of the swine.[3]

Woman, Thou Art Loose

The Gerasene demoniac is a clear example of demonic possession. However, Jesus dealt with oppression as well. On one occasion, he was teaching in one of the meeting places on the Sabbath. There was a woman present who was afflicted by an evil spirit. She was twisted and bent over with arthritis. It was so bad she couldn't even look up. She had been afflicted in this way for eighteen years.

When Jesus saw her, he called her over. "Woman, you are free," he declared. Then he placed his hands on her, and immediately she straightened up tall, giving glory to God.[4]

Later on, Jesus went on to explain that "This dear woman, a daughter of Abraham, [had] been held in bondage by Satan for eighteen years."[5] The woman was clearly not a demoniac. She had control of her faculties. But she was oppressed by the devil and had suffered an affliction for eighteen years!

Unfortunately, this is the reality for many Christians today. This woman, a daughter of Abraham, is a type of today's believer. They love the Lord and are faithful to God. They are not demon possessed, but boy are they oppressed! For whatever reason, they suffer needless pain and affliction. Some even wear their afflictions as a badge of honour, forgetting that Jesus can make them completely free!

EVERY BELIEVER IS A DELIVERANCE MINISTER

Jesus was very clear when he said: "And these signs will accompany those who believe: In my name they will drive out demons."[6] Every believer has this ability. It is part of the package you were endowed with at the new birth. It isn't the exclusive preserve of certain people. All you need is an awareness of who you are in Christ, an understanding of your authority as a believer, sensitivity to the Holy Spirit, and a desire to advance God's kingdom.

People become demon possessed and suffer demonic oppression through a variety of channels. These include generational curses, ancestral covenants, satanic contamination, the power of the spoken word, and personal sin, all of which we will consider in the chapters that follow. It's very possible that some of the difficulties you experience are the result of demonic oppression. The fact is, you already have the victory over these things! You just need to learn to enforce that victory in your life.

Ultimately, deliverance means becoming free. When we are delivered and walk in freedom, we become the ultimate expression of Jesus's victory in the earth. As children of God and victorious soldiers in this spiritual war, it's our job to get free, stay free, and live free, being blessed and walking in triumph!

In the next few chapters, we shall take a look at some of the tactics and evil schemes of the devil and learn how to outsmart him. Are you ready? Let's get right in!

Chapter 5:

LIKE FATHER, LIKE SON?

> "'Rabbi,' his disciples asked him, 'why was this man born blind? Was it because of his own sins or his parents' sins?'"
>
> **John 9:2, NLT**

The rock star and political activist Robert Frederick Zenon "Bob" Geldof, KBE, is a good man. He cares for the poor and down trodden, and he is widely recognised for his anti-poverty efforts for Africa. In 1984, he cofounded Live Aid to raise money for famine relief in Ethiopia. Two years later in 1986, he received an honorary knighthood from Queen Elizabeth II in recognition of his work in organising Band Aid and other concerts that raised millions of dollars for the starving people of Africa. He has been awarded many other accolades. Bob is very wealthy. He is also a very famous celebrity. But he has a problem—a very big predicament. One which neither his fame nor his immense wealth can resolve. It seems there's a curse operating in his family.

On Monday, 7 April 2014, Peaches Honeyblossom Geldof, Bob Geldof's second daughter, died of a heroin overdose. Stashes of heroin, burned spoons, and almost eighty syringes were scattered around the twenty-five-year-old's country home in Kent. Her husband returned from a weekend away to find her slumped dead on a bed, covered in needle-puncture marks. She had been looking after their eleven-month-old son, Phaedra, who was left alone for up to seventeen hours. A used syringe was in a sweets box next to her body, and a pair of knotted tights had apparently been used as a tourniquet.

Thirteen years, six months, and twenty-one days earlier, on Sunday, 17 September 2000, Peaches's mother, Paula Elizabeth Yates, died in similar circumstances. The forty-year-old mother of four—a successful television producer, model, and writer—was found dead in bed from a heroin overdose at her home in Notting Hill, West London. Her four-year-old daughter, Tiger Lily, who was alone with her at home at the time of her death, was the one to discover her.

WHAT IS A CURSE?

One indication of the presence of a curse in a family is a history of unnatural deaths. The Geldof story would appear to be a clear example of a generational curse at work: mother and daughter dying in their prime, with the circumstances of the daughter's death mirroring that of her mother with chilling similarity. Both are found dead of a heroin overdose, on the bed, and with a young child left at home. The mother dies on a Sunday, while the daughter dies on a Monday, nearly fourteen years apart. Unfortunately, unless the curse is broken, this will not be the last such death we will see in this family.

When the disciples asked Jesus, "Why was this man born blind? Was it because of his own sins or his parents' sins?" Jesus didn't rebuke them. He didn't say, "There is no such thing as a generational curse," which he would have done if they were completely off the mark. Instead he told them, "It was not because of his sins or his parents' sins. This happened so the power of God could be seen in him."[1]

So what is a curse? And what is a generational curse?

A *curse* is the opposite of a blessing. It results from the defilement of sin or from occult connections. It is an evil, shadowy force that disconnects the flow of God's blessings from the recipient. The person under a curse can see those around him drenched in the rain of God's goodness and enjoying his blessings, but he is unable to partake of it.

Usually, the problem will continue from generation to generation, becoming a *generational curse*. Unless broken, a generational curse will normally pass to the fourth generation. Many people go through life enduring curses instead of enjoying God's blessings, with no idea what is happening to them and without knowing how to put an end to their troubles.

A curse can arise in a variety of ways. Sometimes it is a shadowy visitation from the past, the consequence of something that took place many generations ago. At other times, it can be the result of choices we ourselves have made in our lifetime. Curses can also be put in place by satanic agents as well as people who have authority over us, such as parents, teachers, and religious leaders. In addition, blood sacrifices and ungodly covenants can also result in curses.

Blessings and curses have more in common than people care to admit. They are both means by which supernatural power is demonstrated, either for good in the case of blessings or evil in the case of curses. More often than not, they are conveyed through the power of the spoken word. An essential feature of both is that they continue from generation to generation until they are either revoked (in the case of curses) or rejected (in the case of blessings). However, while a generational curse would normally cease with the fourth generation, a generational blessing can continue up to the thousandth generation.[2]

The generational nature of curses and blessings is illustrated by the true story of two American families, the Jukes and the Edwards.[3] Max Jukes and Jonathan Edwards both lived in eighteenth-century America.

Max Jukes was of Dutch origin. He was an ungodly man who loved evil. He lived for himself, with no room for God in his life. He didn't have any time for his children either. Max liked nature. He thought he was lots better than towns' people because he knew more about nature. He found a lovely spot on the border of a beautiful lake in New York State, where the rocks are grand, the water lovely, the forest glorious. There was never a more charming place in which to be good and to love God than this place, where Max built his shanty about 1750. But he did not go there to worship or to be good. He went simply to get away from good people, to get where he would not have to work or be preached to, and this beautiful spot became a notorious cradle of crime.

In 1874, about eighty years after Max died, Richard L. Dugdale, an employee of the New York Prison Commission, studied the lives of twelve hundred living and dead descendants of Max Jukes, including 169 people who married into the family. Of this number, 310 died in abject poverty, fifty women were prostitutes, and seven were murderers. The study also found sixty who were habitual thieves and 130 who were career criminals. Only twenty of the twelve hundred learned a trade, and ten of those learned it in prison. They were a great expense to the state, costing more than $1,250,000 in eighteenth- and nineteenth-century money.

On the other hand, Jonathan Edwards was a clergyman who loved God and was devoted to his family. He was originally from Wales. The grandson of a clergyman, he was ordained into the ministry at the age of twenty-three. He was married to a young Christian woman by the name Sarah Pierpont, whose father was a clergyman and one of the principal founders of Yale. Her maternal grandfather was also a clergyman and was instrumental in the First Great Awakening, which was a significant revival in American history.

A similar study was carried out into the lives of fourteen hundred descendants of Edwards. The result was a sharp contrast to the Jukes family. There were 285 university graduates; thirteen presidents of colleges and other higher institutions of learning, including Yale, Princeton, Union, Hamilton, Amherst, the University of California, the University of Tennessee, Columbia Law School, and Andover Theological Seminary; sixty-five professors of colleges; and many principals of important academies and seminaries. In addition, there were sixty physicians, seventy-five military officers, over one hundred lawyers, thirty judges, and more than one hundred clergymen and missionaries. There were also mayors, many ambassadors, three governors, three senators, and one vice president of the United States. That is the power of a family blessing!

UNLOCKING THE BLESSING

In spiritual warfare, as we've already seen, we enforce the victory of Jesus in every area of life. That means that one of our responsibilities as Christians is to be blessed! Blessing displays Jesus's victory, brings glory to God, and empowers us to make his enemies his footstool.

Throughout this book, we will make reference to the blessing of Abraham, sometimes simply referred to as "the blessing." What is the blessing, and how do you get it to operate in your life?

The blessing was God's promise to Abraham and his seed. God told him: "I'll make you a great nation and bless you. I'll make you famous; you'll be a blessing. I'll bless those who bless you; those who curse you I'll curse. All the families of the earth will be blessed through you."[4]

Incorporated in the blessing of Abraham is everything we could ever need to enjoy our ordinary, everyday lives on this side of eternity: health and healing, fruitfulness in all things, victory and dominion in every area of life, abundance—in spirit, soul, and body—prosperity, protection, favour, and the ability to be a blessing to all the families of the earth, including our children after us.

All these promises become ours the moment we become children of God through faith in Jesus Christ. The Bible tells us that Jesus "redeemed us in order that the blessing given to Abraham might come to the Gentiles through Christ Jesus, so that by faith we might receive the promise of the Spirit."[5] The blessing is ours! As heirs of God and joint-heirs with Jesus, we are co-possessors of everything in heaven and earth.

The Bible tells us, "Praise be to the God and Father of our Lord Jesus Christ, who has blessed us in the heavenly realms with every spiritual blessing in Christ."[6] Note the use of the past tense, "who *has* blessed us," and the all-encompassing nature of the blessing in the phrase "with every spiritual blessing."

Quite simply, all the promises God made to Abraham and his seed have been fulfilled in Christ Jesus and made available to us. They are deposited into our heavenly account. We just need to unlock that account and download the blessing from heaven for use here on earth.

Unfortunately, for a lot of people, a curse has acted to block access to their heavenly account and suspend the downloading of these blessings to earth for their use. To have access to them, they first need to break the curse and activate, unlock, or release the blessing.

I like to refer to a person who is blessed as holding a "Master of Situations and Circumstances" degree, or MSc. The imagery is of a person who is exercising authority and dominion in every area of life. The Bible refers to such a person as the head, while a person under a curse is likened to the tail.[7] The head is in control, does the strategic thinking, and makes the decisions, while the tail just gets dragged along. In the journey of life, are you in charge and exercising dominion and authority, or are you being pulled, even dragged along, by situations, circumstances, and unseen forces over which you have no control whatsoever? The blessing can be yours!

As we saw in the preface, God blesses you to be a blessing. You're not a recipient of the blessing for you to show off or for personal aggrandisement. God wants you to be a conduit, not a reservoir. He is the source. Like a tap, your job is to simply release the blessing to ensure his kingdom comes here on earth. Through spiritual warfare, you unblock and unlock the blessing, release the overflow over God's people, and ensure Christ's enemies are made his footstool.

HOW A CURSE COMES

King David sinned many times. But as we saw in chapter 2, there was one sin in his life that was particularly appalling. It was a grievous sin—what you might call an iniquity. It was so bad that God sent Nathan, the prophet, to tell David about it. You will recall that David got Bathsheba, the wife of a man named Uriah, pregnant—and then he killed Uriah in an attempt to cover up his adultery.

Iniquity is perversity or depravity. It is wilful, knowing transgression of God's law. David's sin with Bathsheba was an iniquity that opened a door to generational curses in David's family.[8]

In his book *Free at Last,* Pastor Larry Huch explains how generational curses come about and enter a family:

> The first time the word "iniquity" is used in conjunction with generational curses is in Exodus 20:5. The scene is this: God is giving Moses the Ten Commandments. In verse 3, He commanded us to have no other gods but Him. Then, in verses 4-5, He commanded that we should not make idols or bow down and worship them or else our iniquity will visit our children and grandchildren.
>
> God forbids bowing down and worshipping an idol, which is anything we love and reverence more than Him. What He is saying is that, when we worship an idol, we are allowing something other than Him to rule us, to make us bow down and serve it. When we do that, the spirit that operates through that idol will come into our lives and not only make us bow down to it again and again, but it will pass from us to our children and our children's children, making them bow down to it. So this spirit of iniquity becomes a force on the inside that causes us, and generations after us, to bow or bend to its destructive nature!
>
> A spirit of iniquity could be in your life because of something you did, or it could also be something that has landed on you because of something a member of your family did years before you were

born. It could be an iniquity, or family curse, that has passed from one generation to another because of something that has happened in your family or something that has happened to your family.[9]

A modern example is the Kennedy Curse, which apparently dooms its members to early death. The Kennedys are an American family of Irish descent who are prominent in American politics and government. The glamour, wealth, and photogenic value of the family members, as well as their extensive and continuing involvement in public service, has elevated them to iconic status over the past half-century, making the Kennedys the closest thing to American royalty. Yet, their history of tragedy tells us that something is wrong in the family.

Believers in the Kennedy Curse generally cite the following events as evidence of its presence:

- 1944—Joseph P. Kennedy Jr., the oldest Kennedy son, dies in a plane crash over the English Channel during World War II. The pilot was just twenty-nine at the time of his death.
- 1948—Kathleen Kennedy Cavendish, the Marchioness of Hartington, dies in a plane crash in France at twenty-eight. Her husband, William John Robert Cavendish, the Marquess of Hartington, died in World War II.
- 1963—Patrick Bouvier Kennedy, the second son of President Kennedy and his wife, Jacqueline, dies on August 7, two days after being born almost six weeks premature.
- 1963—President John F. Kennedy is assassinated on November 22 in Dallas, Texas. He was just forty-six.
- 1968—Robert F. Kennedy is assassinated on June 5 in Los Angeles. He had just won California's Democratic presidential primary election. He was forty-two years old.
- 1969—Edward M. Kennedy drives off a bridge on his way home from a party on Massachusetts's Chappaquiddick Island. Mary Jo Kopechne, an aide who was in the car with him, dies in the accident.
- 1973—Alexander Onassis, Jacqueline Kennedy Onassis's stepson following her marriage to Aristotle Onassis, dies in a plane crash in January.
- 1975—Jacqueline Kennedy Onassis's new husband's health begins deteriorating rapidly, and he dies of respiratory failure in Paris, aged sixty-nine.

- 1984—David A. Kennedy, son of Robert, dies of a drug overdose in a hotel in Palm Beach, Florida. He was only twenty-eight.
- 1997—Michael Kennedy, the son of Robert, dies in a skiing accident in Aspen, Colorado. He was thirty-nine. Prior to the accident, Michael made headlines for allegedly having a long-term affair with his children's babysitter.
- 1999—John F. Kennedy Jr., his wife, Carolyn Bessette Kennedy, and his sister-in-law, Lauren Bessette, die when their plane crashes in the waters off Martha's Vineyard, Massachusetts. Kennedy was flying the Piper Saratoga plane, which plunged into the Atlantic Ocean. He was just thirty-eight.
- 2011—Kara Kennedy, the daughter of Senator Ted Kennedy, dies on September 16 of a heart attack. She was fifty-one. She was diagnosed with lung cancer in 2002.
- 2012—Mary Richardson Kennedy, the fifty-two-year-old estranged wife of Robert F. Kennedy Jr., is found dead in the barn of her home in Bedford, New York. She died of an apparent suicide.

Why are the Kennedys cursed? If a curse exists in this family, how did it come? Could it be because of their alleged involvement with the Mafia?

In an article captioned "Was Kennedy Tied to the Mob?" Patrick J. Kiger writes for *National Geographic:*

> Much of the speculation about an illicit working relationship between JFK and the mafia focuses upon Sam Giancana, the former head of the Chicago crime syndicate, who had a number of apparent Venn-diagram intersections with the President. Giancana had longtime ties to the Kennedy clan, going back to JFK's father, Joseph P. Kennedy, who was involved with Giancana in the bootlegging business during Prohibition. Additionally, Giancana was an associate of singer Frank Sinatra, a close Kennedy friend, and allegedly was a donor to JFK's 1960 Presidential campaign, at a time when politicians weren't required to disclose their deep-pockets contributors.
>
> There also have been allegations that Giancana secretly helped JFK win the 1960 West Virginia primary, in which he bested fellow U.S. Sen. Hubert Humphrey, D-Minn. In 2009, Tina Sinatra, daughter of Kennedy friend Frank Sinatra, told the TV program "60 Minutes"

that the legendary singer—at the behest of JFK's father, Joseph P. Kennedy—approached Giancana. Sinatra allegedly asked Giancana to use mob muscle to pressure local union members to vote for JFK. The request was made through an intermediate, Sinatra, because "it would be in Jack Kennedy's best interest if his father did not make the contact directly," Tina Sinatra explained.

In his 1997 book, *The Dark Side of Camelot,* investigative reporter Seymour Hersh alleged that the elder Kennedy eventually did meet with Giancana in Chicago, to solicit his support for JFK in the general election.[10]

If indeed the Kennedys were members of the mob, and we can't say for certain that they were, then they would have taken part in some initiation rituals. And here lies the answer to how the curse may have entered the family.

The initiation ritual used by the mob is said to have emerged from various sources, including the Roman Catholic confraternities and Masonic Lodges in Sicily, Italy, in the mid-nineteenth century. It has hardly changed to this day.

The chief of police of Palermo in 1875 reported that the man of honour to be initiated would be led into the presence of a group of bosses and underbosses of the mob. One of these men would prick the initiate's arm or hand and tell him to smear the blood onto a sacred image, usually of a saint. The oath of loyalty would be taken as the image was burned and scattered, thus symbolising the annihilation of traitors.[11]

These initiation rites involving blood would have established some very robust and tough generational covenants binding every member of the extended Kennedy family. In exchange for the short-term gain of wealth, exemplary public service, and fame, there would be a lifetime of tragedies among different generations of the family, usually up to the fourth generation. This is exactly the pattern we see playing out in the lives of this family.

DISCERNING A CURSE

Curses—whether generational or self-inflicted—are easy to break if you know what to do. The difficulty is in determining whether your problem is the result of a curse. So how do we discern whether or not we're under a curse?

Deuteronomy 28:15–68 and Genesis 3 contain a complete dossier of every type of curse that can befall a human being. It is interesting that the first fourteen verses of Deuteronomy 28 deal with blessings, while the remaining fifty-three verses are devoted to curses. In effect, for every blessing listed in Deuteronomy 28, there are at least three and a half curses!

From these passages, I have put together eleven pointers that are indicative of the presence of a curse. (I've left out plagues and natural disasters, which are more likely to point to a curse on a nation rather than an individual.) While they are not definitive, the more you have of these pointers in your life, the more likely it is that you're under a curse. If you want to be absolutely certain, you will need to ask the Holy Spirit, because he is the expert.

Here's the list:

Phobias. A phobia is a fear that is irrational. In clinical psychology, a phobia is a type of anxiety disorder, usually defined as a persistent fear of an object or situation which the sufferer goes to great lengths to avoid. The fear is typically disproportional to the actual danger posed. In the event the phobia cannot be avoided entirely, the sufferer will endure the situation or object with marked distress and significant interference to social or occupational activities.[12] There are so many phobias that it is impractical to attempt to list them here. However, two interesting phobias are *pantophobia* (the fear of everything) and *panophobia* (a general condition of groundless fear).

Toil. Toil is working like an elephant but eating like an ant. It's painfully labouring without ever being able to get ahead. Man worked hard before the fall, but *toil* came as a result of the fall and the curse on mankind at that time. God told Adam, "Because you listened to your wife and ate fruit from the tree about which I commanded you, 'You must not eat from it,' cursed is the ground because of you; through painful toil you will eat food from it all the days of your life."[13] Although to some extent all people are under this general curse until creation is completely renewed at the second coming of Christ, if you as an individual experience an unusual degree of toil in your life, and you see this pattern throughout your family as well, it may be caused by a curse.

Drug and Alcohol Addiction. Drug and alcohol abuse show no sign of abating around the world. The National Health Service estimates that around 9 percent of men and 4 percent of women in the United Kingdom show signs of alcohol dependence or alcoholism.[14] This means that drinking alcohol has become an important, or sometimes the most important, factor in their lives, and they feel they're unable to function without it. Alcohol dependence can run in families. It shows all the marks of a curse. In general, if parents are dependent on alcohol, their children are four times more likely to develop dependence too.[15]

Mental or Emotional Breakdown. Madness, schizophrenia, manic depression, and emotional breakdown can be forms of demonic oppression. They can also be symptomatic of a curse, especially if widespread within a family. However, like the other pointers in this list, mental or emotional breakdowns are not always indicative of a curse. Pray to discern whether this is a factor in your life.

Disease. This is repeated chronic sickness, especially of a hereditary nature, where the doctors are not sure of the cause. According to the Genetic Disease Foundation, over six thousand genetic disorders can be passed down through the generations, and many of them are fatal or severely debilitating.[16]

Problems with the Reproductive System. This is applicable to both men and women. It includes barrenness, low sperm count, a tendency to miscarry, fibroids, irregular menstruation, and unusually prolonged labour during childbirth. These conditions are not automatically indicative of a curse, but they usually are.

Marriage Breakdown Leading to Family Alienation. This is particularly likely to be a curse where it leads to parental alienation—where the parent with whom the children reside consciously destroys the relationship between the children and the other parent, denying them access to the children.

Continued Financial Lack. We all have periods of lack for all kinds of reasons. Sometimes, God allows us to go through a wilderness experience to humble us and teach us to depend on him.[17] However, what I am talking about here is constant and continuous financial insufficiency and lack, with no end in sight. You can't seem to ever make ends meet. You never have sufficiency for your needs and always live from hand to mouth.

Being Accident Prone. Some people are accidents waiting to happen. A good example is Thomas L. Cook, as reported by the *Denver Post* on 23 September 2006. According to the *Post*, "Cook got off to a poor start in life, and it never got any better." His mother nearly miscarried. As a child, he broke his collarbone, suffered a brain haemorrhage due to a playground accident, and had his spleen removed because of an injury sustained while playing touch football. He then had a go-cart accident while a teenager and a near-fatal car accident before attending university, and while at university, he spent five months in a coma due to another car accident. He broke his back and ribs many times in various car accidents and falls. It was no surprise when he died in a car accident. "Thomas L Cook, who died at 54 when he was fatally hit by a car on 11 September, spent much of his life recovering from the misadventures that plagued him even in the womb."

A Family History of Unnatural Deaths. What do I mean by an unnatural death? Here are some examples:

- Deaths due to violence or the consequences of injuries, including cases of murder, suicide, or accidents.
- Suicide.
- Any sudden death without pre-existing illness, or death that remains unexplained, including sudden infant death syndrome.
- Death due to an act of neglect by any person, including medical staff.

BUT IS THE CURSE GENERATIONAL?

If there is a curse active in your life, it is more likely to be generational in nature if you can answer "yes" to the following questions:

Is this a family-wide problem? Is the problem widespread in your family? For instance, if you're accident prone, are any of your siblings also accident prone? If you're an alcoholic or gambler, do you have other family members with the same problem?

Did you hate these things in Dad? Are there things you noticed in your parents as a child and hated but are now carrying out yourself and over which you seem to have little or no control? Things like gambling, alcoholism, substance abuse, child abuse, spouse abuse.

Like parents, like you? Are you facing the exact same problems and challenges your parents and grandparents faced? For instance, perhaps your father had an extramarital affair, and although you love your spouse, there's something pulling you toward cheating on her, and you know it's only a matter of time before you start an affair too. Perhaps your mother was an alcoholic, and you've become one too.

If you're under a curse, you will need to take appropriate action to be released from the curse and transition into the blessing. Chapter 12, on "Breaking the Curse and Activating the Blessing," offers practical guidance, including prayers. But first, we're going to look in more depth at the spiritual curses and chains that may be active in our lives, how they may have gotten here, and how we can discern their presence.

Galatians tells us that it is for freedom that Christ has set us free.[18] When we pursue freedom and refuse to go back into slavery to sin, we bring the victory of Christ into reality in this sinful world in which we live.

Chapter 6:

FAMILY LAWS AND EVIL PATTERNS

> "Our ancestors sinned, but they have died—and we are suffering the punishment they deserved!"
>
> **Lamentations 5:7, NLT**

Dr Gustavo Nascimento had three ambitions in life—money, money, and more money! He dreamt of the difference untold riches would make to his life. He spent his waking moments planning how he would spend his millions. He worked very hard and did everything he possibly could to become a millionaire at the age of twenty-five, but to no avail. At age fifty-six, he was no closer to his goal. A senior lecturer at the University in São Paulo, Brazil, he was tired of earning only a decent wage and struggling to make ends meet for his wife, six children, and his elderly parents, who had become dependent on him. The oil consultancy firm he ran on the side was struggling. He wanted more.

As a last resort, he paid a visit to an old school friend, Fernando Rodríguez, a former professor of electronics engineering, who was now a very wealthy businessman.

"Drink?" Rodríguez offered as he ushered Nascimento into his lavish drawing room.

"Yes, please!" Nascimento said as he sank into the sofa. "I would love a large dirty vodka martini—with a slice of lemon peel. And since I am not James Bond, can it be stirred, not shaken, please?"

"I think I need a drink myself," Rodríguez said as he returned with two vodka dry martinis.

"Tell me," Nascimento said, almost whispering. "What is the secret to your millions?"

To his surprise, rather than recommending a particular investment or business secret, Professor Rodríguez told him he needed to meet a man who could change his destiny forever.

"Really?" Nascimento asked in disbelief. "You're not drunk, are you?"

"I couldn't be more sober," Rodríguez responded. "We go back a long way, you and I. And I really want to help you!"

Nascimento became all ears as Rodríguez told him about Marcelo, a powerful oracle and priest of the Candomble religious cult, who had a shrine in the rainforest near one of the national parks on the outskirts of São Paulo. He was so powerful that he could give Nascimento whatever he wanted in life, from riches to long life, children, and political power and fame—as long as he was prepared to pay the price.

"I am desperate. I really am," Nascimento said. "I'm ready to do anything, pay any price. I just want to become rich."

Rodríguez agreed to introduce Nascimento to the oracle.

Marcelo was a burly old man, about five feet one, with bloodshot eyes. He was probably in his early seventies. He received Nascimento with a firm handshake and a warm greeting. After the initial pleasantries, Marcelo took a diviner's fee. He then brought out his cowries, threw them on the floor, and consulted his deity.

"You can have anything you want!" Marcelo told Nascimento. "Political power, more money than you could ever spend in your lifetime, fame, children, long life, anything else you can think of—as long as you can satisfy the requirements of the deity. But you have to think very carefully." Marcelo pointed his index finger at Nascimento. "If you agree to go ahead, you will have seven days to return with all the requirements. Just seven days! And if you fail to do so, you will either lose your mind and develop paranoid schizophrenia, or you will die unexpectedly."

"I don't care about power, fame, or longevity," Nascimento told Marcelo. "All I want is stupendous wealth."

Marcelo's eyes glinted. "My deity can make you rich beyond your wildest dreams," he said. "All you need to do is bring me the following items for the ritual."

Counting on his fingers, he ticked off the requirements one by one:

- A freshly decapitated human head.
- One pint of fresh human blood.
- The pubic hair of a lunatic, along with clippings of her fingernails and toenails.
- US$20 as a down payment. The fee would be US$3 billion, with the balance to be paid by his descendants and anybody who benefited from his riches in instalments over their lifetime.

Marcelo said that as part of the ritual, Nascimento would also be required to make a blood covenant with the deity and the altar. The conditions of the covenant would be as follows:

- His first son would die prematurely within thirteen weeks of the ritual.
- All his male descendants to the fourth generation must sleep with a lunatic in a cemetery before their thirtieth birthday or they would go mad when they reached the age of forty.
- All his female descendants to the fourth generation would be married to the deity and the altar. They are therefore forbidden to marry in this world. Any attempted marriage would end up in divorce within thirteen months.
- All his descendants to the fourth generation and anybody who benefited from his riches would be covenanted to repay the US$3 billion in instalments over their lifetime. They would never be able to save as long as the debt remained outstanding.

Nascimento was so desperate to become a millionaire that he told Marcelo he was ready to pay the price and do whatever the deity wanted. He immediately went to work and returned to the shrine five days later with everything the deity had requested. He provided the human head, one pint of human blood, pubic hair, and the finger and toenail clippings of a madwoman.

Finally, he handed over US$20 in cash. In doing so, he mortgaged his descendants and everyone who would benefit from his riches to the deity. He signed, sealed, and delivered a blood covenant with the devil, which he then bequeathed as an ancestral covenant with devastating consequences to his children and their children after them to the fourth generation.

Shortly afterward, his oil services consultancy firm, which had been tottering on the brink of insolvency, took a multimillion-dollar contract with a leading member country of the Organization of the Petroleum Exporting Countries (OPEC). That was his breakthrough. Nascimento became so wealthy it was unreal. Whatever he touched seemed to immediately turn to gold. But his triumph was bittersweet, because soon after acquiring his newfound wealth, he was heartbroken when his first son, Joao, died mysteriously.

Meanwhile, Nascimento continued to attract money. He had so much money he didn't know what to do with it. He built houses all around the country and bought mansions in London's Mayfair, the south of France, and the Upper East Side of New York City. Each of his mansions had an underground car park with an array of luxury cars. Every mansion had a Bentley or a Rolls Royce. He started hobnobbing with the political elite. He became a philanthropist, donating a huge part of his fortune to good causes. Not long after, he was awarded one of Brazil's national honorific orders for philanthropy in recognition of his generous donations to good causes.

Years later, Carolina is a brilliant young lawyer working in the legal department of a multinational oil company. She holds a first-class honours law degree from an Ivy League university in the United States and was head-hunted by her employers in her final year at university.

By all appearances, Carolina is different from others only in her unusual talent and drive. But there's something about her that is distinctly —and dangerously—different. She is Nascimento's granddaughter.

Carolina didn't really know her grandfather, as he died when she was a toddler. She is told Grandpa Nascimento was debonair, handsome, and stinking rich. But she's puzzled by a few things. How come there's no trace of Grandpa's riches now if he was so stupendously wealthy? Why didn't they pass down to her parents and other relatives? And why have so many tragedies befallen the family since he died twenty years ago?

Abject poverty, mysterious and untimely deaths, divorces, and mental illness have become the order of the day in the family. Her dad was a medical practitioner with a thriving medical practice in an exclusive private hospital in Brasilia until he suddenly developed a severe mental disorder. Now the hospital lies in ruins, and her dad is held under the mental health law at a high-security psychiatric hospital. Most of the patients have mental disorders. About a quarter of them have personality disorders and are considered to require high security because of their dangerous, violent, or criminal propensities.

Carolina's three uncles have followed a similar path, all going insane before the age of forty. Her aunties, Jennifer and Suzany, haven't fared any better. Jennifer has been married four times, and each marriage ended in divorce within thirteen months of the wedding. Suzany recently got divorced exactly a year after her fabulous society wedding.

Carolina's employment is a dream job with a fantastic pay package. Yet she is unable to save, no matter how hard she tries. In fact, she can't even make ends meet. She is never able to stick to a budget. There's always an unforeseen expense. She lives from hand to mouth. Most months, she relies on her overdraft facility to carry her through to payday. Her brothers, sisters, and cousins aren't doing much better.

Carolina recently became a Christian and is seeking answers. She is wondering why it seems there's an evil pattern running through her family. In desperation, she went to her pastor for deliverance. To get to the bottom of the problem, she was advised to research her family history. That's how she found out what Grandpa Nascimento did to acquire his vast wealth. Her pastor explained that although her grandfather may not have left any of his vast wealth to his family, he bequeathed a satanic ancestral covenant to future generations of his family!

THE REALITY OF SATANIC COVENANTS

While the story above is fictional, its gruesome details are not. Covenants with the devil and demonic agents involving animal and human body parts are real, and they happen all the time. These covenants don't just take place in Africa and Central and South America, but also in Europe and North America.

In 2001, the headless torso of a little boy, believed to be the victim of ritual sacrifice, was found in the River Thames in London. The boy's head, arms, and legs had been severed with skilful precision, while his lower intestine contained a highly unusual mix of plant extracts, traces of the toxic Calabar bean, and clay particles containing flecks of pure gold. The police named the boy Adam.

Following her investigation into the case, news reporter Ronke Philips confirmed what most people thought in her article titled, "Voodoo and human sacrifice: The haunting story of how Adam, the Torso in the Thames boy, was finally identified":

> Dr Richard Hoskins, a leading expert on African religion then based at Bath University, came in on the case. He said that the Calabar bean was commonly used by African witch doctors for voodoo. It was exceptionally rare to see the bean used in Britain, but its presence in Adam's gut—along with that of the other ingredients found there—convinced him this was something utterly horrific: a human sacrifice.
>
> "Adam's body would have been drained of blood, as an offering to whatever god his murderer believed in," said Dr Hoskins. "The gold flecks in his intestine were used to make the sacrifice more appealing to that god."[1]

Not too long ago, a Brazilian witch doctor claimed that Lord Mandelson, the former British cabinet minister, held a chicken while he cut off its head as a sacrifice to the god of the Candomble religious cult. According to reports,[2] shortly after Peter Mandelson lost his job as British trade and industry secretary in December 1998, the voodoo practitioner was asked by Mandelson's Brazilian boyfriend, Reinaldo Avila da Silva, to put a hex on the politician's enemies in a ceremony that involved the slaughter of a chicken. It is said among other things that the priest was asked do something to make Charlie Whelan, "who is always trying to harm Peter," disappear from politics. The magic man was reportedly sent a photograph of Mr Whelan, and Mr Mandelson was restored to the cabinet in October 1999 as secretary of state for Northern Ireland.

While such sacrifices are horrible in their own right, they also have deep spiritual significance because blood sacrifices bring terrible consequences. Jesus paid the ultimate sacrifice when he died and rose again. By his death, he perfects those who are sanctified. Anybody who now offers a blood sacrifice of any kind is therefore raising a shrine to the devil and inviting calamity to his household.

However, many people do not know this. Faced with challenges and difficulties which they find overwhelming and unable to solve, they seek help from strange places, including the supernatural. Sometimes, their quest leads them to satanic shrines and demonic altars.[3] At these altars, they are manipulated into entering agreements, and ancestral covenants binding their descendants are established. These people are given short-term solutions in exchange for generational problems.

Unfortunately, in this day and age, people are still binding their future generations to the devil in return for temporary enjoyment! In 2014, Italian anti-Mafia police released unprecedented footage of an initiation ritual secretly filmed as part of an inquiry into the deadly southern Italian Mafia known as 'Ndrangheta.[4] Filmed from a distance by a hidden police camera, the pictures show for the first time an initiation ceremony into the group. As part of the ceremony, the new members are asked to swear to their *family's seventh generation* to protect the honour of their wise brothers! Such a covenant will be passed on to their descendants up to the seventh generation. The devil is no longer just limiting his atrocities to the fourth generation!

Because the devil is able to disguise himself as an angel of light,[5] many people are easily deceived. That's why people sometimes go to the devil for help without realising he is the devil. Usually, the devil can't quite believe his luck: a potential target coming under his roof to seek help without realising that he is their sworn enemy! Of course, the enemy pretends to help, even providing short-term solutions. But often in ways unforeseen by the victims, those short-term solutions come at the price of long-term problems.

The magi or band of scholars who visited Jesus from the East shortly after his birth, during Herod's kingship, provide us with a perfect example of this. The story is beautifully captured by *The Message*:

> They asked around, "Where can we find and pay homage to the newborn King of the Jews? We observed a star in the eastern sky that signaled his birth. We're on pilgrimage to worship him." When word of their inquiry got to Herod, he was terrified—and not Herod alone, but most of Jerusalem as well. Herod lost no time. He gathered all the high priests and religion scholars in the city together and asked, "Where is the Messiah supposed to be born?"
>
> They told him, "Bethlehem, Judah territory. The prophet Micah wrote it plainly: It's you, Bethlehem, in Judah's land, no longer bringing up the rear. From you will come the leader who will shepherd-rule

> my people, my Israel." Herod then arranged a secret meeting with the scholars from the East. Pretending to be as devout as they were, he got them to tell him exactly when the birth-announcement star appeared. Then he told them the prophecy about Bethlehem, and said, "Go find this child. Leave no stone unturned. As soon as you find him, send word and I'll join you at once in your worship."
>
> Instructed by the king, they set off. Then the star appeared again, the same star they had seen in the eastern skies. It led them on until it hovered over the place of the child. They could hardly contain themselves: They were in the right place! They had arrived at the right time! They entered the house and saw the child in the arms of Mary, his mother. Overcome, they kneeled and worshiped him. Then they opened their luggage and presented gifts: gold, frankincense, myrrh.
>
> In a dream, they were warned not to report back to Herod. So they worked out another route, left the territory without being seen, and returned to their own country.[6]

The magi started out in the Spirit, being led by God through a star all the way from the East. However, on the way, they lost contact with God. For whatever reason, they couldn't see the star, and they panicked. They failed to hold on to God and believe that he wouldn't have led them so far only to abandon them. In their anxiety, they decided to try a bit of self-help. They started asking around for assistance, only to end up seeking help from Herod, their enemy—and worse, the enemy of the infant Jesus. They might as well have gone directly to the devil for help! If God hadn't intervened, Herod would have killed Jesus.

When he realised that the scholars had tricked him, Herod burned with fury. He decided to kill Jesus, commanding the murder of every little boy two years old and under who lived in Bethlehem and its surrounding villages. But Jesus was not harmed, because an angel had instructed Joseph to take him and Mary by night into Egypt for safety.[7]

Not every person who seeks help from the devil is manipulated, however. There are those like Dr Nascimento who know exactly what they are doing when they seek help from satanic agents. These people knowingly and willingly consult shrines and demonic altars, knowing what they are getting into but not really worrying about the consequences. Some do it for political power; others for career progression, fame, or wealth. Then there are those who dabble in the occult, either out of curiosity or due to peer pressure, without any real understanding of what they are getting into. They go through the rituals of initiation only to discover that the deeper they go, the more diabolical and Mephistophelian it becomes. Doorways into the occult include the Freemasons and Masonic Lodges, the mob, and various fraternities, sororities, and similar secret societies.

Whether a person consults satanic agents knowingly or out of ignorance, however, the outcome is the same: covenants with consequences that span generations are created. Once established, these covenants become laws that control the life of the person who entered them. At the time of death, the victim then bequeaths these laws as an inheritance to his or her descendants. This manifests as an evil pattern in the family. This is a means of control by the devil. Ancestral covenants and evil family patterns give the devil a stake in the family of the person making the covenant. The devil becomes a stakeholder with an open invitation, and he is able to come and go, with his legion of demons, at will.

One way the devil stakes his claim in a family is through dreams. Dreams are a series of vivid images occurring in a person's mind during sleep. They are a means by which God communicated and sometimes still communicates with man. Being the impersonator that he is, the devil also communicates through dreams. The devil exerts his rights, often flexing his muscle through terror in the form of nightmares, where members of the family are pursued by snakes, dogs, tigers, wolves, or monsters of some kind.

SUPERNATURAL LAWS IN CITIES

Although readers may be tempted to doubt, spiritual forces are real and have a real impact on cities, families, and individuals. Sometimes, this happens through the instrumentality of law.

All of us are governed by laws. For the purposes of this book, we can define *law* as a system of rules and guidelines that are enforced through social institutions to govern behaviour. An example of an international law is the Universal Declaration of Human Rights. An example of a national law is the Constitution of the United States. Laws can be both written and unwritten. The United States has a written Constitution.

The United Kingdom has an unwritten Constitution. However, they are both equally valid! Laws regulate various professions. Doctors, attorneys, accountants, teachers, and nurses are subject to their rules of professional conduct and can be struck off their professional registers if they violate these rules.

But it's important to understand that laws are limited in their jurisdiction. A teacher in the United States cannot be disciplined by the National Council of State Boards of Nursing because he is not subject to their laws. Nor can a doctor in England be struck off by the Solicitors Disciplinary Tribunal, because he is not a solicitor. In like manner, there are laws regulating various nations, cities, families, clubs, and individuals.

Many of the laws governing our lives are supernatural—they are spiritual and unwritten. For instance, there are villages, towns, and cities around the world where nobody has ever amounted to anything in life. There is a kind of unwritten law that people from that neck of the woods generally don't do well. Anybody who attempts to break the mould loses everything, and if he persists, he dies an untimely death! On the other hand, there are cities and even countries known for positive traits.

Let's look at the city of Recife in Brazil. Recife is one of the major cities of Brazil's tropical northeast, an old city originally built by Dutch sugar planters on the easternmost bulge of South America—the part that fits like a puzzle piece into West Africa's nook. Since the 2001 Asian tsunami, Recife has become the new "Sex Capital" of the world. UNICEF estimates that there are around 250,000 children involved in the sex industry in Brazil, and a lot of them are based around Recife.[8] How could the situation in Recife have become so bad? Is it pure economics, or is there a spiritual component—a supernatural law at work? Specifically, could the situation in Recife have anything to do with Carnival?

Carnival in Recife—and its colonial sister city Olinda—is a celebration in the streets. There are no roped-off areas or expensive tickets, just mass human chaos, with millions of people getting freaky together in the sunshine. Old and young, rich and poor, hippie and playboy, black and white all mix and mingle in the cobblestone streets—drinking beer by the gallon, making out with complete strangers, and dancing until their Havaianas fall off.[9] Sexual immorality is rife on the streets of the city during the Carnival celebrations. Because the festival receives official approval and support from the mayor of Recife, it functions as an official sanction of promiscuity, which in turn has opened the city of Recife to the spirits of lust, promiscuity, prostitution, and sexual perversion.

Or what of New Orleans, Louisiana, which was battered by Hurricane Katrina in 2005? Hurricane Katrina was the deadliest and most destructive Atlantic tropical cyclone of the 2005 hurricane season. It was the costliest natural disaster in the history of the United States as well as one of the five deadliest hurricanes in that nation's past. In fact, Katrina was the seventh most intense Atlantic hurricane ever recorded. At least 1,833 people died in the hurricane and subsequent floods. Total property damage was estimated at US$108 billion, roughly four times the damage brought by Hurricane Andrew in 1992.

The most significant number of deaths caused by the hurricane occurred in New Orleans, which flooded as the levee system catastrophically failed; in many cases hours after the storm had moved inland. Eventually, 80 percent of the city and large tracts of neighbouring parishes became flooded, and the floodwaters lingered for weeks.

Could this have anything to do with a satanic ritual which took place in New Orleans on Wednesday, 16 August 1995, exactly ten years and *thirteen* days before Katrina? I believe so. It was certainly a noteworthy ceremony, significant enough to be reported by the *New York Times*. The ceremony arose from the frustration of the residents living in Bywater, a racially and economically diverse neighbourhood on the edge of the French Quarter, who said the New Orleans Police Department was ineffective in dealing with the brazen drug traffic, burglaries, prostitution, robberies, and assaults plaguing the area. Since the police couldn't help, they decided to appeal to the old spirits who once ruled New Orleans for assistance.

Described as "a New Orleans variety of a community watch" and "a public prayer," the ritual was conducted by Sallie Ann Glassman, a voodoo priestess who invoked Ogoun, said to be the baddest spirit in the voodoo otherworld, to frighten the criminals into stopping their evil activities. It was attended by one hundred people, including the New Orleans police (who showed up late). I believe the presence of the police validated the event, unwittingly making it an official ceremony of the government of the city of New Orleans.

According to the *Times*:

The voodoo priestess used a mix of gunpowder and old graveyard dirt to draw a magic symbol on a crossroads in the Bywater neighborhood, opening a spiritual door through which a fearsome deity could pass and save her community from the evil of crack cocaine.

For two hours... as drums pounded along Piety Street and orange flames of fire-eaters and torch carriers danced in the dark, the white-gowned priestess, Sallie Ann Glassman, enticed Ogoun La Flambeau, a voodoo god of war and fire, to prowl among the rows of shotgun houses and punish the dope peddlers and other criminals.

She offered rum, cigars, incense and music, and called out to him in French, respectfully but firmly, since it is unwise to appear weak-willed in the presence of spirits.

Once [someone] uncorks the stopper on the spirit world, they are at the mercy of the god they summon, she said. "You can always regret something that you set in motion," she said. "This is a little precarious, like setting off an atom bomb. You hope Ogoun will play fair. But who knows what his morals are."[10]

There is no doubt that this ritual opened up New Orleans to satanic influences in the years leading up to the deadly hurricane. Ms Glassman summed it up graphically when she said the ritual was dangerous and could open up the city to the devil, with an effect as devastating as setting off an atomic bomb! No wonder Hurricane Katrina was so deadly!

Now to Benin City, a city in Midwestern Nigeria, with streets of red dust and low houses.[11] For some reason, human trafficking from Nigeria is strongly concentrated from Benin City. According to the United Nations Interregional Crime and Justice Research Institute (UNICRI), Italy is now the main destination for more than ten thousand Nigerian prostitutes, the majority of them trafficked from Benin City to European cities and criminal hubs.[12] A survey by the Women's Health and Action Research Centre in Benin City some years ago showed that one in three young women in the city had received offers to go to Europe.[13] While most are trafficked, some travel abroad of their own volition to work as prostitutes.

Why girls from Benin? It's not poverty or deprivation causing this imbalance, because many other communities in Nigeria and the Third World are blighted by economic deprivation, yet their young women are not readily and easily trafficked for sexual exploitation. Could there be a supernatural law at work? Specifically, could this have anything to do with Benin's bloody past?

As long ago as 1897, R.H. Bacon, commander of the British Punitive Expedition, said of Benin City, "Crucifixions, human sacrifices, and every horror the eye could get accustomed to, to a large extent, but the smells no white man's internal economy could stand . . . Blood was everywhere; smeared over bronzes, ivory, and even the walls."[14]

Not much has changed in today's Benin City, as ritual sacrifices with human body parts are still commonplace. It's very common to see blood sacrifices at road junctions, especially at points where three roads meet.

The death of a monarch in Benin and the installation of the crown prince as the new king are usually marked with a lot of rituals. Joseph Nevadomsky reported on the rituals of kingship following the death of Oba Akenzua II in 1978. According to Nevadomsky, following the formal announcement of the king's death, all males in the city were required to shave their heads to mourn the dead king. He continues:

> On the seventh day, priests anointed the prince's head with the blood of sacrificial animals...Sometime later, the heir apparent "planted a shrine" to his father's memory that would be watered with the blood of sacrificial animals...During the burial rites, the palace banned cooking in the city and pregnant women left town...In contrast to the joyous rites of installation as crown prince, the [burial rites] generated anxiety, panic and fear...*Stories abounded about human sacrifice*. The forcible head-shaving of non-Edos brought army units from Lagos. Markets and buildings mysteriously burned.[15] (emphasis mine)

Nevadomsky said the new king reactivated more shrines. "Under the present Oba, royal ceremony has reacquired some of its public potency and magnificence. The rituals of kingship during the latter part of Oba Akenzua II's reign had diminished and some had lapsed altogether. Erediauwa has rallied his people by revitalizing archaic kingship rituals and reactivating the city's major shrines."[16]

SUPERNATURAL LAWS IN FAMILIES

Like the laws that affect cities or nations, the laws regulating families may be written or unwritten. Unlike laws affecting cities, they usually apply only to members of a particular family, not the general public. If a member of the family steps out of line, he becomes a lawful captive and is made to suffer the consequences of breaking the law. A lawful captive is someone whose freedom has been restricted according to law. Here are some examples of supernatural family laws and regulations:

- Nobody is allowed to marry—the consequence is divorce. All the marriages in these families end up in divorce.
- Nobody is allowed to have children or have more than a certain number of children—there is usually a history of miscarriages or child deaths.
- Nobody is allowed to travel abroad—they never do well in a foreign country.
- Nobody is allowed to live beyond a certain age—they all die by a certain age.
- Nobody is allowed to do well—their progress in life is always up and down. Nobody in the family makes consistent progress.
- Sickness and disease will be rampant—every member of the family has diabetes and heart disease, every female member has breast cancer, every male has prostate cancer, etc.
- Nobody is allowed to eat certain foods (e.g., nuts). If you do, you have a severe allergic reaction.
- Every male becomes an alcoholic.
- Every male is a wife beater.
- Every male ends up in prison.
- The females cannot get married before a certain age.
- The men don't get married.
- All the females have bisexual relationships.
- Nobody is able to complete a project. Everyone abandons their projects halfway.

Often, family laws develop into patterns, which in turn become moulds into which the future generation of each family is born. The patterns can be good or evil.

As stated in the preface, when a child is born into this world, he or she is loaded with everything necessary to succeed in life and every resource he or she needs to make the world a better place. But that's not all that comes with birth. The truth is, nobody is born without a family. Regardless of how gifted we are at birth, the family shapes us into what we eventually become. The family turns into a mould, in the sense of a rigid frame or matrix used for shaping fluid or plastic, while the newborn baby is the malleable substance poured into it. Naturally, the new life hardens and sets inside the family mould, adopting its shape. If the family mould is negative or includes curses and covenants with evil, the child's life will fit into those things—sometimes even negating the gifts given by God at birth.

At the new birth, you are poured into a new mould—the family of God. But that doesn't mean the devil won't try to assert his old claims. Part of your warfare is getting free from those old chains and curses so that you can live fully in your new identity in Christ.

DISCERNING A COVENANT

Life is full of challenges, and we all have our fair share of them, whether we admit it or not. You may not believe it, but even Her Majesty the Queen of England has her share of problems, even if they're different from the type you're used to! It is in the nature of life that we all have difficulties. So how do you determine whether or not your problems are the result of an ancestral covenant? Here are some clues to help you. Ask yourself whether the following pointers exist in your life and family:

Recurrent Financial Problems. Do you and all your siblings have serious recurrent financial problems? Is it the case that when money comes into your hands, you don't receive any more until what you've received is spent?

Family Taboos. Do you have family taboos? Foods you can't eat, places you can't visit, or investments you can't undertake?

Satanic Contamination. Did either of your parents or grandparents have any form of satanic contamination in their lives?

Similar Problems in the Past. Is the problem you're facing generational in nature? In other words, did your parents or grandparents have similar problems?

Any Other Family Affected. Is the problem affecting anybody else in your family, or is it restricted to you? Are your brothers, sisters, or cousins going through similar problems?

Recurrent Problem and/or Timing. Is the problem recurrent in nature? It is in the nature of generational curses and ancestral covenants that you will experience the same or similar kinds of problems at particular times, seasons, or periods during the course of the year.

Nightmares. Do you constantly have nightmares where you're pursued by animals like dogs, bears, or tigers? Do you dream and see yourself either in prison or held against your will? Do you eat in your dreams? Any of these dreams might indicate demonic influence. As we stated earlier, an ancestral covenant gives the devil a stake. And he will often stake a claim to his entitlement through dreams.

If you can answer yes to majority of these questions, it is likely that what you're going through is the result of an ancestral covenant and the supernatural laws it has brought into effect in your life. In that case, you need to be made free. You need deliverance. Of course, we can't be 100 percent certain. Only the Holy Spirit can provide precise discernment. However, even if you're not completely sure, going through deliverance will rule out ancestral covenants as the source of your problems.

Sometimes deliverance happens instantly; at other times it's a process. While the Bible tells us to resist the devil and he will flee from us,[17] we are not told *when* he will flee. He will flee from you, but it may not happen immediately. So you need to resist and keep on resisting him until he flees. The blood of Jesus can make you completely free. And living completely free has got to be one of the primary objectives of spiritual warfare!

You will find practical guidance for undergoing deliverance, including prayers, in Chapter 12, "Breaking the Curse and Activating the Blessing."

Chapter 7:

UNDERSTANDING THE ALTAR

"A family altar can alter the family."

Anonymous

Aisha was born into a Muslim family. The fourth of ten children, she was witty, amiable, and very intelligent. Her father, Hajji Mohamed bin Zaid, was extremely wealthy and one of the most powerful men in the United Arab Emirates. Aisha's mother was the first of his four wives. He married her when he was so poor he could barely rub two pennies together. The birth of Aisha coincided with Mohamed bin Zaid's financial breakthrough and his rise in social standing in the Emirates. Not surprisingly, he lavished Aisha with everything money could buy.

Growing up, Aisha enjoyed the finest things in life. She lived in stately homes and had servants at her beck and call. She wore designer clothing and expensive jewellery and travelled first class around the world. She was privately educated in Europe's most exclusive boarding schools. After her university education at a top Russell Group university in Britain, she joined the family business. However, she had become a Scientologist while at university.

Hajji Mohamed wasn't too worried about Aisha's conversion to Scientology because he had betrothed her to Sheikh Abdullah bin Khalid, the crown prince, when she was a baby. In his thinking, once married to the prince, Aisha would end up recanting Scientology and returning to Islam.

Unknown to him, Aisha wasn't really serious about her new religion. She would have given up her faith had he put any pressure on her.

Marriage, however, was an altogether different proposition. She could bet the sheikh would have more than one wife, and although she'd grown up Muslim, she abhorred polygamy and couldn't imagine sharing her husband with up to three other women. On top of that, she wasn't prepared to marry somebody she barely knew, and certainly not Sheikh Abdullah, who although the most eligible bachelor in the Emirates was a well-known playboy.

Aisha decided to marry John, a young man she had met at university, who also happened to be a Scientologist. To her father, her conversion to Scientology was infuriating enough—what would the imam and the rest of the Muslim community think of him? But for Aisha to refuse to marry the prince and choose to marry an *infidel* instead! That was the height of insolence. What would he tell HRH the Emir, whose benevolence had contributed to his enormous wealth? No, this would only happen over his dead body!

When she insisted on marrying her Scientologist boyfriend, Aisha was kicked out of the family business and evicted from her palatial home. Her father then disowned her and took steps to disinherit her.

Notwithstanding everything her family did, Aisha pressed ahead with her decision to marry John. They eloped to Europe, got married, and started a family, eventually having four children—three boys and a girl. The children were beautiful and brilliant, but very sickly. The marriage was at best tempestuous. At worst, it felt like life imprisonment with hard labour! They came close to separating many times. However, they remained married because they didn't want to give Aisha's father the pleasure of seeing the marriage breakup.

Shortly after their marriage, Aisha and John set up a business. They approached a popular and well-known multinational fast-food chain to explore the possibility of joining the franchise and setting up a restaurant under their brand. The franchise business started out very well. However, for some reason they couldn't explain, both the business and their finances became highly seasonal from the second year. During the spring and summer months, their business and investments would do exceptionally well. However, during the autumn and winter months when trees shed their leaves, their business and investments would lose so much money that they would nearly go bankrupt! This happened every year without fail.

Unbeknownst to Aisha and her husband, her father had not stopped at disowning and disinheriting her. Hajji Mohamed bin Zaid was so hurt by his daughter, he felt the only way to remove the opprobrium she had brought on the family was to destroy her. To him, this was a kind of honour killing. She had brought dishonour to the family. She didn't deserve to live. He had no choice.

He went to see a well-known witch doctor. The punishment he wanted for Aisha was as follows:

- To impose financial hardship on her
- To make her marriage turbulent
- To make her a widow at the age of forty
- To make all her children from her marriage to John die in their early teenage years
- To make her die by the age of fifty

The oracle, a notorious and fearsome marabout, asked Hajji Mohamed bin Zaid to provide an unblemished ram, cowries, a full set of lion's teeth, US$1000, and a pair of Aisha's underwear to enable him to raise an altar to the deity Ṣàngó, the god of fire, lightning, and thunder. Using the ram's blood, the oracle tied Aisha's and her husband's destiny to the four seasons, pronounced a death sentence on John and their four children to be executed before Aisha turned forty, cast a spell of turbulence on their marriage, and pronounced a death sentence on Aisha to be executed by the time she turned fifty![1]

About fourteen years into the marriage, and shortly before her fortieth birthday, Aisha attended a three-day healing and deliverance conference at the invitation of her neighbour, a born-again Christian. The guest preacher was a seasoned Nigerian deliverance minister. On the second day, the pastor gave a word of knowledge[2] about somebody whose life was being controlled by an evil altar. He said their marriage was turbulent and their finances seasonal. Worst of all, a death sentence was hanging over their family.

THE SPIRITUAL POWER AND PRESENCE OF ALTARS

Since the fall in the Garden of Eden, God has never allowed man to approach him without a blood sacrifice. In the process of time, the people of God built altars of stone upon which they offered sacrifices to God. The first recorded altar in the Bible was built to God after the flood by Noah.[3] From that time, whenever people drew near to God, whether to offer praise or to seek forgiveness and mercy, they built an altar and offered a sacrifice of blood.

Today, you can find altars in places of worship like churches, mosques, temples, and shrines. An altar can be built or raised practically anywhere—on a tree, on an island, in a house, at a road junction, in a river, on a mountain, or even physically in a human being.

Fundamentally, altars are places where sacrifices are made. They are sacred places where spirits congregate because the sacrifices they carry invoke the presence of spirits. For God's people in the Old Testament, altars were places where sacrifice was carried out, where atonement for sin was made, where the people had communion and fellowship with God, and where covenants were established. Shortly into his covenant relationship with the people of Israel, God restricted them to approaching him *only* through the altar in the temple in Jerusalem. This pointed to the future exclusivity of Jesus Christ, who said that "No one comes to the Father except through me."[4]

The entire focus of sacrifices and altars in the Old Testament was to point to the need for a perfect sacrifice, namely Jesus Christ. Jesus paid the ultimate sacrifice when he died and rose again. By his death, he perfects once and for all those who are sanctified.[5] Though churches today often have symbolic altars at the front of the auditorium near the pulpit, this is not really necessary, as Jesus himself has become our sacrifice at the heavenly altar!

> And every priest stands ministering daily and offering repeatedly the same sacrifices, which can never take away sins. But this Man, after He had offered one sacrifice for sins forever, sat down at the right hand of God, from that time waiting till His enemies are made His footstool.[6]

> We have an altar from which those who serve the tabernacle have no right to eat.[7]

Fact: the devil is a copycat. He apes, impersonates, and copies whatever he sees God do. Because of this, the devil also has altars. Satanic altars exist both in the physical and spiritual realms.

Satanic altars are places where people exercise influence, dominion, and control over their enemies. They are meeting places where human beings meet with, commune with, and have fellowship with the devil and his demon spirits, and where spiritual things are exchanged for physical things, such as blood, money, or cowries. They are places where spiritual marriages are conducted, where people make satanic covenants and seal spiritual contracts. These altars are satanic dining tables where evil spirits and demons are served food by fetish priests. The evil spirits can be served their usual or desired food to attract their "blessings"[8] upon the person offering the sacrifice, or they can be given the wrong type of food in order to entice the spirit to afflict the supplicant's enemies.

At these evil altars, ancestral covenants are established, people's destinies are changed, and generational curses are pronounced. Sacrifices are offered to Satan and his demons to appease them, seek their assistance, or thank them for their assistance. There is a sense in which satanic altars represent a seat of power—places where peoples' destinies are deliberated upon and decisions are made about their future. They are marketplaces where people buy and sell. People, programmes, and events are monitored and controlled at these altars. There are people who are monitored and whose lives are influenced and manipulated by satanic agents based on altars—people like Aisha and her family.

By his death and resurrection, Christ fulfilled all requirements for sacrifice, and in so doing, abolished any need for the sacrificial altar. Never again will any type of blood sacrifice be needed in order for us to commune with God, as Christ's perfect and completely sufficient act is all that will ever be needed. Anybody who now offers a blood sacrifice *of any kind* is, therefore, raising an altar to the devil. Simple as that!

People raise evil altars in various ways. As we have seen, one way is by making blood sacrifices. Why is blood so important? The Bible tells us that in a sense, blood never dies, because the life of every creature is in its blood.[9] The life in the blood gives it a voice, and so blood speaks. For instance, the Bible says the sprinkled blood of Jesus speaks a better word than the blood of Abel.[10] When blood is placed or sprinkled on a satanic altar; the blood empowers the altar and gives the altar a voice. How does this come about? Again, the devil, who has no original ideas, is copying from God's institution of the Day of Atonement[11] and perverting it.

Dr Charles L. Feinberg, the late professor of Semitics and Old Testament at Biola University and an authority on Jewish history, languages, customs of the Old Testament and biblical prophecies, explains the ritual as follows:

> Only one person ministered in the priestly office on the Day of Atonement, Aaron himself. Bathed and properly attired (v. 4), he took the designated offerings. "And he shall take of the congregation of the children of Israel two he-goats for a sin-offering, and one ram for a burnt-offering. And Aaron shall present the bullock of the sin-offering, which is for himself, and for his house. And he shall take the two goats, and set them before Jehovah at the door of the tent of meeting. And Aaron shall cast lots upon the two goats; one lot for Jehovah, and the other lot for Azazel. And Aaron shall present the goat upon which the lot fell for Jehovah, and offer him for a sin-offering. But the goat, on which the lot fell for Azazel, shall he set alive before Jehovah, to make atonement for him, to send him away for Azazel into the wilderness." (Leviticus 16:5-10, ASV, margin of which reads "removal" for "Azazel"). The bullock of the sin offering Aaron offered for himself and his house; in the incense-filled holy of holies *he sprinkled of the blood of the bullock on the mercy seat seven times,* an indication of complete atonement. *The goat for the Lord was then slain, and the same ritual was carried out with its blood in the holiest of all, this time for the sins of the children of Israel.* After the sacrifice of the first goat, Aaron laid both his hands on the head of the live goat, confessing over him the sins and transgressions of Israel. Then the goat was sent away into the wilderness by a man ready for the occasion.
>
> Both [he] goats were a sin offering to the Lord; one was sacrificed, whereas the other was sent off into the wilderness to convey visibly and strikingly the truth of complete removal and dismissal. The escape goat does not represent Christ any more than it stands for Satan. That which was symbolized by both goats pointed to the finished

work of Christ on Calvary. Blessed be our sufficient Sin Offering.[12] (emphasis mine)

The sprinkling of the blood of the bullock and the he-goat on the mercy seat seven times (which pointed to the seven places where Jesus would shed his blood[13]) is very significant. You will notice that this aspect of the ritual took place before Aaron the priest laid both his hands on the head of the scapegoat, confessing and releasing the sins of the entire nation on him. This *exchange* was possible because the altar, having become empowered by the blood sacrifice, was able to *enforce* whatever Aaron pronounced on the scapegoat.

Satanic altars basically replicate and pervert the same ritual. Empowered by blood sacrifices, they use animals, effigies, totems, etc. to represent their victims, releasing curses and spells and calamities and afflictions over their victims. Because of the blood, satanic altars have voices, and they can speak against you.

People also build demonic altars by communing with the dead, consulting satanic agents, visiting shrines, experimenting with occultism, or joining a white-garment "church"[14] and taking part in demonic rituals. Other methods include palm reading, practicing witchcraft, and practicing divination through tarots. So-called "good luck" charms or charms worn for protection are demonic and invite demons and curses into your life. Some carved objects are representations of deities, and these usually have residual demonic spirits and powers in them. Even things as "innocuous" as taking part in pagan dance rituals and festivals, certain carnivals, Reiki and yoga, Ouija boards, astrology, hypnotism, horoscopes, fortune-telling, divination, gambling, magic, and psychic readings can expose you to satanic contamination and evil influences.

COMBATING AN ALTAR

Many people go through the motions of life with no say over the direction of their lives. Other forces manipulate and afflict them every step of the way. In many cases, these people are controlled by evil altars. You may even be one of them. If you are, you can be set free by the blood of Christ. If you are a Christian, your victory is already won by the death and resurrection of Jesus. You share in his authority, and your warfare is accomplished. But as we have seen, in many ways it is your job to bring the kingdom into active reality in your life, here on earth. You fight *from* victory, not *for* victory, but you still need to fight.

For you to experience this freedom, then, you need to first destroy the evil altar. But how do you do that? Where do you begin?

To understand how to combat an evil altar, think about warfare involving an air base. Is it more important to take out the aircraft, the runway, or the control tower? Look at it this way: Without the control tower, the aircraft cannot take off. If the control tower is destroyed when the aircraft is already in the air, it will crash. It seems to me that air traffic control is the most important of the three because it is the brains behind the operation. Without it, it doesn't matter what other equipment is in place: the enemy mission will fail.

In the kingdom of darkness, a satanic altar is the control tower, the place directing and programming the aircraft to carry afflictions and whatever else the altar wishes to send or project on a person. The aircraft is the spirit assigned by both the altar and the spirits sponsoring the altar to carry out its mission. These include monitoring spirits and spirits of make-sure. As the names suggest, monitoring spirits *monitor* the intended victim and report back to the altar with up-to-date information. The afflicted person is placed under constant surveillance. This ensures that the afflictions are customised to suit the circumstances of the victim. Spirits of make-sure ensure that whatever the altar sends is delivered to the intended recipient. More often than not, these spirits will be witchcraft spirits. Because a causeless curse cannot alight,[15] there must be a connection between you and an affliction in order for it to land on you. Sometimes it's your blood link to the family member who has built an altar or visited a satanic altar for assistance. Sometimes it's your own choice in seeking help from an altar. That link or connection is the runway on which the demonic aircraft lands.

You can spend time trying to tear down the runway or shoot individual spirits out of the sky. But if you destroy the altar, you take out the air traffic control. When that happens, the entire satanic operation will crash-land, catch fire, and be completely destroyed! Take out the satanic altar, and you're more or less okay!

FREEDOM IN JESUS

Although satanic altars are incredibly powerful, Jesus can provide true freedom from their grip, as Eghosa found out recently. She was petite and extremely pretty. Her hair, a rich shade of ebony, flowed in waves to adorn her glowing, porcelain-like, dark-complexioned skin. Her eyes, framed by long lashes, were a bright brown and seemed to brighten the world around her. With a straight nose and full lips, she seemed the picture of perfection. The locals in her native Benin City nicknamed her Beauty.

One of eight children, Eghosa was only seventeen and had just completed her senior secondary education when her parents were approached by Joe, who wished to take her to Europe to be a nanny to his friend's children. His friend was also Nigerian but had been unable to travel back to Nigeria with him.

Joe was one of the local success stories. A local boy, he had gone to Europe twenty years ago and had just completed his fourth two-story building of six three-bedroom flats in Benin City. His friend would look after Eghosa, send her to university, and pay her wages in euros. Eghosa and her parents saw no reason not to trust him.

However, because of the cost of financing her immigration papers and the journey, Joe wanted to be sure she wouldn't run away when she got to Vienna. He told Eghosa and her parents that he just needed to take her to Ohen, a local *juju* priest, to ensure she would keep her side of the agreement. Her parents were sure Eghosa wouldn't run away, but they didn't see anything wrong with this ritual if that is what would reassure Joe.

Ohen asked for clippings of Eghosa's fingernails and toenails, as well as her armpit hair, pubic hair, and menstrual blood, for the ritual. Her parents accompanied her to the shrine. When they got there, the priest prepared a concoction with the items and made Eghosa swear an oath on the altar that she would pay back the sum of €50,000 that Joe claimed it would cost him to take her to Europe. If she refused to pay, she would go mad, and her parents would die mysteriously. He gave some of the concoction to Joe. He then made her swallow a miniature clay gourd containing some of the potion.

Soon, word spread that Eghosa was travelling to Europe. She became the envy of her friends, who made her promise not to forget them when she began to swim in foreign currency.

Shortly afterward, Eghosa and Joe travelled. On arrival in Austria, Joe took her passport from her. She was taken to a house where she was shocked to discover she had been sold to a madam and that prostitution on the cold streets of Vienna awaited her. She would be subject to her madam and would have to stand on the streets for hours in the nightly cold, half-naked in short skirts, soliciting men until she repaid the "debt" of €50,000.

Eghosa's madam put the fear of the devil in her when she showed her a powdery concoction and said, "This powder contains your hair, your pubic hair, and clippings of your fingernails. I will blow it into the air to invoke a curse that will make you mad and kill your parents if you make any attempt to run away!"

The day after her arrival, Eghosa was taken to an asylum reception centre to apply for asylum with a fake story. She was issued a white card by the Federal Asylum Office, enabling her to work while her claim was being considered. In time, her asylum claim was rejected. Her appeal to the Asylum Court was also rejected. After three years of working to pay her madam, she was deported back to Nigeria with nothing to show for her time in Europe. At the time she still had €10,000 to pay!

On her return to Nigeria, a nongovernmental organisation gave her a grant of $1000 to set up a shop in Benin City. However, she was very worried about the €10,000 she had to pay Joe and her madam. Now back in Nigeria, where €1 exchanged for ₦210, she reasoned that it would take her a lifetime to repay that kind of money! What was she to do? She remembered two girls who had worked with her in Austria who suddenly went mad for no apparent reason. Madam said they'd gone mad because they tried to run away. She didn't want to go mad. She started having sleepless nights and developed high blood pressure. Whenever she managed to catch a bit of sleep, she would have terrible nightmares. She was in a very bad state.

In her desperation, she met somebody who introduced her to Pastor Igbinosa. He had worked with his father as a *juju* priest and was in line to inherit the shrine from his father, who was the chief priest, when he met Jesus and became born again nearly ten years ago. Now a minister of the gospel, he leads a vibrant church in Benin City.

The pastor led Eghosa to the Lord and then proceeded to minister deliverance to her. Through prophetic declarations in the place of prayer, Pastor Igbinosa destroyed the grip of the altar holding her captive at Ohen's shrine, revoked all the evil covenants she had entered into, blinded the monitoring spirits, and silenced any blood sacrifice speaking against her. In the course of the prayer, Eghosa vomited many things, including the clay gourd she had swallowed at the shrine before she went to Vienna!

The moment she threw up the gourd, she knew she was completely free! That night, for the first time in a very long time, Eghosa slept like a baby. No more nightmares. No more high blood pressure. No more sleepless nights. She was truly free, and she could now concentrate on rebuilding her devastated life.

RESCUED BY A HIGHER POWER

Back to Aisha. After giving the word of knowledge, the man of God invited the affected person forward for prayers. Aisha responded. She gave her heart to Jesus and was baptised in the Holy Spirit. She returned the following day with John and their four children. This started the process of salvation, deliverance, healing, and breakthrough for the whole family. The chains were broken. The death sentences were revoked. The spells and curses were broken. The blood sacrifices were silenced and the evil altars destroyed. Eventually Aisha and her family were fully set free, and they are now beginning to enjoy their everyday lives as God intended.

During this period, Aisha's father had some near-death experiences that led him back to the oracle. These experiences shook him to the core of his being. Initially, all the oracle was prepared to divulge was that a higher power was now protecting his daughter.

One day, after a particularly terrifying ordeal when he thought he was going to die, Hajji Mohamed returned to the oracle and demanded he do something. The oracle brought out his magic mirror and decided to summon Aisha and John to appear before the altar. He called their images to appear in the mirror, but not even the oracle was prepared for what happened next.

Just as he was finishing his incantations, both men could tell the wind had picked up slightly by the noise in the trees around the shrine. Hajji Mohamed bin Zaid looked out through the window to see dark clouds looming in the distance. Suddenly, rain and a thunderstorm blew up. The mirror was struck by lightning and shattered into tiny pieces. The oracle was not spared either. He was struck on the left arm, which became instantly paralysed. He fell to the ground in shock. He had never experienced anything like this in over forty years as a fetish priest. He became so angry that his face flushed as he spoke, his voice trembling with anger. He told Hajji Mohamed bin Zaid to leave his shrine immediately, never to return.

Hajji Mohamed was confused, bruised, and traumatised as he left the oracle. In the end, he called Aisha and told her everything he had done, seeking her forgiveness and asking her to introduce him to this "higher power" that was now looking after her. Aisha was all too happy to forgive her father and reconcile with him and the rest of the family. She is now praying that her parents and siblings will come to know Jesus as Saviour and become born-again children of God.

IS AN ALTAR SPEAKING AGAINST YOU?

Have you ever stopped to ask why it is that you're in an unending cycle of financial hardship? Why does money seem to run away from you? Why do you experience calamity after calamity? Why is your marriage so turbulent despite your best efforts to make it work? How is it that no matter how hard you try, money never meets money in your hands? How come you can never save? Why is disease or death haunting your family? Could it be that like Aisha, an altar is speaking against you?

It can be helpful to understand the following principles:

Altars Enforce Agreements and Covenants. If your parents found it difficult to have children and went to see a white witch, herbalist, or witch doctor for help, and after that you were born, there will be consequences. It may be that part of the exchange that took place during the visit was that you became married to the altar. In this case, because the altar is controlled by a jealous deity or demonic spirit, your physical marriage will always be turbulent unless the spirit marriage is annulled and the altar is taken out.

Altars Demand What is Legally Due to Them. Your parents or grandparents may have visited an altar and paid a diviner's fee. Whatever was paid would normally be miniscule in comparison with the actual amount due to the devil. What then happens is that future generations are covenanted to pay the debt to the devil in instalments. That's why you can never save and money will always desert you, no matter how much you earn. You're paying off a debt in the spirit world.

Altars Bind. Perhaps you're destined for greatness but bound. There are times when the devil decides not to destroy a person, choosing instead to steal or destroy that person's destiny or purpose in life. He achieves this by tying their destiny to an altar and thereby placing them under house arrest and under the control of the specific deity behind the altar. Through the altar, the devil determines what they can or cannot do, where they can or cannot go, what they can or cannot eat, and how far they can go in life. These people are prisoners held captive by the enemy. As he has no desire to kill them, the devil makes use of ropes that won't cut into their flesh when restraining them, employing several turns of the rope to spread the pressure without preventing blood flow. He makes use of long ropes that he doubles over for effectiveness, with the altar determining the precise details of the bondage using feedback from monitoring spirits.

The rope with which the devil ties a person places a restriction over that person's life. This rope is controlled by the altar. As long as such prisoners operate within the parameters set by the altar and don't attempt to go beyond the limitation, they're good. However, if they make any attempt to break the limit and go any further in life, all hell will break loose and their captors will *violently* yank the rope holding them to show they're the ones in charge. Every time your captors tug at the rope, you suffer an inexplicable catastrophe which sets you back years. It's like you try to take two steps forward to improve your lot in life, but you end up going back ten steps and having to start all over again. And again and again! This is the kind of power an evil altar can have over your life.

REACHING YOUR DESTINY

Let me tell you about somebody who was destined for greatness, but who was tied—bound by ropes that kept him back. He was born for a special purpose: to carry Jesus Christ into Jerusalem in the triumphant entry. And because of his special mission, nobody had ever ridden him. Yes, *he was a donkey.* You could say the donkey was born great. But even if he wasn't, he certainly had greatness thrust upon his strong shoulders!

> "Be not afraid of greatness. Some are born great, some achieve greatness, and others have greatness thrust upon them."
>
> **William Shakespeare, *Twelfth Night***

There is no higher honour for any beast of burden than to carry the Lord of Glory himself. And to carry him in the triumphant entry into Jerusalem—nothing can beat that! This was the whole reason for the donkey's existence. He was born for such a time as this. He was born for this specific task.[16]

However, for the donkey to carry out his mission, he first had to get to where Jesus was, on the outskirts of Jerusalem. Unfortunately, the donkey was tied and held back in the village across from Jerusalem, at a point where two streets met! There are people destined for greatness who live in large cities all around the world, but whose lives and destinies are tied up in the villages where they were born, and just like the donkey, some of them are tied at points where two or three streets meet.

Aware that *something* out of the ordinary was preventing the donkey from getting to where he was, Jesus decided to intervene. He sent off two of his disciples with instructions: "Go to the village across from you. As soon as you enter, you'll find a donkey that has never yet been ridden, tethered. Untie him and bring him. If anyone asks, 'What are you doing?' say, 'The Master needs him, and will return him right away.'"

The disciples went as instructed by the Lord, found the donkey tied to a door at the street corner, and untied him. Some of those standing there said, "What are you doing untying that colt?" The disciples replied exactly as Jesus had instructed them, and the people let them alone. They took the donkey to Jesus. As soon as the donkey got to where Jesus was, people spread their coats on him. Some even threw their coats on the street, with others spreading out branches they had cut in the fields. Running ahead and following after, they shouted, "Hosanna! Blessed is he who comes in the name of the Lord! Hosanna in the highest!"

If Jesus hadn't intervened, the poor donkey would have missed his destiny. He was so close, yet so far away! Not only was he tied, but there were enforcement people on the lookout to ensure that he remained in captivity. In the same way, those who are bound to altars have spiritual watchers or spirit guards keeping watch over them to ensure they remain perpetually bound. It took the anointed words of Jesus, "The Master needs him," *not only* to bring deliverance to the donkey, but also to silence the enforcers who were put there by his captors. Thankfully, he was rescued by a higher power and able to fulfil his destiny in the end.

The Master needs you. So what is holding you down? What's holding you back? What's preventing you from being the best you can be? And what are you tied to, that is competing with your love for God? No matter what binds your life, you can be free, and you can fulfil your destiny.

DISCERNING AN ALTAR

If you can identify with the donkey's experience, feeling restrained and unable to go beyond certain parameters, it appears your future has been compromised. Of course, it is not the case that an evil altar is behind every form of oppression. Some people are simply the victims of man's inhumanity to man. Others are reaping the consequences of bad decisions. But altars are real, their power is great, and deliverance is available from them. If there is an altar active in your life, it needs to be dealt with!

So how do you know if the source of your troubles can be traced to an altar? If you or someone from your past has erected a satanic altar—either physically or spiritually—you may be experiencing the effects of that. To determine whether you're affected by a satanic altar, you need to ask yourself these questions:

Do You Know of Any Satanic Altars? This is the obvious one! Have you or your parents (or if you're married, your spouse or in-laws) raised a satanic altar in any of the ways highlighted in this chapter?

Is the Issue Long-standing? Is the problem long-standing, with no apparent end in sight? Any problematic situation that lasts longer than normal can be considered longstanding. So for instance, a couple who want children and have been married for three years without conceiving, or somebody who is looking for work and yet remains unemployed for more than nine months.

Is There a Debt Incurred in the Spirit? Are you paying off a debt incurred to an altar by your ancestors? Are you having problems in your marriage because every woman in your family is married to an altar that is attacking your marriage out of jealous rage? This pattern should be visible throughout your family. You may also have sexual dreams indicating something like this. (See below for more on this.)

Are You Unable to Close Any Deals? Is it the case that you're never able to close a deal? You always get so close, but it never works.

Does the Problem Defy Logic? Does the problem you're facing defy logic? Does it happen over and over again? For instance, you never have a shortage of boyfriends, but just when the relationship is about to get serious, it ends with no logical explanation. Shortly after, you meet another man, and the same cycle begins.

Is It a Common Family Issue? Do other members of your family have similar problems? Is this something family members have come to accept as their "cross"?

Do You Have Sex in Dreams? Do you have dreams where you have sexual interaction, including gay sex? This could be a sign of marriage to a demonic spirit.

Do You Have a Family in Your Dreams? Do you see yourself getting married in your dreams, having a spouse in your dreams? Do you see yourself having a family in your dreams and living in a large house—especially a house under the water—with a spouse, children, and servants?

If your response to most of these questions is yes, it is most likely that an evil altar is speaking against you. And you need deliverance! Jesus, the Power higher than all other powers, can make you free—today. He can set you free right now! If you belong to him, the victory is already yours. You just need to claim it. All you have to do is follow the guidance provided in chapter 12, "Breaking the Curse and Activating the Blessing." The chapter offers practical guidance and prayers. But before we go there, let's continue to look at the curses that may be affecting your life.

Although deliverance should be sought from satanic bondage, it is important to remember that as a believer, you already have eternal victory over Satan and his demons. As you walk in this reality, you advance God's kingdom and demonstrate his manifold wisdom to the devil.

Chapter 8:

THE POWER OF THE SPOKEN WORD

"Words kill, words give life;
they're either poison or fruit—you choose."

Proverbs 18:21, MSG

"You will live to regret this, Bill. This bank will fall to its knees!"

With those words, James Patterson stormed out of the office of Bill Jeremiah, the group CEO of Wall Street banking giant Alliance Barnes, on Friday, 13 October 2006.

Patterson was a senior vice president in the investment division of Alliance Barnes. Earlier that morning, he'd been summoned by the group CEO and told his services were no longer required. A victim of office politics, he was given one hour to clear his desk and leave the building. Not only was he dismissed, but Jeremiah made an example of him. Distraught, Patterson decided he'd teach Alliance Barnes a lesson.

James Patterson decided to contact Tony Tan, his trusted Malaysian *bomoh* or soothsayer, in downtown Los Angeles. Tan had been the brains behind his meteoric rise in Alliance Barnes. Now, he wanted to exact revenge. That night, he flew from New York to Los Angeles. He told Tan he had been terribly mistreated by Alliance Barnes and he wanted the bank brought to its knees, whatever the cost.

Tan gave his thin smile two extra creases. "You can count on me, buddy," he answered as he set about preparing the ritual to give effect to Patterson's request.

"Take this," he said, handing Patterson a powdery substance. "Stand in front of the bank's headquarters in daylight, holding the powder in your right hand. Blow the powder toward the building and declare, 'Alliance Barnes, you treated me unfairly. I won't let you get off scot-free. I have come to exact revenge. I command you to go bankrupt.' You must do this within seven days. The bank will collapse within twelve months."

At the time Patterson was relieved of his job, Alliance Barnes was one of the giants of Wall Street, with seventeen thousand employees and assets of $558 billion. Shortly after Patterson performed the ritual prescribed by Tony Tan, Alliance Barnes was caught up in the subprime mortgage crisis. In the wake of the crisis, Alliance Barnes collapsed spectacularly when other banks lost confidence in the value of their investments in subprime mortgages. Alliance Barnes filed for Chapter 11 bankruptcy protection in late 2007 and was bought by a rival bank for a mere $100 million in June 2008!

The ability to speak words is a unique and powerful gift from God. What happened to Alliance Barnes shows that words are incredibly powerful. They have far more power and capability than we usually attribute to them. Spoken words do more than merely convey information. They are not simply sounds caused by air passing through our larynx. They have real power.

God spoke the world into existence by the power of his words,[1] and because we are made in his image, our words can be quite potent too! Whenever I dedicate babies to the Lord, I beg and plead with the parents never to utter anything negative concerning their children. The reason is simple. Parents can profoundly influence the direction of their children's lives both by the words they say to them and what they say concerning them.

The focus in this chapter is on the ability of the spoken word to generate a negative outcome—i.e., a curse. The words under consideration range from the all-too-common negative comments many of us make from time to time to the carefully selected words chanted as part of a ritual with the intention of casting a spell, causing harm, or creating a predetermined outcome.

THE CREATIVE POWER OF WORDS

As stated earlier, our words have the ability to create. They have the capacity to call into existence things that are not yet in existence and to destroy things that already exist. Words have such power that, whether we want to or not, we give life to what we're saying, either good or bad. We should never speak negative, destructive words toward anybody, especially toward people over whom we have authority or influence. One way or the other, we end up getting what we say!

Powerful as words are, they have no effect until they are spoken into the atmosphere. A curse is not a curse, and cannot be effective, until it is released, usually by being spoken. In the same way, a blessing is not a blessing until it is spoken. Once uttered, the speaker loses control of the words, which then assume a life of their own. Jesus said, "The words that I have spoken to you are spirit and are life."[2]

When God speaks, whatever he says comes to pass. *The Message* tells the story of creation like this: "God spoke: 'Lights! Come out! Shine in Heaven's sky! Separate Day from Night. Mark seasons and days and years, Lights in Heaven's sky to give light to Earth.' And there it was."[3]

Being the copycat that he is, the devil empowers words spoken in certain carefully orchestrated circumstances, especially where a blood sacrifice is involved. Sometimes an effigy is brought before the altar, and whatever is done to the effigy automatically happens to the victim—if the effigy is tied, the victim's progress is limited; if the effigy's legs are broken, the victim develops a mysterious ailment that leads to amputation. Now and again, the victim is summoned to appear before the altar in a magic mirror, where things can be done to him. At other times, incantations are made—spells or chants where curses are released.

Spells work in two ways. They can be "lucky charms," which people seek for their own benefit and protection, such as the so-called love spells, luck and money spells, health and protection spells, and candle spells offered by some marabouts and modern witches' covens. On the other hand, spells can also be used for binding someone else and making them do something they wouldn't normally do. Often, binding someone with a spell by the use of spoken-word formulas involves the use of invocation, a form of incantation used to summon a deity or the supernatural.

Many of the laws and evil family patterns referred to elsewhere in this book arise through the power of the spoken word. Proverbs 6:1–2 says, "My son, if you become surety for your friend, if you have shaken hands in pledge for a stranger, you are snared by the words of your mouth; you are taken by the words of your mouth,"[4] while Proverbs 18:21 tells us, "Death and life are in the power of the tongue, and those who love it will eat its fruit."[5] Some of us are subject to curses and negative words spoken into our destinies by people who had authority over us or even by people we offended. These have become laws against us.

Even our names can affect us. Jabez was affected by his name. His name meant *pain*. He was so named because his mother gave birth to him in pain. His life was a paradox: he was honourable, yet held back by his name and the circumstances of his birth. To overcome the curse of his name, he prayed a prayer of deliverance to God: "Bless me, enlarge my coast, place your hand on me for good, keep me from evil, and help me not to cause pain to anyone." And God granted him what he requested.[6]

Like Jabez, some of us have been trapped by the negative words spoken into our atmosphere by those with authority over us, such as parents, teachers, and religious leaders. But also like him, there is hope for us in the greater power of Jesus Christ.

A long time ago, a man of God by the name of Joshua was entrapped into signing a treaty with the people of Gibeon. Gibeon was a mighty city whose men were great warriors. They were said to be greater than the nearby city of Ai. Now, at that time, Ai had a king, so presumably Gibeon also had a royal family. They would have had governors, police and law enforcement agencies, teachers, doctors, midwives, nurses, judges, university professors, engineers, builders, journalists, scribes, and soldiers.

When Joshua found out that the Gibeonites had entrapped him, he placed them under a curse. In *one day*, the Bible tells us Joshua made the Gibeonites water carriers and woodcutters.[7] Can you imagine the king and the queen of Gibeon, the princes and princesses, the governors, the police and law enforcement people, the teachers, doctors, midwives, nurses, judges, university professors, engineers, builders, journalists, scribes, and soldiers all becoming water carriers and wood cutters in *one* day? How? By the power of the spoken word! Joshua simply said, "May you be cursed! From now on you will always be servants who cut wood and carry water for the house of my God."[8] With those words, Joshua changed the destiny of an entire nation.

Does it appear as if your destiny has been tampered with, changed, or compromised in any way? Perhaps somebody pronounced a curse which has landed on you. The good news is, any such curse can be revoked by the blood of Jesus.

CURSES AND BETRAYAL

Sometimes when we are betrayed, the things we say out of the depths of our hurt, pain, and anger can act to create a curse against those who have hurt us. That is precisely what happened with the Benfica curse.[9] Béla Guttmann was a Jewish Hungarian footballer and coach. He played as a midfielder for MTK Hungária FC, SC Hakoah Wien, Hungary, and several clubs in the United States. However, he is perhaps best remembered as a coach and manager of some the world's leading football teams. His greatest success came with Benfica, whom he guided to two successive European Cup wins in 1961 and 1962.

In 1962, Guttman had just led Benfica to back-to-back European Cup victories, and the Portuguese club looked set to rule the international stage for years to come. However, shortly after steering his side to victory over Real Madrid, he quit when his request for a pay raise was turned down. He felt betrayed. On leaving Benfica, Guttman cursed the club, declaring, "Not in a hundred years from now will Benfica ever be European champion again."

Those words must have come from the depths of Guttman's pain at being so badly treated by Benfica despite all he'd done for the club. And so far—in over fifty years—Benfica has never risen above that curse despite playing in several European cup finals!

The last European Cup final Benfica was involved in was held in Vienna, where Guttman is buried, and Benfica legend Eusebio da Silva Ferreira even went to the grave of his former manager to pray for the curse to be lifted. It had little effect, and Benfica remains jinxed.

Now, before you get too worried, these types of curses are easy to break. However, you need to do more than just pray on the grave of the person who pronounced the curse!

THE POWER AND SCOPE OF CURSES

Curses can be powerful, and their effect is often quite broad. Sometimes, curses don't just land on the individual concerned. They are worded in such a way as to make them affect the descendants of the recipient as well. They become an inheritance received by future generations. Unless and until they are specifically broken, they continue to run through the bloodline of the original recipient of the curse.

A good example is the curse that was pronounced on Gehazi by his master, Elisha, the Old Testament prophet.[10] Elisha said to him, "Because you have done this, Naaman's leprosy shall be upon you and upon your children and your children's children forever." The curse took immediate effect, because suddenly, Gehazi's skin became white with leprosy.

That's pretty tough, some might say! So what happened? What made the man of God release such a deadly curse on his aide?

In this case, the curse was brought on Gehazi through his own corrupt actions. General Naaman was the commander-in-chief of the Syrian army. He was a great hero, but he was a leper. Naaman's wife had a young Israeli maid who told her, "Ma'am, I wish my lord the general would go to see the prophet Elisha in Samaria. He would heal him of his leprosy!" The general made his way to Elisha, who told him to go and wash in the River Jordan seven times and he would be healed of every trace of his leprosy.

After much hesitation, he did it. As he came out of the water after the seventh time, Naaman's skin was healed like the skin of a little baby. He was as good as new! Naaman wanted to show his appreciation, but Elisha wouldn't accept any gift from him. However, Gehazi, Elisha's assistant, thought to himself, *The prophet shouldn't have let this fellow get away without taking his gifts. I will go after him and get something from him.*

So he went after Naaman and lied to him, claiming that Elisha had sent him to receive a reward after all. He returned to the house and hid the money and other rewards Naaman gave him.

Elisha said, "Didn't you know my spirit was with you when you ran after the general and he stepped down from his chariot to greet you? Is this a time to look after yourself, receiving gifts? You've been very foolish, and because of what you've done, Naaman's leprosy will now be on you and your descendants forever!"

How did that work out in practice? I believe Naaman didn't have leprosy until late in life, because there's no way he would have become a general and the commander-in-chief of the Syrian army as a leper. In effect, Gehazi's descendants would be normal at first, but they would develop this horrible skin disease later in life, say in their forties or even fifties.

Can you imagine falling in love with the delicately beautiful Miss Samaria, four generations down the line, long after Gehazi's death? It's so far down the line, nobody remembers the curse. You notice that her father had leprosy, but you think nothing of it, since leprosy isn't hereditary. Plus, you're so much in love you don't take much notice of your pastor's advice that not all that glitters is gold. You decide to get married to her and start a family, not realising that she is Gehazi's great-granddaughter, with the curse of Naaman's leprosy hanging over her. Fifteen years into your marriage, your wonderful life turns into a living nightmare when your beautiful wife unexpectedly develops leprosy!

TAKING SOMEBODY ELSE'S POSITION

Sometimes an enemy can orchestrate to take somebody else's position through the power of the spoken word. This happens all the time, especially in sports, the media, public office, and high-profile positions in large corporations. It happens in two ways. The first is through injury (mainly in team sports), where two people are competing for the same position. If one player is doing extremely well and playing consistently, the player not playing won't get a chance unless his teammate is injured. An effigy of the teammate is taken to an oracle, who uses the power of words to invoke an injury.

The second way it happens is when an oracle releases a spirit of error into a person holding a position where the stakes are high, again through the power of words. This can be a government minister, the president or CEO of a multinational corporation, an ambassador, a sports coach, a bank manager, a university head—the list goes on. The post holder begins to make embarrassing mistakes, schoolboy errors, and it is not long until he is taken off the position, paving the way for the person behind the sacrifice to take over.

"It claps its hands in derision and hisses him out of his place."
—Job 27:23

DEATH SENTENCES

Some people have death sentences hanging over them. A death sentence is a decree that a named person will die by a specified date. It is often made in a shrine. It operates by the power of the spoken word, so even if it is written, somebody will read it out loud, usually as part of a chant in a ritual. Once released, a death sentence will hang over a person's life like the Sword of Damocles, seeking an opportunity to land. Unless it is revoked, it will lead to the individual's death.

If a death sentence is hanging over a person, opportunistic demons and sicknesses will want to take advantage and kill the person. Let me illustrate this with a *fatwa* (an Islamic legal decree) calling for someone's death. If such a fatwa is issued against an individual, all kinds of people around the world will seek to execute it and kill the person. Unfortunately, there's no shortage of people wanting to kill others. This plays into their hands and gives them justification to commit their dastardly acts.

Probably the most well-known death fatwa was proclaimed in 1989 by the late Ayatollah Khomeini, at the time the spiritual leader of Iran, against British author Salman Rushdie over his novel *The Satanic Verses*. The publication of *The Satanic Verses* in September 1988 caused immediate controversy in the Islamic world because of what was seen by some as its irreverent depiction of the prophet Muhammad.

The title of the book refers to a disputed Muslim tradition that is related in the novel. According to this tradition, Muhammad (Mahound in the book) added verses to the Qur'an which he believed were dictated to him by the angel Gabriel and which said that the pagan goddesses worshipped in Mecca were "exalted females whose intercession is to be desired"—a contradiction to nascent monotheistic Islamic orthodoxy. Only later did Muhammad repudiate these verses, argues Rushdie, saying he was deceived by the devil disguised as the archangel.

The book was banned in many countries with large Muslim communities, including India, Bangladesh, Sudan, South Africa, Sri Lanka, Kenya, Thailand, Tanzania, Indonesia, Singapore, Venezuela, and Pakistan.

On 14 February 1989, a fatwa requiring all "zealous Muslims" to execute the author was proclaimed on Radio Tehran by Ayatollah Khomeini, who said the book was blasphemous. The following day,

Rushdie went into hiding under the round-the-clock protection of Scotland Yard's Special Branch. Not long after, the United Kingdom and Iran broke diplomatic relations over the Rushdie controversy. His protection officers suggested he choose another name to increase his security when he turned up at a new home (though being flanked by four armed men in bulletproof Jaguars usually did the trick). So he took the pseudonym Joseph Anton, becoming more or less invisible.

The fatwa sparked violence around the world. Muslim communities in several nations in the West held public rallies, burning copies of the book. Bombs exploded in bookshops in the United States and the United Kingdom. The book's Japanese translator was shot and killed, its Italian translator was stabbed, its Turkish translator was attacked, its Norwegian publisher was shot, and two clerics in Saudi Arabia and Tunisia who spoke out against the fatwa were shot and killed. The threat of assassination wasn't lifted until 1998, when the Iranian government finally modified its position in a move to restore ruptured diplomatic relations with the United Kingdom.

In Salmon Rushdie's case, the whole world was aware of the death sentence on his life, so the United Kingdom government took steps to protect him. But most people are unaware that there's a death sentence hanging over their lives. Because they don't know it's there, they don't do anything to counteract it.

This is similar to what happens to people who are HIV positive. Without treatment, a person who is HIV positive is susceptible to opportunistic infections that come on the heels of a declining immune system. Opportunistic infections are the most common cause of death for people with HIV/AIDS. They are called "opportunistic" because they take advantage of the sufferer's weakened immune system and can cause devastating illnesses.[11] A person who knows he or she has HIV can guard against them, but one who is ignorant will not raise a defence.

A biblical example of somebody with a death sentence is Moses. The story is found in Exodus 1 and 2. This was the death sentence issued by Pharaoh against the Hebrew people: "Every Hebrew boy that is born you must throw into the Nile, but let every girl live."[12] Because Moses was a Hebrew boy born when Pharaoh's decree was in force, the sentence automatically attached to him.

Through the faith of his mother, sister, and the Hebrew midwives who refused to kill him at birth, Moses's life was spared. God miraculously directed events so that he actually became adopted into Pharaoh's household. But although he was now in the palace, the death sentence was never revoked. It was still active and looking for an opportunity to take effect.

Where there is a death sentence, the recipient's decision-making abilities are often corrupted such that he takes unnecessary risks, makes inexplicably stupid decisions, and takes unbecoming and uncharacteristic actions that place his life in danger. For some reason, Moses decided to kill an Egyptian who was mistreating an Israelite. He didn't need to do that. However, because the death sentence needed to come to pass, it was as if something was remotely controlling his actions. When Pharaoh heard that Moses had killed the Egyptian, he decided to kill him! Moses escaped into the wilderness and lived on the run for forty years until he met with God in the burning bush. This encounter with God finally nullified the death sentence, enabling Moses to live to a ripe old age!

REAL-WORLD CONSEQUENCES

The real-world consequences of curses are real, and they're nothing to make light of. In or around 1986, a teacher in my old high school came into a lot of money. With his new wealth, he bought a brand-spanking-new car without a loan and moved into a new house. Shortly after buying his new car, he—we'll call him Ambrose—began an affair with a married woman we'll call Alice.

Somehow, Alice's husband became aware of the affair, and as would be expected, he didn't find it funny. He sent emissaries to Ambrose asking him to break off the affair and leave his wife alone. They told Ambrose in no uncertain terms that if he didn't leave Alice, he'd pay with his head.

Ambrose told them he wouldn't break off the affair because he was in love with Alice and that his head could handle whatever was thrown his way. A few weeks after the meeting, he died in a head-on collision involving his new car.

Why did he refuse to stop seeing a married woman in the face of a threat on his life by the aggrieved husband? I can't be sure, but I would say there was most probably a death sentence on him. That curse made him unable to see sense, and it ended up driving him to his untimely death!

In January 2013, a twenty-seven-year-old New Zealand lawyer who was visiting London with his girlfriend was crushed to death when a thirty-foot metal hoarding collapsed on top of him as he walked along a busy street in Camden, North London, on a Monday afternoon. The deceased had arrived in London the previous September as part of an around-the-world "trip of a lifetime."[13] I don't know much about the circumstances of the deceased, but I can't help wondering why somebody would travel halfway around the world only to die such a miserable death. Did he have a death sentence on his life?

Where there is a death sentence, the cursed individual can become tragically susceptible to human error. People have been known to die from errors by surgeons and other medical personnel. Motor accidents happen all the time due to driver error. And sometimes, the effects can extend beyond just the person who is cursed.

On Sunday, 31 May 2009, as night enveloped the Rio de Janeiro International Airport, the 216 passengers waiting to board a flight to Paris could not have suspected that they would never see daylight again, or that many would sit strapped to their seats for another two years before being found dead in the darkness, thirteen thousand feet below the surface of the Atlantic Ocean. Air France Flight 447 had a highly trained crew flying an immaculate wide-bodied Airbus A330 for one of the world's premier airlines. Even today—with the flight records recovered from the seafloor, French technical reports in hand, and exhaustive inquests underway in French courts—it remains almost unimaginable that the airplane crashed.

The Bureau d'Enquêtes et d'Analyses pour la Sécurité de l'Aviation Civile concluded that the aircraft crashed when temporary inconsistencies between the airspeed measurements—likely due to the aircraft's pitot tubes being obstructed by ice crystals—caused the autopilot to disconnect, after which the pilots reacted incorrectly. This ultimately led the aircraft to an aerodynamic stall from which they did not recover.

It seems absurd, but a combination of mechanical and human error resulted in an Airbus A330 crashing into the Atlantic Ocean and killing all 288 people on board. Was there somebody with a death sentence on board the aircraft?

Not every curse that comes into our lives has the serious consequences of a death sentence. But they do all have consequences—and those consequences can be detrimental to our lives in countless ways. As God's people, we are invited to live under the blessing. For that to happen fully, we need to get out from under curses.

Living under a curse does not please God, nor does it bring him glory. John tells us Jesus came to destroy all the work of the devil.[14] Why endure a curse when you can enjoy the blessing? Coming out from under a curse into the blessing is another way of enforcing the victory won by Christ at Calvary and making his enemies his footstool.

DISCERNING A CURSE

In this chapter we have looked at the various ways in which our lives and destinies can be affected, even destroyed, through the power of the spoken word. Why not take a moment to reflect and see if you can identify with any of those issues? Does it seem as if your destiny has been compromised or even altered through the power of the spoken word?

Perhaps a curse has been ritualistically pronounced over your life. Or perhaps the spoken word has had negative power in your life in more "ordinary" ways. Perhaps you had a teacher who repeatedly told you that you wouldn't amount to anything in life, and now as an adult you find there's a limit you can't go over no matter how hard you try. Perhaps one of your parents kept telling you as a child that you're so clumsy and stupid, you can never do anything right. Years later, you find that those words spoken have somehow become a reality. Maybe the hurts created by past relationships have given rise to words of cursing that are now affecting your life. It may even be that you betrayed your spouse, and since then things have completely fallen apart in your finances or business or ministry.

If you worry that your life is being held back by the power of the spoken word, then you need deliverance. In order to unlock the blessing and enjoy your ordinary, everyday life, you need to *first* undo the effects of any negative words that may have been spoken into your atmosphere.

The blood of Jesus is available to revoke any spoken curse. In chapter 12, we will walk through practical guidance and prayers to help you get free from the power of negative words and come into the blessing of God!

Chapter 9:

THE SINS THAT ENSLAVE US

"The payment for sin is death, but the gift that God freely gives is everlasting life found in Christ Jesus our Lord."

Romans 6:23, GW

Josef Fritzl led a double life. In public he appeared to be a respectable member of the community, living in the small town of Amstetten in Lower Austria, eighty miles west of Vienna, with his wife with whom he had seven grown-up children. But he had a second, secret family with one of his daughters, whom he kept imprisoned in a cellar below their three-story family house along with her children.

It was Wednesday, 29 August 1984. Fritzl waited until he was home alone with his teenage daughter. After years of meticulous planning, he was ready to act on his plans. This was it. It was now or never.

"Eli-sab-eth, darling!" he called out in a singsong voice.

"Yes, Father?" came the reply from his teenage daughter. She was reading a novel in her bedroom.

"Can you give me a hand, please? I need help carrying a door. It's the last piece needed to seal the apartment I'm building downstairs."

"Of course, Father. Please give me a sec."

Shortly afterward, Elisabeth joined her father in the basement, not knowing what lay in store for her. She held the door in place while her father fitted it into the frame. Then, in a flash, he pushed Elisabeth against a wall and held an ether-soaked towel over her face until she passed out, unconscious. He then locked her in the chamber. She was only eighteen.

So began one of the most despicable crimes in the history of modern Austria. For the next twenty-four years, Elisabeth became her father's sex slave in the cramped and windowless eighteen-square-metre cellar. During that period, her father repeatedly raped her, fathering her seven children, all of whom were born in the basement without any medical assistance.

After Elisabeth's disappearance, her mother filed a missing person's report. Almost a month later, her father handed a letter to the police, the first of several that he forced Elisabeth to write. The letter stated that she was tired of living with her family and was staying with a friend; she warned her parents not to look for her or she would leave the country. Her father told the police that she had most likely joined some religious sect.

In April 2008, Fritzl's crimes finally came to light. Following a four-day trial, he was convicted of enslavement, incest, rape, coercion, and false imprisonment, and he is currently serving a life sentence.

What Fritzl did is not only an appalling crime, but it is also a sin against God and Elisabeth, his daughter. Sin is literally "missing the mark," and few would deny that Josef Fritzl missed the mark of what it means to be a decent human being. Failing to do what we know is right is also sin,[1] which is the general term for anything that falls short of the glory of God.[2] We can sin against God or against another person.[3]

Sin pays. It pays wages. But you don't want to receive payment from sin, because the wages of sin is death!

John Lawrence quotes S.D. Gordon, a Christian author and speaker who lived from 1859–1936, as saying there are seven simple facts that everyone ought to know about sin:

> The first is that "sin earns wages." The second, "sin pays wages." The third, "sin insists on paying. You may be quite willing to let the account go, but sin always insists on paying." Fourth, "sin pays its wages in kind. Sin against the body brings results in the body. Sin in the mental life brings results there. Sin in contact with other people brings a chain of results affecting those others. It is terribly true that 'no man sinneth to himself.' Sin is the most selfish of acts. It influences to some extent everyone whom we touch." Fifth, "sin pays in instalments." Sixth, "sin pays in full, unless the blood of Jesus

washes away the stain." Seventh, "sin is self-executive, it pays its own bills. Sin has bound up in itself all the terrific consequences that ever come. The logical result of sin is death; death to the body, death to the mind, death to the soul![4]

There are no secret sins, no matter how hard we try to conceal them. Sin always leaves a mark. Sin always leaves a trail of crimson and dust. There's always a scar. Nothing is hidden from God. He sees all sin. All sin is open to God, who is all-seeing and all-knowing.

The great astronomer, Professor Mitchell, was one day making some observations on the sun, and as it descended toward the horizon, there came into the rays of his telescope the top of a hill seven miles away. On the hill was an orchard, and in one of the apple trees were two boys stealing apples. One was getting the fruit, and the other appeared to be keeping watch, probably thinking no one could see them. But there sat Mitchell, seven miles away, with the eye of the telescope directed fully upon them, seeing every movement as plainly as if he was with them on the spot. In the same way, people think and act as if what they do is hidden from God.[5]

Because no sin is ever hidden, the devil is able to keep a record each time we miss the mark. This record enables him to accuse us[6] and stake a claim over our lives. Sin creates an open doorway to the devil. And because we all sin, it is the most common way that we become snared by the devil.

Sin is not the only way we invite the devil into our own lives. Other ways include what I have referred to as "satanic contamination" or "defilement" elsewhere in this book, as well as by the words we speak about ourselves. Through these channels we invite curses upon ourselves. These are self-inflicted curses, never mind what you may have inherited from your parents, grandparents, great-grandparents, and great-great-grandparents!

LETTING THE DEVIL IN

Whenever we miss the mark, we sin against God, and unless we repent, we make room for curses to come into our lives. I opened with a story that we would all agree is heinous and horrible—there is no question that Josef Fritzl is a sinner! Yet, the Bible identifies many actions and attitudes that qualify us as sinful people. Repentance and forgiveness are available to all, but if we live in unrepentant sin, we let the devil into our lives just as assuredly as Fritzl did.

Here is a selection of the most common ways[7] by which we self-inflict ourselves with curses:

Not Listening to God. Disobeying or just not listening to God is the primary cause of self-inflicted curses.[8] God expects us not only to listen to him, but also to diligently do what he requires of us. He says if we do this, we will enjoy the blessing. Simple as that!

Idol Worship. God is a jealous God who abhors worshiping or bowing down to false gods.[9] God feels about us worshiping idols the way you would feel about a person having an affair with your spouse. False gods include anything that takes first place in our lives, including money and family. God wants to be number one. He wants to have priority in everything.

Disrespect to Parents. God requires us to honour our parents.[10] We don't have to agree with them, but we must honour and respect them. It's very simple really––the Bible says if you honour your father and mother, "things will go well for you, and you will have a long life on the earth."[11] If things aren't going well with you, you need to check your relationship with your parents.

Unforgiveness. This arises where we refuse, neglect, or otherwise fail to forgive someone who has harmed us, hurt us, or done us wrong. Unfortunately, unforgiveness invites curses and closes the heavens, blocking the blessing. If you want God's forgiveness, you must forgive those who hurt you, as the Lord instructs in Luke 6:28.

Injustice to the Weak and Poor. God abhors any form of injustice, particularly toward those who can't defend themselves––the weak, the poor, and the powerless. The Bible says, "He has told you, O man, what is good; and what does the lord require of you but to do justice, to love kindness, and to walk humbly with your God?"[12]

Wrong Sexual Choices. One of the easiest ways people open themselves to the devil is through their sexual choices. Examples include unnatural sex, including incest and paedophilia. To this you can add premarital sex, extramarital sex, gay sex, and pornography. These are not only doorways but open highways through which the devil and his demons move in and out.[13] (Interestingly, there is a link between pornography and the previous point. Because the demand for porn drives human sex trafficking and rape crimes all over the world, this "personal choice" also involves great injustice against the weak and powerless.)

Anti-Semitism. This is any form of prejudice, discrimination, or attack on Jews just because they are Jews. God hates this. The Jews are God's specially chosen people, through whom the blessing has come to the whole world. God specifically placed the Israelites under supernatural protection when he instituted this spiritual law: whoever blesses Abraham will be blessed, and whoever curses Abraham will be cursed.[14]

Perjury. This is intentionally lying under oath. It also includes being a false witness, providing evidence that you know to be false, and making up a case against somebody who is innocent. Perjury is a very serious offence and often amounts to perverting the course of justice. God hates it; the devil loves it.[15] It opens the door to curses.

Theft. Stealing is taking, keeping, or using property that belongs to somebody else without their consent and with the intention of permanently depriving the rightful owner of its use. God hates theft. The stolen thing is accursed and acts as a point of contact to the devil. As long as it is in your possession, it invites curses into your life.[16]

Self-Reliance. God doesn't like us turning away from him and depending on anyone else. The reason is simple: ordinary flesh cannot compare with the power and might of God. This shift in trust from the almighty God to mere man opens up a highway to curses. The Bible puts it this way: "Cursed is the one who trusts in man, who draws strength from mere flesh and whose heart turns away from the Lord."[17] These are people who claim they "don't do God" and instead place their trust on themselves, other human beings, or the world system. The rich fool in Jesus's parable[18] is a good example. Our trust, hope, and confidence must be in the Lord. Unfortunately, even Christians can be guilty of self-reliance.

Withholding Money from God. Whenever we withhold money that's due to God, we invite curses into our lives. The Bible says, "One person gives freely, yet gains even more; another withholds unduly, but comes to poverty."[19] I am not just referring to the tithe,[20] but to New Testament giving.[21] The apostle Paul says the Macedonian churches "gave as much as they were able, and even beyond their ability"[22] and that they exceeded his expectations in their giving.[23] The Bible tells us, "A stingy planter gets a stingy crop; a lavish planter gets a lavish crop."[24] To reap sparingly or receive "a stingy crop" simply because you've been tight-fisted in your giving is to experience a drought in the midst of abundance. And that's a curse!

Abortion. Abortion is quite controversial, even among Christians. The abortion debate asks whether it can be morally right to terminate a pregnancy before normal childbirth. Some people say abortion is always wrong. Some say abortion is right when the mother's life is at risk. Others believe there are a range of circumstances in which abortion is morally acceptable. Whatever positive spin we want to place on abortion, it is the murder of a defenceless human being. In the sight of God, it is the shedding of innocent blood. And it attracts curses. End of story!

Unconfessed Sin. This is particularly worrying for a Christian. Obviously, only a Christian *can* have unconfessed sin—Christians are the only people who live in a continual confessional relationship with God. This is a child of God who falls into sin through ignorance, through making a mistake, through carelessness, or even by choice, but for whatever reason fails, neglects, or even refuses to repent and make peace with God.

Sadly, some Christians become so disappointed with themselves if they sin that they run away from God instead of confessing their sin and repenting. If we repent immediately, our fellowship with God is unlikely to be broken. The Bible tells us, "If we say that we have no sin, we deceive ourselves, and the truth is not in us. [However] if we confess our sins, He is faithful and just to forgive us our sins and to cleanse us from all unrighteousness. If we say that we have not sinned, we make Him a liar, and His word is not in us."[25]

Not living with unconfessed sin is a no-brainer. If you try to hide from God or run away, not only will your fellowship with God be broken, you will open the back door of your life to the devil.

SATANIC CONTAMINATION

As we saw in chapter 7, we contaminate ourselves and therefore open the door to the devil by making blood sacrifices, communing with the dead, consulting satanic agents, visiting shrines, experimenting with occultism, joining a white-garment church, and taking part in demonic rituals. But there are more innocent-looking ways to get ourselves entangled with the devil as well.

These include palm reading; wearing amulets and talismans; practising witchcraft and divination through tarots or other means; wearing so-called good-luck charms or charms for protection; taking part in pagan dance rituals, carnivals, and festivals; playing with a Ouija board; and dabbling in astrology, fortune-telling, hypnotism, divination, horoscopes, gambling, magic, and psychic readings.

Another danger comes from so-called "holistic healing practices," including esoteric and New Age practices like Reiki, yoga, the lotus position, acupressure, acupuncture, Pranic healing, and reflexology. These are based on Eastern spirituality and mysticism coming from Hinduism and Buddhism, and they can expose us to satanic contamination and open the back door to the devil.

THE WORDS WE SPEAK

In addition to sin and satanic contamination, we also invite curses to ourselves by our confessions and the words we speak. We saw in chapter 8 that words have such incredible power that, whether we want to or not, we give life to what we're saying, either good or bad.

The story is told of Jose Lima, a Dominican right-handed pitcher who spent thirteen seasons in major league baseball with the Detroit Tigers, Houston Astros, Kansas City Royals, Los Angeles Dodgers, and New York Mets.[26] His best year in the majors was 1999, when he won twenty-one games for the Astros and pitched in his only all-star game.

Lima was the star pitcher for the Houston Astros for several years in the late 1990s. A colourful guy, he was best known for coining all his pitching appearances as "Lima Time." His remarkably animated display of emotion on the mound made him a fan favourite. He was an outgoing, energetic, likable young ballplayer who usually exuded a positive attitude. He was also known for his flamboyant celebrations in the face of his opponents after his victories and was once described as a "national anthem-crooning, towel-waving merengue singer who moonlights as a right-handed pitcher."[27]

In 2000 when the Astros moved into their new ballpark, now known as Minute Maid Park, Lima got upset. The fence in this left field was much closer than the fence at the Astrodome, their previous ballpark. In fact, at just 315 feet, Minute Maid Park has one of the shortest distances from plate to the left-field fence of any ballpark in major league baseball. The hitters love it, but the short left field makes it tougher on the pitchers, especially when they are working against right-handed batters who tend to hit to left field.

The first time Lima stepped onto the new diamond, he walked out to the pitcher's mound, and when he looked into the outfield, the first words out of his mouth were, "I'll never be able to pitch in here, the fence is way too close."

Sure enough, the next season, despite the enthusiasm of fans and the excitement of playing in that brand-new ballpark, Lima had the worst year of his career. He plummeted from being a twenty-game winner to being a sixteen-game loser in back-to-back seasons. Never in the history of the Astros franchise had any pitcher experienced such a pronounced negative turnaround. What happened to him? He got what he spoke. Be careful what you say about yourself. Cut anything negative out of your vocabulary.

GODLY SORROW AND REPENTANCE

In the next few chapters, we're going to begin to look at deliverance—what it is and how to get it. But when it comes to personal sin, the only cure is repentance. If you're sincerely sorry with godly sorrow for your sins, and you truly repent of them, God will forgive you and give you another chance. God is not *just* a God of second chances: when we are repentant, he gives us chance after chance after chance to get it right. Like King David, we just need to be completely broken over our sin, because God responds to a broken, contrite, and truly repentant heart.[28] You can't fake this, but God will always respond to authentic repentance.

If you sincerely repent, God will forgive and cleanse you. However, that will not *by itself* automatically remove the effect of self-inflicted curses which have landed on you because of the sin. Having been forgiven by God, you will need to specifically and intentionally break the curse, release yourself from the effects of the curse, and then take appropriate action to transition into the blessing.

True repentance with godly sorrow unlocks the heavens because God does not despise a truly pertinent heart. And that's a surefire key to advancing God's kingdom through spiritual warfare.

You will find helpful guidance, including prayers, in chapter 12. But before then, it's time to look at the foundational truths that lead to deliverance.

Chapter 10:

ROLLING AWAY THE REPROACH

> "When they had completed the circumcising of the whole nation, they stayed where they were in camp until they were healed. God said to Joshua, 'Today I have rolled away the reproach of Egypt.' That's why the place is called The Gilgal. It's still called that."
>
> **Joshua 5:8-9, MSG**

Juliet first arrived in the United Kingdom from St Vincent and the Grenadines in August 1998. She arrived as a tourist, then became a student until September 2006, when she overstayed her visa and became an illegal immigrant. Meanwhile, sometime in 2003, the government introduced a scheme whereby it granted permanent residence to those who had spent fourteen years illegally in the United Kingdom. Juliet became aware of this in 2006 when her visa expired. Her lawyer told her she would qualify as long as she remained in the United Kingdom until September 2012. She was overjoyed.

However, in July 2012, after Juliet had spent a total of thirteen years and ten months in the United Kingdom and was preparing to make her application for permanent residence based on fourteen years of continuous unlawful residence, the unexpected happened. The law was changed from fourteen to twenty years! Not only that, but now, twenty years of continuous unlawful residence in the United Kingdom would entitle you, not to permanent residence, but to thirty months' limited leave to remain. She made the application anyway, thinking she was too close to her breakthrough not to. Unfortunately, her application was refused.

Juliet was inconsolable. She was so very close to her breakthrough. She could almost touch it, and all of a sudden, it was all taken away from her. *Just like that!* As we will see later, this is what's called a *reproach*.

There's another example of reproach in the Bible. After an arduous journey encompassing forty long years in the wilderness, the Israelites finally crossed the River Jordan and entered the Promised Land. The Israelites could see that it was indeed a good land—a land with brooks and rivers, springs and lakes, streams out of the hills and through the valleys. A land full of wheat and barley fields, vineyards, and orchards full of fig, pomegranate, and olive trees, and where there was plenty of milk and honey. A land where there was no scarcity or lack.[1]

However, there was a problem. They were now in the Land of Promise, yet they could not yet eat the produce of the land. Instead, they continued to eat manna—in the Promised Land! They came so close they could describe the produce of the land. They could even smell it. But they couldn't taste it. They were so close, yet so far way!

Clearly, something was not quite right. After four hundred and thirty years of slavery in Egypt and forty years in the wilderness, one would have thought the Israelites would have rid themselves of Egypt. But they had not. They were physically out of Egypt, but Egypt was still in their hearts. They carried with them the scars of Egypt—the reproach, the humiliation, the shame, the sorrow, the degradation, the blood of innocent victims killed by merciless slave masters, the chains and pains of slavery. *The reason they couldn't eat the good of the land was that the reproach of Egypt still clung to them.*

This is the ultimate reproach—to enter the Promised Land yet be unable to enjoy the good of that land. God had to do something. And he did—he intervened to provide a divine solution to the problem of the reproach.

God told Joshua to circumcise all the young men who were born in the wilderness. This was a different crop of people. Born in the wilderness, they chose a different path to their parents, who had perished on the way. They were willing to be circumcised as grown men to enable them renew the Abrahamic covenant with the Lord. Because of their obedience, God was ready to transition them from *wanderers* to *warriors* capable of taking the land. He was going to honour their faith and bring healing and deliverance to the people.

After the men healed from the ordeal of circumcision, the Lord told Joshua, "Today I have rolled away the reproach of Egypt." What did God mean by those words?

The Abrahamic covenant which God established with Israel required all males to be circumcised eight days after birth. The fact that all of these men who were born in the wilderness had yet to be circumcised as adults indicates they were still walking in disobedience and not honouring the covenant with God. They were living in sin, opening the door to reproach. Being circumcised was a sign of their repentance and a renewal of the covenant. When God said their reproach had been rolled away, he was telling Joshua and the people of Israel that the evil consequences of their disobedience had been destroyed. Their deliverance was complete. They were now free: free to worship God, free to be a nation under God, and free to enjoy the Land of Promise.

After God uttered those life-changing words, the people of Israel continued to camp at Gilgal. They celebrated the Passover on the evening of the fourteenth day of the month on the plains of Jericho. The day after the Passover, *for the first time since their arrival* they started eating the produce of the Promised Land. They ate flatbread and roasted grain. And surprise, surprise, the day after they ate the food of the land, the manna *stopped!* As soon as the reproach was rolled away, as soon as they were delivered and they started eating the food grown in the Promised Land, manna ceased for the people of Israel. That year they ate from the crops of Canaan.[2]

In the same way, God has brought us out of the Egypt of our old life and sins. But many of us are still living like slaves. Jesus is on the throne, but we act like the devil is still ruling. We need to get free of the reproach of Egypt and start to live in the Promised Land of our new-creation lives. For starters, we need to move beyond manna.

MANNA TRAITS

What was manna? We know that manna was emergency food provided by God for his grumbling children in the wilderness.[3] It was a wafer that could be made into cakes or bread. It contained all the nutrients they needed, yet it had no preservatives—it would rot after only one day, stinking and filled with maggots. Each morning, the Israelites gathered exactly what they needed, no more, no less (except on the eve of the Sabbath when they were allowed to gather two days' worth). Although it was God's provision, manna was strictly for the wilderness, not for the Land of Promise.

How can we relate this to our lives today? Manna was crisis food. The Israelites could not save it. They could only gather enough for one day. It was provision for the wilderness only. To my mind, manna signifies the following, what I call *manna traits*:

No End in Sight. A wilderness experience that's going on and on, with no end in sight. We all go through wilderness experiences. God allows them to humble us, test us, teach us to trust him for our sustenance, and do us good in the end.[4] Why? Because it is in the valley that growth takes place, not on the mountain peak. However, if the experience is unending, then it is indicative of surviving permanently on what should only be a temporary provision. Something is wrong, and you need to be moved into the fullness of the promise.

Buy Now, Pay Later. In other words, generally living on credit. Some people don't own anything; everything they have is borrowed, leased, or hired—houses, automobiles, partner (yes, partner!), clothes, children, etc. They buy their groceries on credit, pay their rent or mortgage with a credit-card cheque, and generally live on credit cards.

Living Hand to Mouth. This is living paycheque to paycheque and depending on your overdraft facility or even payday loans to tide you over from, say, the middle of the month to payday. In the United Kingdom, the short-term loans market has flourished in recent years, in particular the demand for payday loans. Payday lenders offer short-term, high-interest loans to consumers with the suggestion that the money be paid back within a month when the borrower receives the next paycheque. Unlike standard secured or unsecured loans, payday loans are short-term borrowing solutions aimed at those facing immediate financial difficulty. Loans are generally available for amounts of between £100 and £1000 and are usually used to bridge the gap until the next paycheque.[5] The Public Accounts Committee (PAC) says that about two million people in the United Kingdom use payday loans,[6] some with interest rates as high as 5,853 percent per anum![7]

Can't Save, Won't Save. An inability to save and put something aside for a rainy day, no matter how hard you try. A third of people (36 percent) in the United States have nothing saved for retirement, a new survey shows.[8] In fact, according to a survey conducted by the personal finance website Bankrate.com, 14 percent of people aged sixty-five and older have no retirement savings. Twenty-six percent of those aged fifty to sixty-four, 33 percent of those between thirty and forty-nine, and 69 percent of those aged eighteen to twenty-nine have no savings. In the United Kingdom, figures released by Scottish Widows suggest that one in five people have absolutely no savings at all. According to the report, 20 percent of people polled relied on nothing more than their monthly wages to cope with the needs of life. The report reveals that the number of people with no savings today is the highest seen since 2009.[9]

Irresponsibility. Lacking any sense of responsibility when it comes to your finances is a manna trait. You buy products you can't maintain. You take out loans without a thought as to how you will repay them. For instance, you may be unable to pay child support, yet you own the latest electronic gadgets. You might own the latest mobile or cell phone handset but have to go to a McDonald's restaurant to charge it because you can't afford electricity. You might possess the latest electronic gadgets but eat your breakfast cereal with a fork so you can save on milk!

If you're experiencing any of these manna traits, there's probably a reproach hanging over your life that needs to be rolled away, a curse that needs to be broken, or an ancestral covenant that needs to be revoked.

To enable us to properly unpack this concept, there are some key words and phrases in the Scripture passage we need to look at. These are the *reproach of Egypt, Gilgal,* and *circumcision.*

THE REPROACH OF EGYPT

Reproach is disgrace, discredit, or shame. It is seen in anything that is a cause or an occasion of shame. In the case of the children of Israel, it sounds really bizarre that they had entered the Promised Land and yet still ate manna. They still had the mentality of slaves, and they needed to be emancipated by the Lord. Reproach is being so close to your breakthrough but not able to touch it. Synonyms of reproach include *dishonour, shame,* and *disrepute.* Reproach is anything that causes people to shake their heads in disbelief when they hear your story.

Another example of reproach is what happened to Israel during the time of the judges. Whenever the Israelites planted their crops, Midianites, Amalekites, and Easterners would invade them, camp in their fields, and destroy their crops all the way down to Gaza. They left nothing for them to live on, neither sheep nor ox nor donkey. Bringing their cattle, camels, and tents, the invaders came in and took over like an invasion of locusts. They marched in and devastated the country, reducing Israel to grinding poverty![10]

Lamentations describes another form of reproach in its heart breaking lament: "Slaves rule over us; there's no escape from their grip."[11] Can you imagine a country where those born free are ruled by slaves with an iron grip and the citizens are wondering who will deliver them?

Samuel Doe was a twenty-eight-year-old, uneducated master sergeant when he became the leader of Liberia in a *coup d'état* on 12 April 1980. His parents were poor and uneducated, like most rural Liberians of that era. He had only completed his primary school education when he joined the Liberian Armed Forces. He was in his fourth high school grade and attending night school when he and a group of soldiers seized power, assassinated the American-Liberian president William R. Tolbert Jr., and established, for the first time in Liberia's history, military rule over the country.

Samuel Doe was the highest-ranking non-commissioned officer of the coup plotters, so he became chairman of the People's Redemption Council (PRC) and ruled the country for ten years. A power-drunk master sergeant, with little more than a primary school education, led an entire country for ten years. Talk about reproach!

To many people around the world, America is the land of opportunity. It is said that when America sneezes, Europe catches cold. Michael Lind describes America as the land of promise in his book, *Land of Promise: An Economic History of the United States*. Every year, millions of people from all over the world apply for visas into the United States in pursuit of the American dream. Every year, many thousands illegally cross the United States' borders from Cuba, Mexico, and other countries in search of this dream. The allure is so irresistible that the illegal immigrant population of the United States now stands at a massive 11,700,000, according to a January 2014 estimate of the U.S. Department of Homeland Security.[12]

The American dream is a set of ideals in which freedom includes the opportunity for prosperity and success and upward social mobility achieved through hard work. The idea is that if you stay in school, graduate, work hard, and play by the rules, you will get ahead! The notion of the American dream is rooted in the United States' Declaration of Independence, which proclaims that "all men are created equal" and that they are "endowed by their Creator with certain inalienable Rights" including "Life, Liberty and the pursuit of Happiness."

Yet there are millions of Americans living in America who know nothing about the American dream! They have no idea whatsoever about what these lofty ideals mean. The reality for them is a daily struggle for survival.

The table below is the result of research conducted by the National Law Center on Homelessness and Poverty on homelessness in the United States. It shows that as of July 2014, there were nearly two million homeless people in the States, twelve million children living below the poverty level, and thirty-one million Americans either living in hunger or on the verge of hunger.

American Homeless Poverty Statistics[13]	Data
Number of homeless people in the United States	1,750,000
Average monthly income for a homeless individual	$348
Percent of homeless that do not get enough to eat daily	28%
Percent of homeless that have been homeless for more than two (2) years	30%
Number of Americans now living in hunger or on the edge of hunger	31,000,000
Number of children in the United States who live below poverty level	12,000,000
Annual number of food stamp recipients who are children	9,300,000

Like the Israelites, these Americans live in the land of promise, the land of opportunity, and yet all they eat is manna! They know people who have experienced the American dream, they can describe it, they can even smell it, but they can't touch it. To them, the American dream is little more than a fantasy.

ARE YOU UNDER A REPROACH?

Are you worried that you may be living under a reproach? If you are, you may be wondering, "How does a reproach come into our lives?"

Reproach comes into our lives in one of two ways. We have already looked at both in depth. More often than not, a reproach is the fruit or external manifestation of a generational curse, an ancestral covenant, an evil family pattern, or a satanic altar speaking against us. In chapters 6 and 7, Carolina, Aisha, and Eghosa all had varying degrees of reproach because of the actions of other people. We can also bring reproach on ourselves through the choices we make. This can happen in a variety of ways, but only when we open the back door of our lives to the devil as we saw in chapter 9.

To effectively deal with the problem and roll away the reproach, you have to attack the root cause. There's no use simply destroying the fruit or even cutting the branches from the tree of reproach. You must go further. You must uproot the tree and destroy it. For this to happen, you must have a Gilgal experience, be circumcised in your heart, and shut the door against the devil. These are the foundations of deliverance.

A GILGAL EXPERIENCE

The Israelites were circumcised in Gilgal. The Lord rolled away and removed the reproach of Egypt there, after which it was named Gilgal ("to roll"). They kept the Passover at Gilgal. It was there that they first tasted the good of the land. It was also there that manna ceased!

Therefore, to have a Gilgal experience is first of all to be born again. It is to have a divine encounter with the Most High God, one from which it is difficult to recover!

Are you born again? Have you been redeemed by the blood of Jesus? Have you invited Jesus into your heart and asked him to become your personal Saviour and Lord?

The sin problem originated with the first man, Adam. He disobeyed God in the Garden of Eden, and because of that, every human being is born with an Adamic sin nature. Accordingly, we sin because we are sinners. The Bible says, "Consequently, just as one trespass resulted in condemnation for all people, so also one righteous act resulted in justification and life for all people. For just as through the disobedience of the one man the many were made sinners, so also through the obedience of the one man the many will be made righteous."[14] David said, "Surely I was sinful at birth, sinful from the time my mother conceived me."[15]

Following the fall of man, God sent Jesus Christ, the Son of God, to die for our sin. "For God so loved the world that He gave His one and only Son, that whoever believes in Him shall not perish but have eternal life."[16] Jesus died on the cross of Calvary and rose from the grave on the third day. Through his death and resurrection we are saved, sanctified, and justified. "For God made Christ, who never sinned, to be the offering for our sin, so that we could be made right with God through Christ."[17]

Jesus is the Way, the Truth, and the Life, and the only way by which human beings can have access to God.[18] To be saved, all we have to do is acknowledge that we are sinners and receive what Jesus did on our behalf through his death and resurrection. If you haven't already done so, you can invite Jesus into your heart right now to become your personal Saviour and Lord as you acknowledge that you are a sinner and accept that he died on your behalf and rose for you. Why not pray the sinner's prayer at this very moment?

Please say it out loud:

> Lord Jesus, I acknowledge that I am a sinner. I believe with my heart that you died for my sin and that you were raised from the dead for my justification. Your Word says in Romans 10:9, "If you confess with your mouth the Lord Jesus and believe in your heart that God has raised Him from the dead, you will be saved." I confess with my mouth that you are my Saviour and my Lord. I invite you to come into my heart and make me a new creation. Thank you, Lord Jesus, for saving me. Please write my name in your Book of Life. In Jesus's name I pray. Amen.

As you pray this prayer, may you know Jesus as your Saviour and be saved, as your Healer and be healed, and as your Deliverer and be delivered. If you've just prayed the sinner's prayer, sincerely from your heart, then you're now a born-again child of God. Congratulations! Please write to let me know so I can encourage you in your new faith.

If you are saved and still experiencing reproach, then you are fighting *for* victory in your spiritual warfare. You are not fighting *from* victory! Your spiritual life is backwards. Something is not quite right. Either you are fighting the enemy in your own strength or he is oppressing you for a variety of reasons. And you need to break free.

THE CIRCUMCISION

For the people of Israel, circumcision was not optional. It was compulsory! It represented the covenant between Abraham and God. It was to be performed on the eighth day after birth. Therefore, nobody was ever circumcised before they had experienced one Sabbath—the seventh day of the week, on which rest was commanded for all the people. Spiritual Sabbath is resting in God's ability to accomplish what he has begun in our lives. It is being entirely reliant on God's grace. The eighth day also signifies a new beginning. Something is different after circumcision. Spiritual circumcision is the start of a new thing in our lives.

The Israelites received their deliverance and their reproach was rolled away after they were circumcised. Circumcision therefore *led* to their deliverance. Spiritual circumcision, the cutting away of the "foreskins" of our hearts, is a description of our conversion experience.[19] It can only take place as we experience the spiritual Sabbath by resting on the accomplished work of Calvary.

When we invite Jesus into our lives, the Holy Spirit converts and transforms us, making us new creations in Christ Jesus.[20] Conversion takes place on the inside, in our spirits. Our spirit is transformed and is now able to communicate with God. We become born again, spiritually circumcised and experiencing a new day. If you have accepted Jesus into your life, this is your new day! Your day of deliverance has come.

On the other hand, you can be saved and experiencing reproach, much like the Israelites who were the church in the wilderness. For the Christian, this will be a case of demonic oppression. If this is your situation, there is hope. Jesus can make you free.

SHUTTING THE DOOR AND KEEPING THE DEVIL OUT

Generally, both the kingdom of God and Satan's kingdom operate by legal rights or open doorways. Unless we open the door of our hearts to God, he won't come into our lives to be our personal Saviour, Healer, and Deliverer. Jesus said, "Here I am! I stand at the door and knock. If anyone hears my voice and opens the door, I will come in and eat with that person, and they with me."[21] If you don't let him in, he won't come in!

In much the same way, the devil generally can't come into your life unless the door is opened to him. Unlike God, who only comes in by our personal prayer of invitation, there are many ways the door can be opened to Satan. He is very sly and will take advantage of the slightest opening that he can detect in our lives. He crouches like a wild animal at the door waiting for an opportunity, an opening to enter into our lives.

> As the most dangerous winds may enter at little openings, so the devil never enters more dangerously than by little unobserved incidents, which seem to be nothing, yet insensibly open the heart to great temptations.[22]

As we saw in chapter 9, we open the door to the devil mainly through the choices we make in the areas of sin, the words we speak, and satanic contamination. If we break the hedge, the serpent will bite us.[23] Unless you close those doors, the devil has a legal right to operate in your life and to steal, kill, and destroy your blessings.

We close the doors through repentance and deliverance. Once these doors have been shut, we have to be diligent in keeping them shut. Satan will to try to get those entryways into your life open again. Don't let him in! He is very subtle and crafty and can appear as an angel of light.[24] He will try his best to find a way back in, but thank God, we are not ignorant of his evil schemes.[25] Glory to Jesus!

In chapter 14, we will look in more detail at how to keep the door shut against the devil *for good*. But before we get there, let's look at an unexpected but common obstacle to complete deliverance—thinking you don't need it because you're already born again.

Chapter 11:

BUT I'M BORN AGAIN!

> "In the same way, faith by itself, if it is not accompanied by action, is dead."
>
> **James 2:17**

Jane and Peter got married nearly seven years ago. They're both born-again children of God who are very active in their local church. Peter is an associate pastor, while Jane heads the children's church. Jane's parents are Christians.

Jane and Peter wanted to have children, but for some reason Jane couldn't seem to carry a pregnancy to full term. The doctors weren't sure why she kept miscarrying. They said there were so many potential factors it was hard to pinpoint the specific cause.

This couple came to see me shortly after my book *Crushing the Devil* was released. They wanted me to pray with them. They wanted to become parents. They wanted the miscarriages to stop.

As I listened to their story, I felt it was abnormal for her to have so many miscarriages. However, we needed to delve into their respective backgrounds to find out if there was anything of interest.

As it transpired, Jane was brought up by her maternal grandparents in West Africa. As a young girl, she was eating and sleeping with men in her dreams. Worried about this, her grandmother took her to the white-garment church just up the road from them, for deliverance. The prophet said she was being tormented by water spirits, and the remedy was for her to take part in a ritual on the banks of the local river.

Jane was asked to take a special bath with a special soap and sponge at the riverside. As part of the ritual, a chicken was killed. She placed the chicken all over her body while the prophet "spoke in tongues." She was then told to walk backwards toward the river, swing the chicken around her head a certain number of times, and throw the chicken and the sponge into the river without looking back.

After this ritual, the problem stopped. However, from time to time, she would see herself in her dreams living in a large house under the water with a beautiful family, including a husband, children, and servants.

Jane later became a Christian and eventually met Peter. Following her marriage, the sex in her dreams returned. This time, though, she appeared to be sleeping with her husband.

I immediately diagnosed marriage to a water spirit. The white-garment prophet had exchanged Jane's glory, beauty, and destiny for ashes. The ritual that took place at the banks of the river when she was a little girl was effectively a marriage ceremony. Jane was married to a jealous water spirit. She had children in the world of the water spirits, and so she would never have children in the real world. Every time she got pregnant, her spirit husband would attack the pregnancy, resulting in miscarriage. The water spirit had a legal right because of the marriage covenant at the riverside.

Peter and Jane couldn't understand how the devil still had a claim on her life after she'd become a Christian. I told them she needed to specifically break the marriage covenant with the water spirit, recover her glory, and claim what Jesus had done for her in order to be truly free. We spent some time in prayer, and I led her to revoke the marriage covenant and to divorce herself from her spirit husband. We then verbally destroyed the spirit marriage, killed her spirit babies, and recovered her glory, beauty, and destiny in the place of prayer.

Shortly afterward, Jane got pregnant again. The doctors also did their part, keeping a close eye on her and the pregnancy. This time she was able to carry the pregnancy to full term. Today, she is the proud mother of a healthy baby!

Jane and Peter are not alone in questioning the relevance of the Deliverance ministry to Christians. In my ministry, I have met two categories of people who struggle with the very concept of generational curses and ancestral covenants. Some, like Jane and Peter, believe that because they're now born again, they should no longer be affected by *any* satanic covenants or generational curses. Others struggle with the idea that somebody can reap what a family member sowed in a previous generation. In this chapter, I will address these two objections.

CURSES AND THE BORN-AGAIN BELIEVER

Can a born-again child of God, redeemed by the blood of Jesus, still be subject to evil family patterns, generational curses, and ancestral covenants? There are two opposing views about this.

Many people believe that once you're saved, you're free from all curses and evil covenants because the Bible says "Christ redeemed us from the curse of the law by becoming a curse for us, for it is written: 'Cursed is everyone who is hung on a pole.'"[1]

Others believe that being saved does not automatically break the curses and revoke the covenants; you have to specifically break them in the name of Jesus. What is the correct position?

Before answering the question, let me point out the common ground between these opposing points of view. They both agree that there's power in the name of Jesus to break every chain. There's power in the name of Jesus to destroy every invisible barrier. There's power in the name of Jesus to tear down every limitation on a person's destiny. There's power in the name of Jesus to revoke every generational curse and rescind every ancestral covenant. There's power in the name of Jesus to destroy evil family patterns. What they are unclear about is whether or not this takes place *automatically* at the new birth or whether something further needs to be done in order to enact this freedom.

To answer the question, I would like to analyse four passages of Scripture which are similar and which tell us about different aspects of the sacrificial death of our Lord Jesus Christ. God is a God of principle. Every area of life is guided by principles revealed in the Word of God. When we look at the principles in these four passages, we can clearly see that it is not sufficient to be saved in order to receive what God has for you. You must also *apply* the principles revealed in the Word.

The first Scripture is a rare gem, a beautifully crafted diamond of a Scripture. It says, "God made him who had no sin to be sin for us, so that in him we might become the righteousness of God."[2] Jesus became sin for the whole world by his death and resurrection so we can become God's righteousness. Does this make the entire world automatically saved?

Of course not! To be saved, you have to admit that you're a sinner, accept that Jesus died for your sins and was raised up for your justification, invite him into your heart as Saviour, and declare that he is Lord.

Salvation is by grace and therefore free. But salvation is only available to those who willingly accept what Jesus accomplished on their behalf on the cross. The Bible puts it this way in the book of Romans:

> If you declare with your mouth, "Jesus is Lord," and if you believe in your heart that God raised Jesus from the dead, you will be saved. We believe with our hearts, and so we are made right with God. And we declare with our mouths that we believe, and so we are saved. As the Scripture says, "Anyone who trusts in Him will never be disappointed." That Scripture says "anyone" because there is no difference between those who are Jews and those who are not. The same Lord is the Lord of all and gives many blessings to all who trust in Him, as the Scripture says, "Anyone who calls on the Lord will be saved."
>
> But before people can ask the Lord for help, they must believe in Him; and before they can believe in Him, they must hear about Him; and for them to hear about the Lord, someone must tell them; and before someone can go and tell them, that person must be sent. It is written, "How beautiful is the person who comes to bring good news." But not all the Jews accepted the good news. Isaiah said, "Lord, who believed what we told them?" So faith comes from hearing the Good News, and people hear the Good News when someone tells them about Christ.[3]

There are millions of people in the world today who are on their way to hell because they haven't accepted Jesus. Whoever believes in him is not condemned, but whoever does not believe stands condemned already because they have not believed in the name of God's one and only Son.[4]

The second Scripture is another piece of quality, a diamond shining brightly among the jewels around it. It deals with poverty. It says, "For you know the grace of our Lord Jesus Christ, that though he was rich, yet for your sake he became poor, so that you through his poverty might become rich."[5]

What does this actually mean? I think it is self-explanatory—it does exactly what it says on the tin! Jesus, though rich, became poor. He was rich in the glory he had before the world was made. His wealth was being in the form of God and being equal with God, being God, the very God. His wealth was the majesty and splendour he enjoyed in heaven.

Jesus became poor through his incarnation. He emptied himself. As the Bible says:

> [He] set aside the privileges of deity and took on the status of a slave, became human! Having become human, he stayed human. It was an incredibly humbling process. He didn't claim special privileges. Instead, he lived a selfless, obedient life and then died a selfless, obedient death—and the worst kind of death at that—a crucifixion.[6]

Why did Jesus do this? "That [you and I] through His poverty might become rich." He did all that for you, for me; for your sake, for my sake. Why? To make poor sinners like you and me rich. Materially rich? Certainly! Spiritually rich? More so! Eternally rich? Even more so!

"But rich with what riches?" somebody may ask. Jesus is God eternal. And as eternal God, he is as rich as God is rich. God created all things and he owns all things. He owns the universe and all that is in it. He owns all power, all authority, all sovereignty, all glory, all honour, all majesty, all that is created, and all that's yet to be created. Jesus's wealth is beyond human comprehension. His wealth is boundless. His wealth is limitless. His wealth is immeasurable. His wealth is inestimable. It is fathomless. It is infinite. Jesus is infinite, and his wealth is as infinite as his being.

Jesus is rich with the same riches he possessed prior to the incarnation and continues to possess. He is rich in salvation, power, forgiveness, joy, peace, life, light, glory, holiness, and honour. He is rich in splendour and majesty. He is rich in silver and gold.

Born-again children of God are also rich. That's why they're called God's heirs and joint-heirs with Christ.[7] They are promised an inheritance incorruptible and undefiled that does not fade away, laid up for them in heaven.[8] They are rich here on earth too because he gives them the ability to acquire wealth.[9] God's children are very rich. They are as rich as he is rich. And to think they were once poor. Really, really, really poor!

It was King David who famously said, "I have been young and now I am old, Yet I have not seen the righteous forsaken or his descendants begging bread."[10] And yet, today, there are many born-again children of God who can't make ends meet. Even though God is their provider, supplying all their needs according to his glorious riches, they still live impoverished lives. Unless they apply the relevant principles of the Word of God, they will remain poor even though they're heaven-blessed and heaven-bound!

The third Scripture I would like us to consider says, "'He himself bore our sins' in his body on the cross, so that we might die to sins and live for righteousness; 'by his wounds you have been healed.'"[11]

As we saw in chapter 7, Jesus shed his blood in seven places.[12] By the stripes on his back, he won back our health, making it possible for those who are redeemed by his blood to live in divine health. It's all been paid for. We just need to claim it by faith! The main principle for healing is faith. Without faith for your healing, you can be born again and heaven-bound and still not receive your healing.

Jesus could have died a relatively painless death and still saved us. On several occasions, the Jews wanted to push him over a cliff,[13] but he would disappear until he was ready to die God's way. And then he died the most brutal kind of death imaginable! He did this to secure our healing, but we will not experience that healing unless we appropriate it by faith.

Now to the fourth and final Scripture. It's another sparkling pearl, a beauty, quietly tucked away in one of the Pauline epistles. It says, "Christ redeemed us from the curse of the law by becoming a curse for us, for it is written: 'Cursed is everyone who is hung on a pole.'"[14]

This is of course the Scripture referred to by those who say that being born again automatically revokes every curse. This passage of Scripture is very similar to the first three we considered. The first said that God made Jesus, who knew no sin, to become sin for us; the second said that Jesus became poor so that through his poverty we might become rich; the third said that by his stripes we have been healed; and here we are told that Jesus became a curse for us.

If, as we have seen, salvation is not automatic but has to be specifically accepted even though it is available to the whole world; and if Christ's riches are available to every Christian through Christ's poverty in his incarnation and yet there are millions of Christians in both spiritual and material poverty; and if we are healed by the stripes of Jesus and yet many believers live with sickness and disease; what makes us think that being a Christian automatically removes the ancestral covenants and generational curses that may be following us?

Here's the truth as I understand it: No matter your ancestry, and no matter what you may have unknowingly adopted as a pattern in your life, the blood of Jesus Christ has already broken its power over you. In Christ, your freedom is already secure. It does not matter what is in your past or what your ancestry is. The cross of Jesus Christ *is* sufficient to cut off all the power of every generational curse, to destroy every evil family pattern, and to revoke every ancestral covenant. *You just need to embrace, accept, and receive what Jesus has done.* You need to do this *specifically*. You do this by faith in the name of Jesus.

And when you do this—specifically break generational curses and ancestral covenants—you are affirming the once-for-all finished work of Jesus Christ when he declared, "It is finished."[15]

Jesus has done what he needs to do. You have to do your part by specifically breaking the curses and revoking the covenants.

Daniel was a prophet of Israel who lived in exile in Babylon. Because everyone in Israel had sinned and stubbornly refused to obey God, the curses and sworn judgments written in the Law of Moses had been poured out on them, bringing great disaster upon them. They were taken captive and were to remain in captivity for seventy years.[16]

How were these curses broken? During Darius's first year as king of Babylonia, Daniel found out from studying the writings of the prophets that the Lord had said to Jeremiah, "This country will be as empty as a desert, because I will make all of you the slaves of the king of Babylonia for seventy years. When that time is up, I will punish the king of Babylonia and his people for everything they have done wrong, and I will turn that country into a wasteland forever."[17] God had also promised to restore his people to their land.

The time was now up, but the people of Israel were still in captivity. So Daniel took it upon himself to fast and pray and repent of the sins of the entire nation.

He told God:

> We have sinned and committed iniquity. We have done wickedly and rebelled, even by departing from your precepts and your judgments.

Neither have we heeded your servants the prophets, who spoke in your name to our kings and our princes, to our fathers and all the people of the land.

He concluded his prayer this way:

Master, you are our God, for you delivered your people from the land of Egypt in a show of power—people are still talking about it! We confess that we have sinned, that we have lived bad lives. Following the lines of what you have always done in setting things right, setting people right, please stop being so angry with Jerusalem, your very own city, your holy mountain. We know it's our fault that this has happened, all because of our sins and our parents' sins, and now we're an embarrassment to everyone around us. We're a blot on the neighbourhood. So listen, God, to this determined prayer of your servant. Have mercy on your ruined Sanctuary. Act out of who you are, not out of what we are. Turn your ears our way, God, and listen. Open your eyes and take a long look at our ruined city, this city named after you. We know that we don't deserve a hearing from you. Our appeal is to your compassion. This prayer is our last and only hope: Master, listen to us! Master, forgive us! Master, look at us and do something! Master, don't put us off! Your city and your people are named after you: You have a stake in us![18]

Covenants, curses, and family patterns can affect you even if you've become born again unless and until you appropriate to yourself what Jesus did for you at Calvary. You've got to specifically break and revoke these covenants and curses in the place of prayer by the blood of Jesus and claim your freedom. You can be a millionaire and yet die of poverty if you don't spend the money you have in the bank!

Although Jesus has paid your debt of sin in full, you can still end up spending eternity separated from God in hell if you don't accept his sacrificial death and receive him as Saviour and Lord. Similarly, you can be on fire for Jesus and be so poor you don't know where your next meal will come from. You can be born again and afflicted with sickness and disease. And you can be a tongues-speaking, hallelujah-singing, demon-casting, heaven-bound, born-again child of God and still be oppressed by the devil if you're ignorant of his schemes. A child of God can be affected by generational curses, ancestral covenants, and the words spoken over him if he doesn't specifically break and revoke them.

REAPING THE SINS OF OTHERS

Now to the second objection: can you really reap what a family member sowed in generations past? The very idea that somebody can be affected by the iniquity committed by another person in a previous generation isn't logical at first glance. And it doesn't sit well with a lot of people.

In his book, *Free at Last,* Pastor Larry Huch provides some useful insight:

> In our Western-world mind-set, we can accept the fact that someone is paying a price because of something they did. We understand that a man reaps what he sows. What we're not taught is that we may reap something sown by our family many generations ago. The disciples knew that curses were passed on to future generations. They understood that the supernatural could transcend all reason and logic. And we must understand this truth to be set free from generational curses!
>
> > Like a flitting sparrow, like a flying swallow,
> > So a curse without cause shall not alight. (Proverbs 26:2)
>
> I am amazed when I hear or read about birds migrating to distant continents at various seasons of the year. A bird can fly out of North America and find its way across the equator to South America, find the exact nest it had before, stay there for the winter season, and then fly home to Alaska and find its way back to the exact nest it left there.
>
> This is a tremendous illustration of the spiritual principle behind curses. Proverbs 26:2 tells us to look at the swallows that fly thousands of miles every year, if not tens of thousands of miles, and return to the same nest. How does that happen? They don't have a map, a GPS unit, and they're not following road signs. The birds are not guided by radar or air traffic control. They're not just flapping their wings, flying around, and then suddenly, somehow, happen to find their way

to the right nests. It is not a coincidence. There is something inside those birds that guides them to return to exactly the same place they were born.

Here in the Northwest, a salmon can be born in one of thousands of streams or rivers and will go downstream into a bigger river, that will empty into a bigger river, that will empty into a bigger river, and eventually go out into the ocean. It will spend a couple of years in the ocean, but when it's time for that salmon to spawn, it will swim back from the ocean to the main river, up another river, up another river, and go to the exact stream where it was born years before. How does that happen? Something on the inside draws the salmon home.

In a similar way, a curse doesn't just float around in the atmosphere and then, for no apparent reason, land somewhere. Just as there is something that directs the salmon and the swallows, there is something that directs a curse to a person, city, church, or nation. That curse is guided by a spiritual force.

There is a reason why a child grows up to become an alcoholic. There is a reason why an abused child becomes an abusive parent. There is a reason why a young man ends up in prison. There is a reason why a person goes through divorce after divorce.[19]

Generational curses are alive and well. As Christians, we can't bury our heads in the sand and pretend they're not there. And praise God, Jesus has made adequate provision to take care of the problem they pose. Beth Moore puts it this way:

Exodus 20:5 says, "You shall not bow down to [idols] or worship them; for I, the Lord your God, am a jealous God, punishing the children for the sin of the fathers to the third and fourth generation of those who hate me."

The word punishing in this verse proves a stumbling block for some people. The King James Version translates this as "visiting," which is more reflective of the original Hebrew word *paqadh*, meaning to inspect, review, number, deposit, or visit in the sense of making a call. It's also used for taking a census.

Ezekiel 18 assures us God doesn't punish children for their parents' sins. God clearly says, "I will judge you, each one according to his ways" (v. 30). I believe God is numbering or reviewing those who have been adversely affected by the sins of their parents and grandparents. For instance, if a pollster took a census of the number of alcoholics in three generations of an alcoholic patriarch's family, the head count likely would be very high. Why? Because alcoholism was deposited in the family line. It came calling, and an unfortunate number of children and grandchildren answered the door.

Can you think of any negative traits or habits in your life that have been in your family line for generations? Perhaps you can identify negative patterns such as alcoholism, verbal or physical abuse, pornography, racism, bitterness, or fear. These areas of bondage are anything you may have learned environmentally, anything to which you may be genetically predisposed, or any binding influence passed down through other means. Whatever the bondage may be, the Lord wants to rebuild, restore, and renew these areas of devastation.

We must face generational strongholds head-on. If we don't, they can remain almost unrecognizable—but they don't remain benign. Family strongholds continue to be the seedbed for all sorts of destruction. Oftentimes we've grown up with these chains and they feel completely natural. We consider them part of our personality rather than a strangling yoke.

Thankfully, Christians aren't doomed to live with our families' sins. The Cross of Calvary is enough to set us free from every yoke; God's Word is enough to make liberty a practical reality, no matter what those before us left as an "inheritance."

Before we parents die of fright, let's remember God is the only perfect parent. He's not cursing three or four generations over a little parental irritability. In fact, I don't believe He's calling a curse down on anyone. As believers under the New Covenant who have been cleansed by Christ's blood, I think the concept of generational sin applies to us through its powerful repercussions instead. I believe God is referring to a natural phenomenon described poignantly in Hosea 8:7, "They sow the wind and reap the whirlwind." Parents and grandparents must be very careful what they sow because it may reap the wind in their own lives and a whirlwind in the lives that follow.

> Never underestimate, however, God's power to redirect and bless an entire family line for generations to come when we humble ourselves before Him, confess our sins, and petition Him for full redemption.[20]

Notice the "when" in the sentence above. Something is required from you in order to become free! If you don't resist and repel the devil, he won't run away from you. God has done his part in defeating the devil, disarming him, and making you not just a conqueror, but *more* than a conqueror. Now you've got to do your part, which is to enforce Jesus's victory!

> Therefore submit to God. Resist the devil and he will flee from you.[21]

That's all you've got to do. Enforce Jesus's victory! For this to happen, you've got to be smart. Jesus said, "I am sending you out like sheep among wolves. Therefore be as shrewd as snakes and as innocent as doves."[22] The devil has been around for a very long time, and although a defeated foe, he is incredibly crafty and sly. The apostle Paul urges us to be aware "so that Satan will not outsmart us. For we are familiar with his evil schemes."[23]

DEALING WITH OUR DEBTS

Though we are free in Christ, some of us continue to accrue debts in the spirit realm. But how do these debts arise, and how do we deal with them?

Debts in the realm of the spirit can arise in a variety of ways. Here are some of them:

Satanic Benefit. This is a situation where we received a benefit from the devil, but just before payback time, we became Christians. The debt is still there! For instance, some of us were sickly as children, and our parents took us to a shrine, herbalist, or soothsayer and made some sacrifice for our healing. We received a short-term solution from the devil in exchange for future long-term problems. The devil doesn't give anything for free. Now he wants his pound of flesh, but we've become Christians. There is still an agreement here that must be broken. If your parents found it difficult to have children and they went to the local shrine and things were done that resulted in your birth, again, the devil would have offered a short-term solution in exchange for future long-term problems. However, just before payback time, you became a Christian. The debt must still be cancelled through the power of Christ.

Parents Helping Out. You are a Christian but are having a challenge in one area of your life. Maybe it's in your health or your career. You tell your parents. They then take your name to the local oracle and do things on your behalf. You now owe the devil.

Stepping Out of Line. You are a Christian. You're going through a particularly difficult and turbulent time. You decide for whatever reason to step out of line and seek divination or help from the enemy's camp. You then realise your folly and repent before the devil can take his payment. You still owe him big-time!

Neglecting Your Duty of Care. Debts can also arise if you have a duty or responsibility to take care of somebody and you don't. For instance, if you neglect your children, give them up for adoption, or abandon them, you accrue spiritual debt.

Although as a child of God you are free through the cross, you need to specifically deal with these situations. It is like having millions of dollars in the bank but not paying your bills: if you do this, you will end up in court. One reason the devil is always accusing some people before God is because of unpaid debts. Imagine if somebody owes you money and is refusing to pay. However, you see he is doing very well, building houses and driving flashy cars. What would you do? I am sure you would do everything you could to get your money, even if it meant making yourself a nuisance. The devil is no different!

So how do you pay these debts? *Simply by offering the blood of Jesus to the devil in full and final payment of any debt you owe him and then forbidding him from ever troubling you about it again.*

The blood of Jesus has more power than the human mind can ever comprehend. The source of the power of God for every area of your life is in the shed blood of Jesus Christ. The blood of Jesus is precious and of eternal significance. It is greater in value than silver and gold and the blood of animals.[24] Through the blood of Jesus, you become completely free.

Chapter 12:

BREAKING THE CURSE AND ACTIVATING THE BLESSING

> "For who is powerful enough to enter the house of a strong man like Satan and plunder his goods? Only someone even stronger—someone who could tie him up and then plunder his house."
>
> **Matthew 12:29, NLT**

Kenneth E. Hagin once told how the Lord Jesus Christ appeared to him in a vision and talked to him for about an hour and a half about the devil, demons, and demon possession.[1] The year was 1952. Toward the end of that vision, an evil spirit that looked like a little monkey or elf ran between Jesus and Pastor Hagin and spread something like a smoke screen or dark cloud. Then the demon began jumping up and down, crying in a shrill voice, "Yakety-yak, yakety-yak, yakety-yak." Because of the interference of the demon, Pastor Hagin couldn't see Jesus or understand what he was saying.

He couldn't understand why Jesus allowed the demon to make such a racket. He wondered why Jesus didn't rebuke the demon so he could hear what he was saying. He waited a few moments, but Jesus didn't take any action against the demon. Jesus was still talking, but he couldn't understand a word—and he needed to, because Jesus was giving instructions concerning the devil, demons, and how to exercise authority. Pastor Hagin thought to himself, *Doesn't the Lord know I'm not hearing what he wants me to? I need to hear that. I'm missing it!*

Pastor Hagin said he almost panicked. In desperation he cried out, "In the name of Jesus, you foul spirit, I command you to stop!" The minute he said that, the little demon hit the floor like a sack of salt, and the black cloud disappeared. The demon lay there trembling, whimpering, and whining like a whipped pup. He wouldn't look at Pastor Hagin.

"Not only shut up, but get out of here in Jesus's name!" Pastor Hagin commanded. The demon ran off.

At that point, Pastor Hagin was still thinking, *Why didn't Jesus do something about that? Why did he permit it?*

The Lord knew exactly what was in Pastor Hagin's mind. Jesus looked at him and said, "If you hadn't done something about that, I couldn't have. Not one single time in the New Testament is the church ever told to pray that God the Father or Jesus will do anything against the devil. In fact, to do so is to waste your time. The believer is told to do something about the devil."

The Lord continued, "The reason is because you have the authority to do it. The church is not to pray to God the Father about the devil; the church is to exercise the authority that belongs to it. The New Testament tells believers themselves to do something about the devil. The least member of the body of Christ has just as much power over the devil as anyone else, and unless believers do something about the devil, nothing will be done in a lot of areas."

Jesus then referred Pastor Hagin to Matthew 28:18, Mark 16:15–18, James 4:7, Colossians 1:13, 1 Peter 5:8, and Ephesians 4:27, all Scripture passages I encourage you to read.

What God was telling Kenneth Hagin is this: In spiritual warfare you fight *from* victory, not *for* victory! The devil is a defeated foe. You don't need to try to defeat him. Simply exercise your authority as a believer and take back what is rightfully yours! Don't waste your energy trying to defeat a defeated foe.

IT'S TIME TO EXERCISE OUR AUTHORITY

Now that we have gone through foundational teaching on the believer's authority and the need for deliverance and have understood that our deliverance comes through the blood, blessing, and power of Christ, I'd like you to *now* exercise your authority over the devil. Let's take back from the devil what rightfully belongs to you by breaking the curse and activating the blessing! Let's do some warfare in the place of prayer.

A skilful hunter has his quiver full of arrows of varying sizes and shapes. When he sees a potential target, he picks out an arrow that's most appropriate for it. In the same manner, as a child of God, you have a variety of weapons available to you for spiritual warfare. God expects you to use the appropriate weapon based on the nature of the challenge that faces you. This knowledge comes with experience in your walk with God.

The Bible makes it clear that "the weapons we fight with are not the weapons of the world. On the contrary, they have divine power to demolish strongholds."[2]

For our purpose, I encourage you to make use of the following weapons from your supernatural arsenal:

The Name of Jesus. This is one of the most powerful weapons available to you in spiritual warfare. God elevated Jesus to the place of highest honour and gave him the name above all other names, that at the name of Jesus every knee should bow, in heaven and on earth and under the earth, and every tongue confess that Jesus Christ is Lord, to the glory of God the Father.[3]

The Blood of Jesus. This blood is no ordinary blood. It is a powerful weapon of spiritual warfare. First of all, it cleanses us from all unrighteousness. Then it speaks. Not only does it speak for you, it also speaks against any sacrifice that may be speaking against you.[4]

The Fire of God. This is a must-use weapon when attempting to take out a "control tower," a satanic altar controlling the attack on your life. Not only is our God himself a consuming fire, but a fire also goes before him to consume his enemies.[5] Although in spiritual warfare you cannot destroy the devil, you can demolish and destroy his *work,* including satanic altars, with fire.

Earthquakes. The Bible says, "God's temple in heaven was opened, and within his temple was seen the ark of his covenant. And there came flashes of lightning, rumblings, peals of thunder, an earthquake and a severe hailstorm."[6] There are certain satanic strongholds which can only be taken out by an earthquake—literally or in the spirit realm. For such demonic problems, there's ample provision in our spiritual armoury.

Fasting. There is a place for fasting in spiritual warfare. It is one of the weapons God has provided to his church. Fasting and prayer go side by side. The Bible tells us, "But when you fast…"[6a] The use of the word "when" suggests that it is not a question of *if* we fast, but when and how often.

STEPS TO DESTROYING EVIL FAMILY PATTERNS, SILENCING SATANIC ALTARS, BREAKING GENERATIONAL AND SELF-INFLICTED CURSES, AND ANNULLING ANCESTRAL COVENANTS

First, recognise you've got a problem. As a child of God, the first step in receiving your freedom is realising that you've got a problem and coming to terms with that. No use pretending it's not there. No use trying to sweep it under the carpet. The problem with people of faith is that many are not faithful! Faithfulness generally signifies wholehearted devotion to God and his service. However, sometimes, to be faithful to God and yourself is to come to terms with a problem and seek help.

Samson, though chosen by God, was a man of compromise who lived a lifestyle of disobedience.[7] He was a man of faith, but he wasn't faithful. He had a problem with women and repeatedly gave in to lust. Unfortunately, he neither recognised that he had a problem nor did he come to terms with it and seek help, and this ultimately led to his downfall.

If you're an alcoholic, there is no use saying "The devil is an alcoholic" instead of "I'm an alcoholic" because you don't want to make a negative confession when *you're* the one with the drinking problem! Recognise that you've got a problem, and even if it appears to be a generational problem, don't blame anyone else for it. Instead, take full responsibility for it. Don't keep it hidden. Bring it out into the open. In the prayer of Daniel we read earlier, Daniel took responsibility for the sins of his forefathers and the whole nation of Israel.

Speak to a trustworthy person who can pray with you. The apostle James puts it this way: "Make this your common practice: Confess your sins to each other and pray for each other so that you can live together whole and healed."[8]

Do you want to destroy that evil family mould? Do you want that generational curse broken? Do you want to revoke that ancestral covenant? Jesus asked a similar question of an invalid who had been ill for thirty-eight years.[9] He said, "Do you want to be made well?" I mean, *seriously?* This man had been an *invalid* for thirty-eight years, and Jesus is asking if he wants to be made well? I don't want to sound like a jerk, but *really?* Yet, Jesus's question is a valid one. I think Jesus wanted this man to come to terms with his situation and take responsibility for himself!

Second, establish a scriptural basis for your release from that reproach or that curse. The Bible is the final authority on all things spiritual. The best way to know God's heart concerning your freedom is to allow the Bible to speak for itself. You may want to start with the words of the Lord Jesus in John's gospel, where he said, "If the Son sets you free, you will be free indeed."[10] You may then move on to Paul's epistle to the Corinthians, where he declared, "Therefore, if anyone is in Christ, he is a new creation. The old has passed away; behold, the new has come."[11] And from there to Galatians, where the Bible informs us, "Christ redeemed us from the curse of the law by becoming a curse for us, for it is written: 'Cursed is everyone who is hung on a pole.' He redeemed us in order that the blessing given to Abraham might come to the Gentiles through Christ Jesus, so that by faith we might receive the promise of the Spirit."[12]

Here are a few other passages of Scripture that provide a basis for your freedom from curses: Colossians 1:12–14, 1 John 3:8b, Luke 10:19. Study them. Interact with them. Know them by heart. Meditate upon them and make them a part of your daily experience.

Third, research your past if necessary. Every so often, for a wound to heal properly, the medics must open it up and cleanse it thoroughly before closing it again, thus achieving a wound environment that is conducive to healing. In the same way, to get to the root of our problems, it is sometimes necessary to know our family's past. Understanding our background can help us make sense of who we are today.

Researching your ancestors may feel like a daunting task, but it may not be as difficult as you think. Here are some ideas that you may find helpful:

1. Write down everything you know about your family history. Jot down everything you can remember about any apparent medical or evil patterns in your family, particularly any evidence of the following: Alzheimer's disease/dementia, arthritis, asthma, blood clots, cancer, depression, mental disorders, diabetes, heart disease, high cholesterol,

high blood pressure, pregnancy losses and birth defects, stroke, alcoholism, drug abuse, barrenness, child abuse, and divorce.
2. Speak to your family. You may need to ask some difficult questions. Ask about any devil worship, pagan worship, membership in secret societies or cults, blood sacrifices, etc. Living family members can be a wealth of knowledge. Start with parents, aunts, and uncles, and then work back a generation if you can. Somebody once said, "If your grandparents can tell you about their grandparents, you will have access to a hundred years or more of family history." Make notes and record the interviews if your relatives don't mind. Look out for rumours or hazy recollections.
3. Look for physical clues. You'll be amazed at how much you can uncover by looking through drawers and boxes in your parents' home. Obvious documents such as wills can provide valuable information about your ancestors. Letters can be another valuable source of personal information.

Fourth, repent if necessary. When Daniel discovered there was a curse upon Jerusalem and the exiles of Israel, he identified with the sins of the nation and repented, telling God in the place of prayer, "We have sinned, we have done wrong."[13]

Notice his wording: "we... we..." Some people have a problem with saying sorry for the wrongs of previous generations. However, as it happens, it's not that unusual a thing to do. Governments, for example, are known to apologise for the errors of previous governments. This happens even when the present administration has nothing in common with the former regime! They recognise that in a way, the responsibility for the crime is inherited. In February 2008, the Australian government made a formal apology for the wrongs caused by successive governments to the Aboriginal population. Prime Minister Kevin Rudd apologised in parliament to all Aborigines for the laws and policies of successive parliaments and governments that inflicted profound grief, suffering, and loss on them. He said, "For the indignity and degradation thus inflicted on a proud people and a proud culture, we say sorry." The apology was beamed live around the country on TV.[14]

Sometimes, to receive our breakthrough, we need to identify with the iniquities of our ancestors and repent in the sense of viewing or thinking of their actions with deep regret or remorse, telling God we are sorry, determining not to follow in their footsteps, and asking him to show mercy.

Fifth, forgive. Unforgiveness is one way by which we invite curses into our lives. Forgiving those who hurt us can be really difficult, especially if they don't show any remorse for their actions. That is probably why Alexander Pope wrote, "To err is human, to forgive divine." Unfortunately, to receive God's forgiveness we must first forgive others. Jesus put it this way: "In prayer there is a connection between what God does and what you do. You can't get forgiveness from God, for instance, without also forgiving others. If you refuse to do your part, you cut yourself off from God's part."[15]

I believe Jesus's words are self-explanatory, and if we want to know true freedom, we must learn to forgive everyone who hurts us whether they deserve it or not.

Sixth, renounce all contacts with the occult by you and your ancestors. This is a fundamental part of the deliverance process. The devil will hold on to any agreement or covenant that gives him a right into your life unless and until you specifically break it. Through some of the prayers in this chapter, I will guide you to revoke and renounce all occultic contact and contamination.

Seventh, get rid of all accursed things that may act as a point of contact for the devil. There's no point in seeking deliverance and freedom if you have any object that belongs to the devil in your possession. It won't work. Simply get rid of it, no matter how expensive it is. No matter how emotionally attached you are to it. Borrow a leaf from the new believers in Ephesus. The Bible tells us that a number of them who had been practicing sorcery brought their incantation books and burned them at a public bonfire. The New Living Translation says, "The value of the books was several million dollars."[16]

Eighth, speak to the cause of the reproach and tell it to be broken. This is crucial. By the authority in the name of Jesus, speak to the root cause of the problem and command it to be broken. This is not the time to plead, nor is it a time for diplomacy. No way! This is the time to forcefully take what rightfully belongs to you. This is the time to exercise your authority as a child of God. Jesus said, "From the days of John the Baptist until now the kingdom of heaven has suffered violence, and the violent take it by force."[17]

DELIVERANCE PRAYERS

The prayers below are divided into different sections and will mainly take the form of declarations and decrees. This is because you are exercising your authority as a believer. You are not struggling with the devil; instead you are enforcing your victory. Jesus said, "Behold, I give you the authority to trample on serpents and scorpions, and over all the power of the enemy, and nothing shall by any means hurt you."[18]

Are you ready? Let's go.

First Things First. Let's Pray the Sinner's Prayer if You are Not yet Saved. Here's a health warning for anyone who has yet to know Jesus as Lord and Saviour: Please don't proceed any further in this chapter without first receiving Jesus into your heart by praying the sinner's prayer. If you do, you may open yourself to demonic attacks. *This is not a gimmick or a game. It's deadly serious, and the powers we are dealing with are real.*

If you would like to invite Jesus into your heart to become your Lord and Saviour *right now,* you will need to pray the sinner's prayer. Please say it out loud:

- Lord Jesus, I acknowledge that I am a sinner. I believe with my heart that you died for my sin and that you were raised from the dead for my justification. Your Word says in Romans 10:9, "If you confess with your mouth the Lord Jesus and believe in your heart that God has raised Him from the dead, you will be saved." I confess with my mouth that you are my Saviour and my Lord. I invite you to come into my heart and make me a new creation. Thank you, Lord Jesus, for saving me. Please write my name in your Book of Life. In Jesus's name I pray. Amen.

Now Let's Begin. *Please say out loud:*

- Dear Jesus, I believe you are the Son of God, you are the only way to God, you died for my sin, and you rose from the dead. I now confess to you any sins of which you've made me aware. [Take a moment to reflect and mention any sins the Holy Spirit brings to your remembrance.] I now confess the sins of my ancestors [again, please take a moment to reflect, and be as thorough as you possibly can.

For instance, if your parents were idol worshippers or cultists, mention that specifically].
- Lord, I repent of all sins I have ever committed. I hate them and turn from them. I turn to you, Lord Jesus, for mercy and forgiveness. If I have been involved with the occult, I repent and renounce it and sever myself from it through the blood of Jesus. If I have any occult objects in my possession, I commit myself to get rid of them. [Make sure you get rid of any such object at the earliest opportunity after these prayers.]
- Lord, I forgive any person who has ever harmed me or wronged me or hurt me. I forgive them as I want you to forgive me. [Take a moment to reflect and name the people you need to forgive.]
- Lord Jesus, to the best of my ability I have met your conditions, and I now claim your promise in Joel 2:32 that whosoever shall call on the name of the Lord shall be delivered. I am calling on you now. In the name of the Lord Jesus Christ, I claim my deliverance from all evil spirits. I hate them. They are not my friends, they are my enemies, and I command them to go from me now in the name of Jesus.

Let's Deal with Generational Curses. *Please say out loud:*
- I break every generational curse operating in any area of my life, and I revoke every ancestral covenant affecting any area of my life in the name of Jesus.
- I destroy, revoke, and undo every evil family law operating in my family, whether written or unwritten, in the name of Jesus.
- I destroy every evil family pattern manifesting in my family and break free from every limitation on any area of my life in the name of Jesus.
- Satan, I resist you and your demon spirits, and I put you to flight from me in the name of Jesus. I command you to take your hands off my affairs, take your hands off my finances, take your hands off my spouse, take your hands off my children, and take your hands off everything that pertains to me in the name of Jesus.
- Every arrow of affliction, tragedy, and untimely death that is sent in my direction, I divert and deflect back to its sender by the anointing of the Holy Spirit and in the name of Jesus.

Next, Let's Take Out the Satanic Altars. *Please say out loud:*
- Lord, if any member of my family—past or present—has brought a demonic altar into the family, I repent on behalf of the entire family and ask for mercy. If I have visited any satanic agent to seek divination, to offer sacrifices, to speak to the dead, in pursuit of wealth, to seek health, or for any other reason, I repent and ask for mercy and forgiveness in the name of Jesus.
- I declare that I am a child of God. I have invited Jesus into my heart as my Saviour and Lord. I have been redeemed by the blood of Jesus. I am the righteousness of God in Christ Jesus.[19] Jesus has set me free, therefore I am free indeed.[20]
- Right now, in the name of Jesus, I destroy every satanic altar that has been raised up against me, against my spouse, and against my children. Be destroyed by the fire that goes before God to consume his enemies.
- Altars in my ancestral home, altars in my place of birth, altars connected to the lakes, rivers, and body of waters in the place of my birth, I address you right now. By the blood of Jesus, I silence you and destroy you by fire. I undo everything you have done in my life. I undo whatever you have set in motion in my life in the name of Jesus.
- Any shrines connected with my family, and any altars connected with those shrines, I destroy you right now by fire in the name of Jesus.
- Altars connected to my placenta, connected to my umbilical cord, I address you in the name of Jesus, and I command you to be destroyed in the name of Jesus.
- Any altars connected with and sponsoring childlessness or barrenness in any shape, form or manner, be destroyed by fire in the name of Jesus.
- Altars from my mother's side of the family; altars from my father's side of the family; altars against my destiny; altars against my marriage; altars against my career; altars against my finances; altars sponsoring financial limitation, inconsistent progress, and sickness; any altar where my name or any member of my family has ever been mentioned for evil; any altar where my destiny has been discussed: be destroyed by fire and earthquake in the name of Jesus.
- Any spirits on assignment from any of these altars, I terminate your assignment, and I blind you by the blood of Jesus in the name of Jesus.

I bind you and decree that you shall not have any reinforcement in the name of Jesus.
- In the name of Jesus, I take authority over every witchcraft spirit operating around me, and I bind all evil touching the senses—sight, smell, touch, taste, and hearing—and the emotions; all evil against the seven points of the body used by witchcraft (the base of the spine, spleen, navel, heart, throat, between the eyes, and the top of the head). I bind all evil on my bodily systems (reproductive, skeletal, muscular, digestive, excretory, endocrine, respiratory, nervous, and circulatory).

Let's Deal with the Power of the Spoken Word. *Please say out loud:*
- I revoke every negative word that has ever been spoken into my destiny, whether by my parents, my teachers, or anybody who had authority over me. I undo them, I repeal them, and I destroy them in the name of Jesus.
- I identify every spell cast in my direction and every incantation spoken into my destiny, and I declare them revoked by the blood of Jesus in Jesus's name.
- I stand on the Word of God that says, "No weapon that is formed against you will prosper,"[21] and I declare that I will not be hissed out of my position, my role, or my destiny in the name of Jesus. I resist and stand against every spirit of error and break your hold over me in Jesus's name.
- Lord, let all my adversaries become confused and begin to fight themselves in the name of Jesus.
- I release the spirit of error upon any hidden enemies who are fighting me, and I cause you to begin to make mistakes that will expose you and move me forward in Jesus's name.
- In the name of Jesus, I revoke any death sentence handing over me.
- I break the power of spoken curses over my family and speak blessing instead. My children, I command you to arise and shine. I empower you to disobey every satanic programme and instruction in Jesus's name.

Let's Roll Away the Reproach. *Please say out loud:*
- I address every reproach, past and present, operating in my life and any hidden reproach waiting to manifest. I locate you by the anointing

of the Holy Spirit, and I command you to be removed and rolled away in the name of Jesus.
- I stand in the righteousness of Christ, and I break free from any form of financial hardship and declare that henceforth I will operate in supernatural breakthrough in the name of Jesus.
- I overcome the stagnancy of life, I overcome hidden destructive covenants operating in any area of my life, and I break the power of recurrent problems in my life by the blood of Jesus in Jesus's name.
- I declare that this is my season, and therefore I will enjoy the goodness of the Lord in the land of the living in Jesus's name.
- In the name of Jesus I speak into my destiny, and I declare, decree, proclaim, and prophesy that henceforth I will no longer labour in vain.
- I stand on the Word of God, and by the blood of Jesus, I destroy and break any covenant of poverty, any vow of poverty, any yoke of poverty, and any curse of poverty in my life in Jesus's name.
- I renew my mind with the Word and declare that I am not poor. I have been redeemed by the blood of Jesus. It is written, "For you know the grace of our Lord Jesus Christ, that though He was rich, yet for your sake He became poor, so that you through His poverty might become rich."[22] I am not poor. Poverty is not my portion.
- I shut every door open to the devil in the name of Jesus. I put the blood of Jesus at the root of any opening where the enemy has come in. I shut those doors, seal them with the blood of Jesus, and send the evil spirits who took advantage of those doors to the waterless places, forbidding them from ever coming back to me or touching anyone else on the way. Go, immediately, now, in the name of Jesus!
- I release and sprinkle the blood of Jesus to purify and cleanse my body, soul, and spirit, my conscious and subconscious mind, my memory bank, the chambers and inner recesses of my mind, and the memory bank of my heart, and I erase every satanic picture, every emotional trauma, and every hurt in the name of Jesus. Father God, I call on you to please place your healing balm of Gilead in all of my memory in the name of Jesus!
- I cancel all documents that the devil has about me, all assignments that have been placed on me, and all pacts, oaths, and dedications I may have made with the devil, either knowingly or unknowingly. By the blood of Jesus, I cancel and revoke them right now in Jesus's name.

- I speak to the ground (the place from which I get my provision): Because Jesus died for my sins and wore the crown of thorns, I declare in the name of Jesus that no longer:
  - Will you, the ground, sprout thorns and weeds for me.
  - Will I get my food the hard way.
  - Will I eat through painful toil.
  - Will I eat by the sweat of my brow.
  - Will I struggle to scratch out a living.

Let's Exercise Authority in Relation to Delay and Long-Standing Problems. *Please say out loud:*
- Satisfy me early with your mercy, O Lord, that I may rejoice and be glad all the days of my life. In Jesus's name I pray.
- I stand in the righteousness of Christ, and I command my glory, which may have been hidden and covered, to manifest by fire in the name of Jesus.
- I empower my Destiny Helpers in Jesus's name. My Destiny Helpers, hear me. Wherever you are, locate me and fulfil the purpose for which God planted you in my life in the name of Jesus.
- Delay, past and present, and any future delay seeking an opportune time to manifest in my life, I command you to expire by fire in the name of Jesus.
- Today, I surrender my will to God. Lord, from this moment and for the rest of my days, have your way in every area of my life, in Jesus's name.
- I stand in the righteousness of Christ, and I plead the blood of Jesus over every area of my life where I am struggling with my willpower in the name of Jesus.
- By the blood of Jesus, I break the power of every addiction and every besetting sin that is holding me captive, and I proclaim my freedom in the name of Jesus.
- By the blood of Jesus shed on my behalf in the garden of Gethsemane, I redeem and take back my willpower, which I lost when Adam sinned in the Garden of Eden. I declare that Jesus has set me free, therefore I am free indeed in Jesus's name.
- I stand in the righteousness of Christ and declare that I am redeemed by the blood of Jesus. Every affliction, sickness, and disease operating in and around my life, I command you to develop ears and hear the Word

of the Lord. It is written, "Surely there is an end."[23] Standing on the Word of God, the Scriptures which cannot be broken,[24] I command you to expire right now by fire in the name of Jesus.
- Every spiritual coffin built for my sake, and every spiritual grave dug for me, I command you to be destroyed by fire in the name of Jesus.
- By the anointing of the Holy Spirit, I identify every debt I owe the devil. Satan, Jesus has paid off every one of these debts on my behalf. Therefore, right now, I offer you the blood of Jesus in full and final payment of any debt I owe you, and I forbid you henceforth from ever troubling me in the name of Jesus.
- Thank you, Father God, for the blood of Jesus that cleanses me and frees me from sin. I declare that I have been redeemed by the blood of Jesus, and I am God's property! I am trusting in the Lord who protects me from harm and provides for all my needs. Every step I take is ordered by the Lord. His angels have charge over me. They watch over me and keep me in all my ways. My life, my health, my finances, my family, my friends, my work, and my property are protected by the blood of Jesus. I draw a line around them with the blood of Jesus and declare them off-limits to the enemy. Devil, you can't have them, so I command you to get your hands off! In Jesus's name I pray. Amen!

Let's Get Some Help with Maintaining Your Freedom. *Please say out loud:*
- Lord, I approach the throne of grace[25] and ask for the grace not to give the devil any opportunity or foothold in Jesus's name. I declare that I will not give the devil a foothold in my life in the name of Jesus.
- Lord, I ask that you open my eyes to enable me to understand the evil schemes of the devil in the name of Jesus.
- Lord, I ask that you open the heavens, your good treasure house upon me, and pour your blessings upon me that I would not have sufficient room to contain them. Lord, I receive the overflow in Jesus's name.
- Lord, I ask that you teach me to live like an overcomer. Help me to live fulfilled, to live life to the full, to enjoy everyday life, to be on top of things, and to be far from oppression at all times in Jesus's name.
- Lord, you who make the winds your messengers and the flames of fire your servants,[26] dispatch your angels of fire and war to search the

land of the living and the dead, locate my stolen blessings, and restore them to me in Jesus's name.
- From the east, from the west, from the north, and from the south, O Lord, raise up intercessors and destiny helpers to stand in the gap for me in the name of Jesus.
- Every astral projection against me, I frustrate you and destroy you by the blood of Jesus and in Jesus's name.
- Every complicated evil network working against me, I command you to be eaten up by the elements in the name of Jesus.
- I bind every power pulling anything in my body toward evil by means of energy drawn from the sun, the moon, and the stars. Fall to the ground and be destroyed in the name of Jesus.
- I bind every power pulling anything in my body toward evil by means of energy drawn from the planets, constellations, and the earth in the name of Jesus.
- I bind every power pulling anything in my body toward evil by means of energy drawn from the air, wind, fire, water, light, darkness, and the elements in the name of Jesus.
- Any power drawing energy against me from evil lines and circles, fall down and be completely destroyed in the name of Jesus.
- By the blood of Jesus, I break and revoke all evil soul ties affecting my life in the name of Jesus.

Now Receive Your Freedom by Faith. *Please say out loud:*
- Lord Jesus, having received your forgiveness by faith, with the authority I have as a child of God, I now release myself and those under my authority from any curse over our lives, right now in the name of Jesus. I declare release. I claim it. I receive it by faith in the name of Jesus.

Finally, Let's Activate the Blessing of Abraham!
Congratulations! You have now destroyed evil family patterns, silenced the satanic altars, broken the curses, revoked ungodly covenants, and released yourself from all of their effects! But wonderful as that is, it is not enough just to be made free. There is now a vacuum in your life, and it needs to be filled with blessing! You need to begin to enjoy the blessing of Abraham.

In chapter 5, we saw that the blessing of Abraham encapsulates everything we need to enjoy our ordinary, everyday life here on earth: health and healing; victory and dominion in every area of life; abundance in spirit, soul, and body; and the ability to be a blessing to all the families of the earth, including our seed after us. When we enjoy this blessing *instead of enduring a curse,* we honour and give glory to Jesus, who sees his kingdom becoming a reality here on earth through us.

We said in that chapter that the blessing has been deposited into our heavenly account and is waiting to be downloaded to the earth for our everyday use. It is now time to transition from the curse into the blessing by activating and downloading the blessing. These blessings will pursue you and overtake you. However, the blessing won't begin to pursue you automatically! In the same way that you specifically revoked the curses, you have to intentionally invoke and release the blessing into your life and the lives of those under your authority.

Steps to Activating the Blessing

First, receive and take hold of what Jesus has done. It was theologian and first editor-in-chief of *Christianity Today* Carl F.H. Henry who famously said, "The whole secret of abundant living can be summed up in this sentence: 'Not your responsibility but your response to God's ability.'"[27] What is your response to God's provision? Jesus has done everything that needs to be done. Just before he breathed his last breath on the cross of Calvary, Jesus said, "It is finished," meaning it's all been paid for and there's nothing more for God to do![28] All that's left is for you and me to willingly and freely accept and receive what Jesus has already done.

In September 2003, the government of the United Kingdom launched a major advertising campaign to encourage retired people to claim the new pension credit. The credit aimed to reward people who had made modest savings for their retirement. The government estimated about half of the eight million pensioner households would be eligible for the credit, gaining an extra £400 a year on average. The campaign featured pensioners at coffee mornings, allotments, and in the street seeing money and being told to "Pick it up, it's yours."[29] In the same way, all we have to do is pick up and take hold of what Jesus has already done for us! The blessing is yours. Just pick it up, it's yours!

Second, begin to see yourself the way God sees you: as blessed. To activate and release the blessing, you've got to see yourself the way he sees you: blessed, victorious, triumphant, and highly favoured. In the words of Joel Osteen, "How do you tap in to what God has already done? Very simple: just act like you're blessed, talk like you're blessed, walk like you're blessed, think like you're blessed, smile like you're blessed, dress like you're blessed. Put actions behind your faith, and one day you will see it become a reality."[30] In other words, you must let the truth of God's Word become part of your daily routine.

Now, Let's Receive the Blessing. If you're ready, let's pray together. *Please say out loud:*

- Through the sacrifice of Jesus on the cross, I have come out from under the curse and entered into the blessing of Abraham, whom God blessed in all things. I release this blessing—in particular health and healing; victory and dominion in every area of life; abundance in spirit, soul, and body; prosperity; supernatural protection; divine favour; and the ability to be a blessing to all the families of the earth—into my life and into the lives of my children and my children's children to the thousandth generation. I claim it, declare it, and receive it by faith in the name of the Lord Jesus Christ!
- Therefore I declare:
  - My household is blessed.
  - My finances are blessed.
  - My spouse is blessed.
  - My children are blessed.
  - My parents are blessed.
  - My siblings are blessed.
  - All my debts are cancelled.
  - I am blessed in my going out and my coming in, from this time and even forever. Amen!

Now, begin to thank the Lord for transitioning you from the curse into the blessing. Glory to Jesus! Amen.

Chapter 13:

SURELY THERE IS AN END!

> "For surely there is an end; and thine expectation shall not be cut off."
>
> **Proverbs 23:18, KJV**

A young Christian went to his pastor and said, "My meditation on Scripture is horrible! I feel so distracted, and I'm constantly falling asleep. It's just horrific!"

"Do you know what the Bible says in Matthew 7:28?" the teacher asked.

"I do," the student responded. "It says, 'And it came to pass—"

"That's it," the teacher said, cutting him short. "It will pass."

A week later, the student came back to his teacher. "My meditation is wonderful! The Scriptures are so alive. I feel so peaceful, so connected to God! It's just wonderful!"

"I wouldn't dwell on that," the pastor replied matter-of-factly. "It may pass too."

Nothing in this world lasts forever. Nothing—good or bad! However good or bad a situation is now, the one thing you can count on is that *it will change*. Change is the only thing that's constant in life.[1]

You may have struggled in an area of your life for a long time. Maybe the challenge has been in your health, finances, career, ministry, or relationships. And because "delayed hope makes the heart ill,"[2] you may have wondered if it will ever end. I've got good news for you! God says, "Yes, because you're now completely free from the curses and covenants that held you captive, change is on its way." Whatever you're going through has an end date, an expiry date! It shall *come to pass*. It's not a dead end; you're simply *going through* it!

It doesn't really matter how you got into this mess in the first place. It may have been a dark shadow from previous generations. You may have made a mistake. You may have been negligent. It may have been an attack of the enemy. You may even have sinned. With the best will in the world, things sometimes happen. But it really doesn't matter. Remember, there is no glory without a story!

As long as you've made your peace with God, he is willing and able to turn your mess into a message and your test into a testimony. Why? Because now that you've identified and broken off the curses, you have entered a new season. It is a season of favour, mercy, and the fullness of the blessing of Abraham.

> Thou shalt arise, and have mercy upon Zion: for the time to favour her, yea, the set time, is come.[3]

The Bible puts it this way: "'Not by might nor by power, but by My Spirit,' says the Lord of hosts."[4] The word *Spirit* in this passage is the Hebrew *ruwach*, which can be translated *breath*.[5] In other words, the Lord is saying the breakthrough won't happen by your hard work, your experience, your talent, or even your connections. It is happening because God has decided to breathe in your direction. *That's called favour!* God is reworking the winds and blowing deliverance, healing, promotion, restoration, favour, and much more your way.

THE MINISTRY OF THE BLOOD

Supernatural protection is included in the package coming your way. In terms of protection for us as children of God, there are at least five areas of our lives that are covered by the blood of Jesus.[6] Did you know that the blood of Jesus has a ministry? Yes, the blood speaks and works on your behalf in heaven!

You should make a regular habit of verbally sprinkling the blood on these five areas. They are:

- You. Me. Us. The blood covers us as individuals.
- Your house and family. The blood covers your home and your family.
- Your possessions and property.
- Your endeavours, i.e. your undertakings, the work of your hands, your businesses, etc. The blood covers this as well.
- Your sphere of influence. This has to do with your social interactions. The blood of Jesus is also available to cover this.

We are told that the blood speaks better things than the blood of Abel, who of course, was killed by his brother Cain.[7] So what else does the blood of Jesus do for us? Here are a few things:

1. The blood provides forgiveness. Jesus shed his blood to enable us obtain forgiveness for our sins.[8] The blood brings everyone, regardless of race or nationality, age or gender, social status or background, into a right relationship with God. It brings us into a relationship with God that we didn't have before and could never have had on our own.[9] Thus, it enables reconciliation between God and us.
2. The blood buys us out from the control of the enemy. The blood was the price Jesus paid. Jesus bought us from the control of Satan and sin by his precious blood.[10] His blood was the price he paid. As a result, we now belong to God and are no longer under Satan's control.
3. The blood justifies us. The blood of Jesus justifies us and makes it possible for us to appear blameless before God, who is holy and cannot behold sin.[11] Furthermore, there is no longer any question of being at odds with God in any way because the blood makes us acceptable to God.
4. The blood redeems us. We are redeemed by the blood of Jesus.[12] The Bible describes our redemption as follows: "Because of the sacrifice of the Messiah, his blood poured out on the altar of the Cross, we're a free people—free of penalties and punishments chalked up by all our misdeeds. And not just barely free, either. Abundantly free!"[13]
5. The blood purifies us. The blood of Jesus purifies our consciences from sinful deeds so that we can worship the living God. The Bible says that if "animal blood and the other rituals of purification were effective in cleaning up certain matters of our religion and behavior, think how much more the blood of Christ cleans up our whole lives, inside and

out."[14] The blood cleanses us from all sin, washes away our sins, and sanctifies us.[15]

6. The blood of Jesus brings us peace. The Bible says God "made peace with everything in heaven and on earth by means of Christ's blood on the cross."[16] This is the peace that transcends all human understanding.[17] Perhaps Jeanette Windle had this in mind when she said, "Safety is not the absence of danger, but the presence of God."[18]
7. The blood gives us access to God. Following the fall, the human race lost access to God. The Bible puts it this way: "Listen! The Lord's arm is not too weak to save you, nor is his ear too deaf to hear you call. It's your sins that have cut you off from God. Because of your sins, he has turned away and will not listen anymore."[19] The blood of Jesus rectifies this problem by providing us access into the Most Holy Place before the throne of God.[20]
8. The blood validates the New Covenant. Jesus came to enact a New Covenant between us and God. The blood of Jesus seals and ratifies this New Covenant.[21] It is the blood that makes the new agreement valid. Because of the blood we can rely on the New Covenant.
9. The blood helps in spiritual warfare. The blood of Jesus is a weapon of spiritual warfare in our battles against the devil. The Bible says the devil is defeated by the blood and the testimony of God's people.[22] The blood also offers supernatural protection against the attacks of the devil.[23]

Many of us are used to pleading the blood of Jesus—that is, relying on it. Let me offer a new perspective. From today, learn to also apply the blood of Jesus by *sprinkling* it. This is like dipping your hands into the blood and actually applying it to the various areas of your life.

When you get to your car today, touch the car and say, "I sprinkle the blood of Jesus on this car." As you lock or unlock your front door, place your hand on your door and say, "I sprinkle the blood of Jesus on this door and on this house." When you go to work, place your hand on your desk and say, "I sprinkle the blood of Jesus on my employment/business." In this way, we apply the blood to all these areas of our lives.

Pleading or applying the blood of Jesus is our opportunity to enforce the efficacy of the blood over darkness, evil, and sickness. It is our opportunity to wield it as a weapon of warfare against every work of darkness.

IT'S COMING SUDDENLY

There is power in the name of Jesus to break every chain. And now, the long-standing chains are falling. The invisible obstacles are breaking and falling apart. The mountains that have become synonymous with your life are being moved out into the sea. The generational problems, well-established difficulties, and long-established challenges are receiving divine solutions.

You may have learned to live with these problems, modifying your lifestyle to accommodate them where necessary. The diabetes has become such an integral part of your life that you've learnt to live with it. You've had the asthma for so long you've personalised it; now you say, "I need the inhaler for *my asthma*." The back pain, the migraines have become such a regular part of your life that you always have painkillers on you. You've endured so much pain, heartbreak, and humiliation in life, you unconsciously expect them at certain times of the year. When the seasons change, you expect the flu or hay fever. You've become so used to lusting after women that you've lowered your standards—now you say there's nothing wrong with lusting as long as you don't take it any further!

The Bible tells us though weeping may last through the night, joy comes in the morning.[24] The New Living Translation says "joy comes *with* the morning." If joy merely comes *in* the morning, it can come at any time between twelve midnight and twelve noon. However, if joy comes *with* the morning, as I believe it does, then your joy will come with the first break of dawn. No matter how long your night may have been, as the earth remains, your morning will definitely come. There is a spiritual law established by God that says, "While the earth remains, day and night shall not cease."[25] So don't you dare give up! Change is coming your way. You're closer than you think. It is written, "For surely there is an end; and thine expectation shall not be cut off."[26]

If you've followed the teaching in this book and identified and broken off any curses, covenants, and evil family moulds that previously held you back, you're standing on the threshold of your breakthrough. You're ready to receive the blessing of Abraham. God is opening to you "his good treasury, the heavens, to give the rain to your land in its season and to bless *all the work* of your hands."[27] And you need to get ready, because it's going to happen *suddenly*.

> Sing, barren woman, who has never had a baby. Fill the air with song, you who've never experienced childbirth! You're ending up with far more children than all those childbearing women. God says so! Clear lots of ground for your tents! Make your tents large. Spread out! Think big! Use plenty of rope, drive the tent pegs deep. You're going to need lots of elbow room for your growing family. You're going to take over whole nations; you're going to resettle abandoned cities.[28]

On the day of Pentecost, the disciples were all with one accord in one place when *suddenly* there came a sound from heaven, as of a rushing mighty wind, and it filled the whole house where they were sitting.[29] The apostles received the Holy Spirit quickly and unexpectedly. Get ready for a similar experience. You will experience a "suddenly" moment when things will happen *quickly and unexpectedly*. What should take weeks, months, or even years will happen *suddenly*. By breaking off ancestral chains, you have opened a door for blessings you have never experienced.

Suddenly, that job will come. Suddenly, the breakthrough is here. Suddenly, the prodigal child will return home. Suddenly, the healing will take place. Suddenly, the broken marriage will be mended. Suddenly, reconciliation will take place. It will be so sudden, for some, that it will be like a dream. "It seemed like a dream, too good to be true, when God returned Zion's exiles."[30] Right now, even if you are a prisoner or prey *lawfully* captured by the enemy, the Lord says you're coming out! You're free! Jesus has set you free, and you're *truly* free.

Here's what the Lord says:

> Shall the prey be taken from the mighty, or the lawful captive delivered? But thus saith the Lord, Even the captives of the mighty shall be taken away, and the prey of the terrible shall be delivered: for I will contend with him that contendeth with thee, and I will save thy children. And I will feed them that oppress thee with their own flesh; and they shall be drunken with their own blood, as with sweet wine: and all flesh shall know that I the Lord am thy Saviour and thy Redeemer, the mighty One of Jacob.[31]

We will recover all. Starting with everything the devil has stolen from us. And then everything we've ever lost! Our debt has been fully paid. All of it! We owed a debt we couldn't pay. Jesus paid a debt he didn't owe. It's done. All fully paid for!

IT IS FINISHED

How can we know this is true? Let's look at the Scripture:

> When He had received the drink, Jesus said, *"It is finished."* With that, He bowed his head and gave up his spirit.[32]

The word *finished* is the Greek *teleo*.[33] It means:

To end; *i.e. to*

Complete (a payment). Jesus has completed it all. There's nothing more to be done. Nothing more can be done!

Execute (a deed). Jesus purchased us from the devil and from the clutches of sin. All signed, sealed, and executed by his blood.

Conclude (a transaction). Not only did Jesus redeem us from paying the penalty for our sin, he also bought us out of the slave market, so we don't need to go back into slavery.

Discharge (a debt). Every debt owed to the devil was nailed to the cross and fully paid.

To accomplish. He accomplished and completed the work of salvation on the cross. There's nothing more to be done. He did it all.

To make an end. Jesus put an end to every curse, generational or self-inflicted, and all ancestral covenants.

To expire. As Jesus died on the cross, every affliction past, present, and future expired on the cross. We just need to *confess* it to *possess* it!

To finish. It was all done on the cross. There is nothing more for God to do. Salvation is complete through Christ. That's why Jesus is the only way back to God!

Performed. Jesus performed and fulfilled all the requirements of the law. Not only did he do this for us, he overcame the devil, made us victorious, and made us *more than* conquerors.

In other words, when Jesus said "It is finished," he was basically proclaiming that whatever debt you owed has expired, having been fully paid by him. Your affliction has ended. The problem of sin is finished. Sickness is over. Poverty has ended. Death has been conquered. Fear is dead! And this is the reason you can now fight the devil *from* victory, not *for* victory!

IT'S TIME TO RECEIVE

Now, you've got to believe. You've got to be expectant, because this is your moment. This is your season of breakthrough, healing, and deliverance. This is your time. You're next in line for a miracle!

Now that you have recognized and dealt with generational curses and covenants, you're closer than you've ever been to your breakthrough. If you will believe, you will see the salvation of the Lord your God. Not next year. Not next month. Not next week. No, not even tomorrow! But *today,* right now. You've heard of twenty-four-hour miracles, but you can receive a *right now* miracle!

Why not begin to thank the Lord for your miracle? Give him some good quality praise. Tell him, "Lord, I thank you for my breakthrough. I receive it right now, according to your riches in glory. Amen!"

The anointing of the Holy Spirit makes the difference. "It shall come to pass in that day that his burden will be taken away from your shoulder, and his yoke from your neck, and the yoke will be destroyed because of the anointing oil."[34] Yes, every yoke placed by the devil and every satanic burden will be destroyed by reason of the anointing. The blood of Jesus is available this very minute. And where the blood of Jesus is, the anointing follows!

Yes, there is an end. You can claim the victory of Jesus right now, this minute.

> "Do not be afraid. Stand firm and you will see the deliverance the Lord will bring you today. The Egyptians you see today you will never see again."
>
> Exodus 14:13, NIV

Chapter 14:

MAINTAINING YOUR FREEDOM

"So I say, live by the Spirit, and you will never fulfill
the desires of the flesh."

Galatians 5:16, ISV

The Right Honourable Lord Templeton, the twenty-fourth Earl of Lamberton in the Scottish border country, was only ten years old when he inherited the earldom, including the lavish Templeton Castle. His father, the late earl, died of a mysterious illness aged just thirty-eight, as did his grandfather and great-grandfather, who all died of similar illnesses before the age of forty. His great-great-grandfather was said to have sexually assaulted a minor and taken his own life shortly afterward when it became public knowledge. He was only thirty-nine when he died. In all, the four previous earls had all died from mysterious illnesses between the ages of thirty-five and forty.

Lord Templeton's mother, the Dowager Countess of Lamberton, a widow at only thirty-one, was understandably very protective of her son. She became very worried for him when he began to approach the age of thirty-five. She ensured that the earl married early so he could have an heir just in case he died early like his ancestors.

But unlike his father, grandfather, great-grandfather, and great-great-grandfather before him, Lord Templeton has lived past the age of forty. In fact, he recently celebrated his fiftieth birthday. However, although Lord Templeton and Lady Mary have been married for over twenty years, they don't have any children. The earldom has no heir.

One day Lord Templeton met Roger, an old school friend of his, at the Oxford and Cambridge Club in Pall Mall, in the heart of London. They hadn't seen each other in a long while. After the initial pleasantries, their conversation drifted to the earl's plight. Roger told him he could introduce the earl and the countess to a white witch in Kensington, West London. He would massage Lady Mary's abdomen, and that should result in her getting pregnant and having a baby!

Although not a religious person and so not against the idea in principle, the idea of going to a dingy coven to have his beautiful wife massaged by a witch doctor with grubby hands seemed a little odd to the earl. Should he or shouldn't he?

As we can see from the life of Lord Templeton, the devil doesn't like to let go! But under ordinary circumstances, he can only enforce his grip over a family until the fourth generation. The generational problems will end unless the family members either renew an ancestral covenant or open the door to a new curse. So, in most cases, the devil gifts the fifth generation with a problem that will bring them right back to him for short-term solutions. He then gives them short-term solutions in exchange for new generational problems—and the cycle starts all over again.

God doesn't just want you free; he wants you to maintain your freedom. He wants you to stay free, because that's the only way you can receive the blessing and enjoy your everyday life. God wants you to enjoy your life today, right now. Not when you're older. Not when you graduate from high school or college or university. Not when you land that dream job. Not when you get married. Not when you have children. Not when the children leave home. Not when you become a millionaire. No, he wants you to enjoy life *right now*. The reality is, God wants us to enjoy our lives every *single moment* of *every day*. Did you know that?

If you didn't know, or if you just aren't sure whether God approves of people enjoying their lives, take a look what the Bible says:

> Warn the rich people of this world not to be proud or to trust in wealth that is easily lost. Tell them to have faith in God, who is rich and blesses us with everything we need to *enjoy life*.[1] (emphasis mine)

This is an absolutely incredible Scripture because it shows us very clearly that God doesn't just want us to be alive, he actually wants us to *enjoy* being alive! Jesus put it this way:

> The thief comes only in order to steal and kill and destroy. I came that they may have and enjoy life, and have it in abundance (to the full, till it overflows).[2]

In other words, God wants us to live with joy—abundant, overflowing joy! Quit putting your life on hold and start enjoying your normal, everyday life!

At the new birth, Jesus liberates us from the shackles of sin, sickness, poverty, and death. If you're a child of God, he has made you free! And if Jesus has truly set you free, then you are free indeed. Free to love God. Free to live for him. Free to realise your full potential and fulfil your purpose. Free to make a difference to the world around you. Free to overcome every challenge life throws at you. Free to enjoy the blessing. Free to enjoy everyday life. Free to be a blessing to those around you. Free to bequeath the blessing to your children and their children's children. Free indeed!

> It is for freedom that Christ has set us free. Stand firm, then, and do not let yourselves be burdened again by a yoke of slavery.[3]

The Americans say, "Freedom ain't free." The phrase, engraved into one wall at the Korean War Veterans Memorial in Washington, DC, was coined by retired US Air Force colonel Walter Hitchcock to express gratitude for the service of members of the military, because the freedoms enjoyed by many citizens in many democracies are only possible through the risks and sacrifices made by those in the armed forces. We too owe our gratitude to the One who paid for our freedom with his own suffering and death.

Through his death and resurrection, Jesus purchased our freedom, redeeming us from Satan's monstrous grip and freeing us from the chains of sin.

> When you were stuck in your old sin-dead life, you were incapable of responding to God. God brought you alive—right along with Christ!

> Think of it! All sins forgiven, the slate wiped clean, that old arrest warrant canceled and nailed to Christ's cross. He stripped all the spiritual tyrants in the universe of their sham authority at the Cross and marched them naked through the streets.[4]

Freedom is an aspect of grace, freely given to us through Christ's sacrifice at Calvary. The best definition of *grace* I can find is from Brennan Manning, who said:

> God loves you unconditionally, as you are and not as you should be, because nobody is as they should be. It is the message of grace... My life is a witness to vulgar grace—a grace that amazes as it offends. A grace that pays the eager beaver who works all day long the same wage as the grinning drunk who shows up at ten till five. A grace that hikes up the robe and runs breakneck toward the prodigal reeking of sin and wraps him up and decides to throw a party, no ifs, ands, or buts. A grace that raises bloodshot eyes to a dying thief's request—"Please, remember me"—and assures him, "You bet!" A grace that is the pleasure of the Father, fleshed out in the carpenter Messiah, Jesus the Christ, who left His Father's side not for heaven's sake, but for ours, yours and mine. This vulgar grace is indiscriminate compassion. It works without asking anything of us. It's not cheap. It's free, and as such will always be a banana peel for the orthodox foot and a fairy tale for the grown-up sensibility. Grace is sufficient even though we huff and puff with all our might to try and find something or someone that it cannot cover. Grace is enough. He is enough. Jesus is enough.[5]

With this free gift comes a huge responsibility. God has a purpose for his blessings—they are always for his glory. The gift of freedom is no exception. God demands a response from us. He expects us to receive his gift *and remain free*. Jesus shed his precious blood to release us from every chain. It is for *freedom* that he made us free. Therefore, we must never again enslave ourselves to the sins that so easily entangle us. We should seek to always glorify God with our whole being—spirit, soul, and body.

As we've seen, our freedom in Christ isn't free. Jesus gave his life to give us his freedom in exchange for our chains. *Yes, our freedom cost Jesus his life.* If we take our freedom for granted, we run the risk of losing it. Jesus said, "If you abide in My word, you are My disciples indeed. And you shall know the truth, and the truth shall make you free."[6] Therefore, the least we can do is give his Word first place in our lives, making it the final authority in order to maintain our freedom in him.

MAINTAINING AND SUSTAINING OUR FREEDOM

The Bible tells us, "So Christ has truly set us free. *Now make sure that you stay free,* and don't get tied up again in slavery to the law"[7] (emphasis mine).

When we talk of maintaining our freedom in Christ, it's certainly not about *working* to keep our salvation. Having begun in the Spirit, we cannot afford to end in the flesh![8] We must depend on the Holy Spirit and hold on to the truth of God's Word to keep us free.

Throughout this book, we've seen that there are born-again children of God today who are not experiencing the abundant, joy-filled life that Jesus died to give them. Many are held in satanic prisons where the devil controls their destiny through the evils of generational curses, ancestral covenants, evil family patterns, satanic altars, and their own sins. Their lives are full of reproach.

Others are still ruled by the flesh, giving in to worldly lusts and sensual feelings. They are tossed back and forth from day to day, controlled by their feelings and behaving as though they have no power against sin. God has given them freedom, yet they are still living like slaves. This is the essence of dying to self which we mentioned in the A to Z of spiritual warfare. When we are Spirit-controlled, our bodies become vessels of honour available for God's use.

So how do we sustain our freedom in Christ?

We Must First Be Free! Are you born again? Have you been redeemed by the blood of Jesus? Has Jesus set you free? This has got to be the starting point—our salvation. We can't even begin to consider sustaining or maintaining a freedom we don't have! Having been made free, we can then begin to look at how we sustain this freedom.

We Must Learn to Listen to God and Obey His Voice. This is probably the most important way to stay free and keep the blessing. The Bible tells us, "If you fully obey the Lord your God and carefully keep all his commands...the Lord your God will set you high above all the nations of the world. You will experience all these blessings if you obey the Lord your God."[9]

We Must Stay Alert, Yield to God, and Shut the Door Against the Devil. The devil, the enemy of souls, seeks to take us back into bondage. That's why God counsels us:

> Stay alert! Watch out for your great enemy, the devil. He prowls around like a roaring lion, looking for someone to devour. Stand firm against him, and be strong in your faith. Remember that your family of believers all over the world is going through the same kind of suffering you are.[10]

To effectively combat the devil, we must first draw near and submit ourselves to God, resist or stand firm against the devil, and ensure that we don't give him any opportunity or foothold in any area of our lives.[11]

How do we submit to God? In my book, *Crushing The Devil: Your Guide to Spiritual Warfare and Victory in Christ*, I made the following point:

> To submit to God is to surrender and yield our hearts, our wills, and our lives to him. It is to:
>
> *Obey Him.* To obey God is to do as God tells you. It is to comply with God's instructions to you as an individual. It is to act upon his Word, abide by his commandments, and conform to his will. Essentially, you are to just do what God wants you to do, how he wants it done, and when he wants it done. No more, no less!
>
> *Be faithful.* Faithfulness requires total, full, and wholehearted devotion to God and his service. Be loyal to God. Be so dedicated to God that you are sold out to him. Be fully, completely, and totally committed to him. Be trustworthy in whatever he has committed into your hands, recognizing the fact that someday you will be required to render an account of your stewardship to him (1 Corinthians 4:2). Be reliable; be dependable.
>
> *Entrust yourself to Him.* Rely on God. Trust him. This trust should come from the revelation that God is able to do whatever he has promised, and secondly that God is your source—not your job, not your business, not even the economy of your country. He has

promised, and he will never fail. He is dependable. So hang on him. Depend totally upon him.

Yield yourself to Him. God desires to have precedence in all things. You must seek him first. Surrender completely, totally, and absolutely to God. He wants to be your Saviour and your Lord, not just your Saviour. Be in total submission to his will in all things. Yearn for him in the same way that the deer pants and longs for the water brooks (Psalm 42:1).

To submit to God is to trust and obey. Put differently, to yield to God is to *walk* the *talk*. Without total surrender and complete submission to God, we cannot firmly resist and stand firm against the Enemy.[12]

RESISTING THE DEVIL

We resist the enemy by standing firm against him in prayer and opposing him with the Word of God, just like Jesus did when he was tempted.[13] Whenever he was tempted, Jesus responded by saying, "It is written" and quoting an appropriate passage of Scripture. And because the Word of God is the sword of the Spirit[14] when spoken in faith, every time Jesus said, "It is written," he was launching an attack on the devil—he was going on the offensive!

Notice that Jesus didn't ignore the devil, because that isn't the solution. Burying your head in the sand and pretending the problem isn't there won't make it go away! He didn't argue with the devil, because the devil doesn't see reason; the only language he understands is the language of force—based on the Word of God and backed by the blood and the name of Jesus. He didn't rationalise with the devil, nor did he weigh the pros and cons of the devil's temptations. He simply resisted the devil with the truth of God's Word.

Part of resisting the devil is learning to address the enemy and commanding him to back off in the name of Jesus. Tell him, "I resist you in the name of Jesus, and I command you to take your hands off my life in the name of the Lord Jesus Christ."

We Must Not Give the Devil a Foothold. The Bible says, "And do not give the devil an opportunity."[15] The word "opportunity" (also translated "place" in this passage) is the Greek word *topos*, and it means *spot, opportunity, coast, licence, place, plain, rock, room*.[16] *Topos* is also the origin of the

English word *topography*. Topography has to do with the contour, shape, or surface of the land.

The word in Ephesians 4:27 means God wants us to be sober, vigilant, and alert so as not to:

- Give the devil any room.
- Give the devil a foothold.
- Give the devil a spot to operate from.
- Give the devil any inroad into our lives.
- Give the devil any surface to operate from.
- Give the devil any opportunity into our lives.
- Give the devil a licence to operate in our affairs.
- Give the devil a place, coast, plain, or rock to stand on.
- Give the devil an inlet, a peninsula, a cape, an island, a mountain peak, or a valley.

Why is the Lord counselling us to be so careful? Simply because the devil is very crafty, and although a defeated foe, he is not exactly a toothless bulldog, as some people imagine! Let me explain. The Bible says Satan prowls the earth like a roaring lion, seeking people to devour.[17] If the devil can *devour* the unbelieving, then he can certainly seek to enslave those who give him the opening! He can hurt you if you make room for him in your life. If you give him an inch, he will take a mile. As someone once said, "If you give the devil an inch, he will try to become your ruler!"

We Must Never Forget that We Are in a Battle with the Devil. Yes, the outcome has been predetermined by God—we're victorious. We are more than conquerors. We are overcomers. But we must still fight the war. All we're required to do in this battle is enforce the victory won by Jesus at Calvary and make his enemies his footstool. This is the essence of spiritual warfare. Nonetheless, we must be aware that the devil is ruthless and will take advantage of any crack in our lives, no matter how minute or minuscule. The serpent will bite anyone who breaks the hedge of protection that God has in place over his children.[18] We can't afford to give him a foothold!

> It is Satan's custom by small sins to draw us to greater, as the little sticks set the great ones on fire, and a wisp of straw kindles a block of wood.[19]

Even so, the devil is a defeated foe. In *Crushing The Devil: Your Guide to Spiritual Warfare and Victory in Christ*, I said:

> To help you understand what Jesus did to the devil, let us look at what happens when countries go to war. The Falklands War is a good example. It started on Friday, April 2, 1982, with the invasion and occupation of the Falkland Islands and South Georgia by Argentina. Great Britain under the late "iron" Prime Minister, Margret Thatcher then launched a naval task force to engage the Argentine forces and retake the Falklands. The war lasted only seventy-four days. It ended on June 14, 1982, when Mario Menéndez, the Argentine governor of the Falklands, surrendered to Major General Sir Jeremy Moore, the commander of the British forces. The two countries eventually signed a surrender document.
>
> When Argentina surrendered to Britain, they gave up their arms and withdrew from the Falklands. However, the surrender did not make Argentina incapable of fighting. If the British had given back the ammunition to the Argentines, they could have continued the fight. Also, if the British were to invite the Argentines back into the Falklands, they could stake their claim again.[20]

In fact, despite the defeat in 1982, the Argentines continue to assert their right to the islands. For instance, in an open letter to Prime Minister David Cameron on 3 January 2013, Cristina Fernández de Kirchner, president of the Argentine Republic, accused Britain of having taken possession of the islands—known in Argentina as *Las Malvinas*—in a "blatant exercise of 19th century colonialism."[21] In much the same way, although he has been disarmed, the devil can still operate in the lives of those Christians who *let* him.

YOU'RE AN OVERCOMER

As a born-again child of God, you're an overcomer. The Bible makes it very clear that "whatever is born of God overcomes the world. And this is the victory that has overcome the world—our faith. Who is he who overcomes the world, but he who believes that Jesus is the Son of God?"[22]

The Bible isn't saying you *will* overcome. It says if you're born of God, you've *already* overcome! Yes, it's in the past tense—you have already overcome. You just need to walk in this reality and see yourself as an overcomer. Think like an overcomer. Talk like an overcomer. And act like an overcomer!

To overcome is:

- To be fulfilled.
- To live life to the full.
- To enjoy everyday life.
- To be on top of things.
- To operate under open heavens.
- To be far from oppression.

To walk in this reality, this victory, you need to maintain your freedom in Christ in your ordinary, everyday life, from when you wake up to when you go to bed.

The fact that you're an overcomer doesn't mean you won't have challenges. Challenges will definitely come while we remain on this side of eternity. They come with the territory! However, they won't get you down! Why? Because you have the assurance of God's abiding presence through every challenge the devil and life can throw at you. We won't have to face any challenge on our own. God will be with us in the midst of it, strengthening us, upholding us, and if necessary, making a way where there seems to be none.

God says when we pass through the waters, he will be with us; and when we pass through the rivers, they will not sweep over us. When we walk through the fire, we will not be burned; the flames will not set us ablaze, and even if we walk through the valley of the shadow of death, he will be with us.[23]

Shadrach, Meshach, and Abednego faced an enormous challenge.[24] Should they bow down and worship the gold statue King Nebuchadnezzar had set up? If they didn't, they would be thrown into a blazing furnace. They were sure God would deliver them from the fiery furnace. But even if God didn't, they still wouldn't worship the king's golden image. They were prepared to die for their convictions.

In the end, God was with them in the furnace, and the flames did not set them ablaze. They walked through the fire and were not burned. As Christians, we pass through the fire—figurative and real—everyday of our lives. But we are not consumed by the fire, because God is always with us, ensuring that we come out on the other side better than ever before. When I am tried and tested, I will come forth as gold.[25]

GETTING RID OF THE DEVIL'S CLAIMS

If we want to walk in the blessing every day of our lives, have victory in our warfare, and live as overcomers, *we must make sure the devil doesn't have any claim on our lives.* We've already looked at the concept of legal rights, but this is a good place to discuss it again. One way we give a foothold to the devil is if he has a claim on us. Flies are attracted to garbage. Get rid of the garbage, and the flies will flee.

Jesus said, "I will no longer talk much with you, for the ruler of this world is coming. *He has no claim on me*"[26] (emphasis mine). Jesus was referring to the devil here. The devil didn't have any claim on Jesus. But does the devil have a claim on your life? Does he have a stake in your life?

Any covenants that are still live and unbroken will give the devil a claim over your life. As we've seen elsewhere in this book, these covenants can be ancestral or self-made. Or perhaps he has a hold over you personally, for instance, through an addiction or "besetting sin" you're struggling with.

The emphasis here is on *the little things* we take for granted—the little foxes that spoil the vine. "Take us the foxes, the little foxes that spoil the vines."[27] The fox is a rather peculiar animal. It has a tendency to dig underground to settle in holes or burrows or to feast on grapevines. It is silent and solitary. It has an incredible sense of sight, smell, and hearing. It exhibits tremendous cleverness in going after its prey. At times, it will actually play dead in order to attack a bird that is within its striking range. When hunted, it is very cunning and devious, capable of misleading its pursuers with utmost skill.

Examples of spiritual foxes in our lives include the following:

- Any form of disobedience
- Any unconfessed sin lurking anywhere in our lives

- Unforgiveness
- Gossip
- Backbiting

Does the devil have anything in you? Sin belongs to the devil. He originated it. Sin belongs to him. As an unbeliever, you had a sin nature. You were dead in sin and couldn't help yourself. You sinned because you were a sinner. As a Christian, you've become dead to sin and should *no longer sin habitually.* If there is any unconfessed sin in your life, the devil will grab hold of that. He will also lay hold of anything that is accursed—for example, the proceeds of a crime. Do you have anything that doesn't belong to you? Something you "borrowed" and didn't return? Do you have a prized painting, artefact, sculpture, or figurine that has a link to the occult and to which the devil can lay claim?

Does the enemy have anything to use against you? Remember, he is an accuser.

> Then I heard a loud voice in heaven say: "Now have come the salvation and the power and the kingdom of our God, and the authority of his Christ. For the accuser of our brothers, who accuses them before our God day and night, has been hurled down."[28]

Think of the devil as an extortionist who wants to blackmail you. Is any part of your life hidden and in secret? Is there anything you've done that you regret or are ashamed of but which nobody else knows anything about? He will use it against you. To receive freedom and break the enemy's hold, you need to tell somebody (not just anybody—go to a trusted and mature Christian; your mentor or a peer with whom you have mutual accountability would be perfect). Once you tell and it's out in the open, the enemy's hold will normally be broken!

As long as the devil has a hold over your life, you will not enjoy the fullness of God's abundance in this world. You won't know thorough freedom. There is a level of breakthrough and open heavens you will not experience in this world unless and until you can say like our Lord Jesus, "The Prince of the world is coming and he has nothing to use against me."[29] Examine your life today, and take heed to what you find! "Therefore let him who thinks he stands take heed lest he fall."[30]

WALKING IN THE SPIRIT

Finally, we must walk in the Spirit. To walk in the Spirit is to be led by the Holy Spirit. It is to completely depend on the Holy Spirit in everything. The apostle Paul tells us, "So I say, live by the Spirit, and you will never fulfill the desires of the flesh."[31]

God expects us as his children to depend on the Holy Spirit. God wants us to enjoy the fullness of the ministry of the Holy Spirit in our lives as our *Parakletos*—the Greek word for the Holy Spirit, which can be translated *advocate, defender, protector, helper, comforter, intercessor, counsellor, assistant,* and *teacher*. The Holy Spirit is all of these things for you and me. As we walk in the Spirit, we will become conformed to the perfect will of God and produce the fruit of the Spirit: love, joy, peace, longsuffering, kindness, goodness, faithfulness, gentleness, and self-control.[32]

To Walk in the Spirit, We Must Be Doers of the Word. God expects us to complement our faith with corresponding action. One of the greatest mistakes we make as believers is to confess our faith in the Word of God and at the same time contradict our confession by wrong actions. We say we're trusting God for healing, but at the same time we are worrying about what will happen if we are not healed. We say we are trusting God to make us holy, but we go on living in sin and make the excuse that we just can't help it. There is no corresponding action there! One minute we confess that the Word of God is true, and the very next moment we undo everything we say by wrong actions. Our actions must correspond with our believing if we are to receive from God and preserve our freedom in Christ. The Bible puts it this way: "In the same way, faith by itself, if it is not accompanied by action, is dead."[33]

If we are doers of the Word, our actions will coincide with our confession. When I trust in the Lord with all of my heart and stop leaning upon human understanding, then my actions correspond with my faith. My actions will be in perfect harmony with my confession of faith. This happens as we constantly renew our minds with the Word of God. The more we renew our minds, the easier it is for our actions to correspond to our confession of faith.

Until we get to a level where there are corresponding actions in our lives, we will always experience failure. It is easy for me to confess and declare that God is the strength of my life. However, if at the same time I continue to talk about my weaknesses, my daily struggles, and my lack of faith, I will be defeated because there is no corresponding action supporting, accompanying, and supplementing my confession. What I am doing is resorting to human methods instead of trusting the Lord. This inconsistency or contradiction leads to confusion in my spirit and brings weakness and failure to my life. There is just one thing for us to do, and that is to turn to God's Word and act upon it, in faith, complemented by our corresponding action.

To Walk in the Spirit, We Must Also Watch and Pray. Usually when we pray, we close our eyes as a sign of submission to God and to help us concentrate and avoid distraction. On the other hand, the biblical concept of being watchful in prayer involves staying wide awake, with all our senses and faculties fully awake and alert.[34] The admonition is that we need to be *prayerfully observant* of the world we live in. We must be conscious of the things going on around us because every now and then, God uses them to tell us about the times and seasons. It is therefore not sufficient merely to pray; we must also be vigilant. Both should go hand in hand.

To Walk in the Spirit, We Must Avoid Unforgiveness. There are many people who refuse to forgive. Some fail to forgive, while others neglect to forgive. This is one of the easiest ways to give up our freedom in Christ. Forgiveness makes us *better,* while unforgiveness makes us *bitter!* Forgiveness is a choice. It is the person who cannot forgive who suffers. Unforgiveness is a cancer that nibbles at our relationship with God, causing a deterioration in our fellowship with him. It also eats up the human immune system, causing a variety of diseases and medical conditions.

To maintain our freedom, not only must we forgive those who hurt us, we must also pray for them and bless them. Like Stephen the martyr, who prayed for those who stoned him as he died, we must be able to say, "Lord, do not hold this sin against them."[35]

To Walk in the Spirit, We Must Guard Our Hearts and Minds. As we saw in Chapter 2, the mind of a man is like a big tumble dryer of various thoughts that are constantly in motion. Our thoughts come from different sources:

- From God. He speaks to us!
- From physical stimuli (the five senses: touching, taste, hearing, smelling, and seeing).
- From self (your own memory and your imagination).
- From the powers of darkness (evil spirits). They are very real!

The Bible admonishes, "Guard your heart above all else, for it determines the course of your life."[36] Guard your heart and mind. You've heard the expression: "Garbage in, garbage out." The opposite is equally true: "Virtue in, virtue out." This is why it is always advisable to avoid pornography and any material that glorifies the occult or witchcraft, including books, carvings, paintings, and movies.

The Bible describes it beautifully through the apostle Paul as follows: "Summing it all up, friends, I'd say you'll do best by filling your minds and meditating on things true, noble, reputable, authentic, compelling, gracious—the best, not the worst; the beautiful, not the ugly; things to praise, not things to curse."[37] Be careful what you read and what you listen to!

MAKE UP YOUR MIND

We've come a long way in the pages of this book. We've learned about the war going on in the world, our victory and authority, and our responsibility to enforce the reign of Jesus in our lives. We've recognized the powers of darkness that can bind our lives, and we've taken the steps to break them off. We've called down the blessing of God and committed to maintaining our freedom. But there's one last step we need to look at when it comes to living a victorious life: *we have to make up our minds.*

There are people who have one leg in the church and one leg in with the devil. They have a form of godliness but deny God's power.[38] This is extremely dangerous, because there can be no *in-betweeners* with God. You're either hot or cold. You're either in or out!

I recently came across a report by Catharina Moh, the Bolivia correspondent for BBC News, on the five-hundred-year-old mines of Bolivia's Cerro Rico mountain. These are the mountains that produced the silver that once made the Spanish empire rich.[39] During the Spanish Colonial

Era, two billion ounces of silver were extracted from the mountain. Over the same period, about eight million people are estimated to have died in the mines, earning Cerro Rico the nickname "The Mountain that Eats Men."

Today about fifteen thousand miners work on the mountain, and the local widows' association says fourteen women are widowed each month. Average life expectancy is forty. Now riddled with tunnels, the mountain is a death trap for the men and boys who work there—and who pray to the devil to keep them safe. Yes, they pray to the devil! The high death toll on the mountain fuels superstition. The men and boys chew coca leaves, saying it helps filter the dust. They also make offerings of these coca leaves along with alcohol and cigarettes to El Tio—the devil god of the mines.

Each of the thirty-eight businesses running mines on the mountain has a statue of El Tio in their tunnels. "He has horns because he is the god of the depths," one of the managers says. "Usually we gather here on Fridays to make offerings, in gratitude because he gave us lots of minerals, and so that he will protect us from accidents. Outside the mine we are Catholics, and when we enter the mine, we worship the devil."

How can you possibly think it's acceptable to worship the devil in the mines and God when you're out? *This is having a form of godliness but denying its power!*

And this is perhaps the greatest key to staying free. Who will you serve? Who will you worship? Who will you believe?

You must make up your mind.

Afterword:

FIGHT *FROM* VICTORY, NOT *FOR* VICTORY!

> "Everyone born of God overcomes the world. This is the victory that has overcome the world, even our faith."
>
> **1 John 5:4, NIV**

One of the first things I learned in law school is that a good lawyer is not one who knows the law, but one who knows where to find it!

Sometime ago I handled a case as an immigration lawyer. My client, Richard, had been granted leave to remain in the UK for two and a half years as the spouse of a British national. He and his wife had two-year-old twin daughters. About one year into his visa, they started having serious problems in their marriage. Unknown to Richard, Lucy informed the immigration authorities that she no longer supported his application, and his visa was curtailed.

Six months later, Richard lost a cousin in Barbados and travelled for two weeks. On his return to the UK, he was arrested at the airport by the UK Border Agency. That's when he found out his visa had been revoked six and a half months previously! He was detained and scheduled for deportation back to Barbados on the next available flight, which was in three days.

Richard contacted me and instructed me to act for him. I immediately lodged an appeal against the curtailment of the visa. After lodging the appeal, I contacted the immigration authorities, asking them to cancel the flight and grant him temporary release. The flight was cancelled because of the appeal, but custody was maintained. I continued to press for his release. I reminded the authorities that the appeal was unlikely to be held soon, and his daughters' birthday was imminent—it would break their hearts if Daddy was not there. I also told them he would comply with any restrictions they might impose.

This went on for a few days. Eventually the authorities decided to grant him temporary release with a restriction on working. Mrs Jones, an immigration officer rang me to inform me of the good news.

But just before Mrs Jones rang, I saw *it*! I came across a law that automatically extends a person's curtailed visa as long as he has a pending appeal. The effect of this little-known law was that my client had valid leave! As you can imagine, this discovery changed the case. Previously, I had been pleading with the immigration authorities to grant my client temporary release, when in fact they had no right to detain him in the first place! Armed with this knowledge, I was no longer *fighting for victory*. I was now fighting *from victory*!

"Hello, Mr Okoro, I am happy to inform you that we have decided to grant your client temporary admission," Mrs Jones informed me. "However, there will be certain restrictions on him."

"Thank you, Mrs Jones," I responded. "However, I am no longer asking for temporary admission for my client. I am asking for his immediate unconditional release."

"What do you mean, Mr Okoro?" Mrs Jones interrupted. I could tell she was getting agitated.

"My client has 3D leave," I began with a huge smile. I was trying very hard not to sound triumphant. "Section 11 of the Immigration, Asylum and Nationality Act 2006 added section 3D to the Immigration Act 1971. This is to prevent a migrant from becoming an overstayer while exercising a right of appeal against a decision to curtail or revoke leave to enter or remain. In those circumstances, you have acted illegally in detaining my client. Unless he is granted immediate, unconditional release, without any restriction on his ability to work, we will seek compensation for wrongful imprisonment."

Eventually Richard was released...unconditionally.

As you've seen throughout this book, spiritual warfare is real. But you've got to realise that you shouldn't be fighting a battle you've already won! That's right. You defeated the devil in Christ more than two thousand years ago. You were nailed to the cross of Calvary in him. This became a reality for you the day you received Jesus into your heart as your Saviour and Lord. The Bible puts it this way: "I have been crucified with Christ and I no longer live, but Christ lives in me. The life I now live in the body, I live by faith in the Son of God, who loved me and gave himself for me."[1]

You've got to always remember that the devil is a defeated foe. The battle has been won. You don't need to fight him. So what do you do?

You simply stand and exercise your authority.

All you've got to do is exercise your authority. Simply stand your ground and speak the Word! You see, for the believer, spiritual warfare shouldn't be a struggle.

In the great Bible passage on spiritual warfare,[2] the word *stand* appears four times, while the word translated *wrestle, battle, fight,* or *struggle* appears only once. In essence, God is asking you to spend the majority of your time in warfare standing! But what does it mean to stand?

The word translated *stand* is the Greek *histemi,* which can be defined as "to uphold or sustain the authority or force of anything."[3] That's telling us something, isn't it? God isn't asking you to fight the devil. He is asking you to simply *uphold or sustain* the victory won by Jesus at Calvary and enforce *his* authority over the devil. You're like the traffic warden who raises his hand and the vehicles stop. They don't stop because he can physically bring the vehicles to a halt, but because he is representing and upholding the authority of the state. God is asking you four times out of five, in this beautiful passage of Scripture, to uphold and sustain his authority. He is asking you to do so because you're an overcomer. You've overcome already. You've defeated the devil.

So how do you uphold Christ's authority? This wonderful passage of Scripture begins by enjoining us to "be strong in the Lord and in his mighty power"[4] because as we saw in chapter 1, God is the source of our authority. What you have is delegated authority. So to engage in spiritual warfare, you've got to be strong in the Lord.

The word translated *strong* is the Greek word *endunamoo* and means "to be strong, endue with strength, strengthen, to receive strength, be strengthened, and increase in strength."[5] In other words, to be strong in the Lord is to depend completely on God, relying on his resources and using his strategies. Finding your strength in God is an admission that you have no strength of your own.

To stand against the enemy is to *rest* in what Jesus has already done. It's almost like saying you need to run a race from a position of rest. You make more progress by sitting behind the wheel of a car than by pedalling a bicycle. When you struggle with the enemy, you are pedalling with your own strength. You will have a lot of action but little motion. You won't go very far. However, when you rest in Jesus, you are like an eagle. An eagle soars by using thermal currents of air. These warm air patterns are created by the surrounding terrain. The eagle spreads its wings and tail feathers and lets the wind carry it to new heights. From time to time, it glides down to catch another upward thermal. Soaring saves the eagle energy because it does not have to flap its wings often. It can soar to unimaginable heights without breaking a sweat.

Here's another way to describe it: Resting is like being the pilot of a 747 jumbo jet. He sits down yet is able to fly the plane. He doesn't need to run. He doesn't need to try to push the airplane. He flies from a position of rest. He sits, yet he is able to fly at speeds of 565 mph. That's what God wants you to do: rest in him.

There are four elements to resting in God:

Know who you are. You've been redeemed by the precious blood. You're a chosen generation, a royal priesthood, and a peculiar person. You're a royal ambassador.

Know whose you are. You're a child of the Most High God. You're God's heir and a joint-heir with Jesus Christ.

Know where you are. You're seated in the heavenly places with Jesus Christ, far above principalities and powers.

Know what you have. All of God's resources, paid for by Jesus Christ, are made available to you. There's nothing more to be done. Simply receive what has been freely given to you.

Don't attempt to fight the enemy in your own strength. You will experience burnout, and you will fail. Don't even think about it!

And don't get sucked into thinking that spiritual warfare is a wrestling match with the devil. It isn't. If you try to wrestle with him, you will fail. Unfortunately, that is the sad reality today for many ministers of the gospel who are in the frontline of the enemy's attacks. A 2010 article in the *New York Times* reported that "Members of the clergy now suffer from obesity, hypertension and depression at rates higher than most Americans. In the last decade, their use of antidepressants has risen, while their life expectancy has fallen. Many would change jobs if they could."[6]

The key is to engage in spiritual warfare God's way. And that is by resting in him and fighting *from* victory, not *for* victory!

Appendix:

101 WAYS TO CRUSH THE DEVIL

"The God of peace will soon crush Satan under your feet.
The grace of our Lord Jesus be with you."

Romans 16:20

Although there's only one way to heaven (through Jesus Christ), there are a million and one ways to crush the devil! By this I mean ways by which you can exercise your authority as a believer and enforce the victory won by Jesus at Calvary.

Here are my top 101 ways to ensure the devil remains where he belongs, *under* your feet. Each of them will help you advance the kingdom of God and improve your relationship with God. And the amazing thing is that each one of them also hurts the devil and crushes him in a unique way. It's like destroying the kingdom of darkness on autopilot!

I've compiled this from my understanding of Scripture and my experience of spiritual warfare! To help you, there are infographics which you can download for free at www.pedrookoro.com/101-ways/

This list is by no means exhaustive. Therefore, please feel free to add anything which I may have omitted. Join the conversation on social media using the following hashtag: **#101WaysToCrushTheDevil**.

1. **Give your heart to Jesus**. Be born again. Accept Jesus as your personal Saviour and Lord. You can only exercise authority over the devil in Christ Jesus. This has got to be the starting point, because once you're born again the devil is under your feet!

2. **Have a personal relationship with Jesus**. It's not enough *simply* to be born again! You've got to develop and nurture that relationship. Get to know the Lord. Seek to become more like him. Seek to be transformed into his image. Become more and more like him! There are people who go to church singing "just as I am" and go home just as they came. To avoid being in that crowd, desire to become more and more Christ-like. This is guaranteed to keep the devil under your feet.
3. **Have faith in God**. Without faith you cannot please God. As you study the Scriptures, your faith will invariably grow.
4. **Be on fire for Jesus.** Be sold out for Christ. Be fixated and consumed with Jesus. Breathe, sleep, eat, and live Jesus! When you're on fire for Jesus, the devil will find you too hot to handle!
5. **Read your Bible and pray every day**. The devil hates believers who read their Bibles and pray daily. Remember, seven days without prayer makes *one weak*.
6. **Study the Word of God**. Be a diligent student of the Bible.
7. **Meditate on the Word of God day and night**. Spend quality time ruminating on the Word of God. It will do you good. "How well God must like you, you don't hang out at Sin Saloon, you don't slink along Dead End Road, you don't go to Smart Mouth College. Instead you thrill to God's Word, you chew on Scripture day and night. You're a tree replanted in Eden, bearing fresh fruit every month, Never dropping a leaf, always in blossom."[1]
8. **Renew your mind with the Word**. Let the Word of God transform your thoughts. You're the sum of your thoughts.
9. **Be a doer of the Word**. Apply the Word of God. All Scripture is inspired by God. So don't pick and choose.
10. **Avoid negative confessions**. Align your thoughts and words with what God says about you. Whatever you say will invariably come to pass.
11. **Think on what is lovely, true, and of a good report**. Don't fill your mind with negative, evil, and destructive thoughts. As you think, so you are. Simple as that!
12. **Put on the whole armour of God.** As we saw in chapter 3, the armour has seven pieces. Put on all the armour. You need all the armour to fight the enemy *from* victory.

13. **Bind the enemy in the name of Jesus.** You've got the authority. Make use of it. Put the devil where he belongs, *right under your feet!* "No one can enter a strong man's house and plunder his goods, unless he first binds the strong man. And then he will plunder his house."[2]
14. **Resist the enemy in the name of Jesus.** Trust me. This is one of the easiest ways to crush the devil. Simply resist him! The Bible says, "So give yourselves completely to God. Stand against the devil, and the devil will run from you."[3]
15. **Restrain the enemy in the name of Jesus.** You can stop demonic activities in your neighbourhood. Simply restrain the powers of darkness.
16. **Rebuke the enemy in the name of Jesus.** Like Jesus did, you can rebuke sickness, demons, and the devil himself.
17. **Plunder the enemy's goods in the name of Jesus.** His goods are basically the souls of those who have yet to know Jesus as Saviour and Lord. Rescue them. Open the prison gates for them. Set them free!
18. **Cast out the enemy's evil and demonic spirits in the name of Jesus.** The ability to cast out demons is one of the signs that accompany you as a child of God.
19. **Disrupt the enemy's meetings in the name of Jesus.** Make it your regular practice to pray against satanic meetings in your neighbourhood. You have the authority. Make use of it. It works.
20. **Frustrate the enemy's plans in the name of Jesus.** You can upset the devil's plans. You can destroy them in the place of prayer. Simply speak the word. And it will happen.
21. **Disarm the enemy in the name of Jesus.** You can!
22. **Nullify the enemy's power in the name of Jesus.** As we saw in chapter 1, you have complete authority over all of the devil's power.
23. **Destroy the enemy's yoke and lift off the burdens he has put on you and others in the name of Jesus.** The devil specialises in burdening people with heavy yokes. You've got the power and the anointing. You can destroy the devil's yokes and lift his burdens.
24. **Uproot any seed or tree which the enemy has planted.** The devil likes to sow tares among the wheat. You can uproot them and cause them to wither.

25. **Demolish and tear down the enemy's strongholds in the name of Jesus.** You have the authority. You can do it if you choose to.
26. **Command the enemy to stop meddling or interfering in the name of Jesus.** Is the devil interfering in your life or something you're trying to accomplish for God? Command him to stop meddling. Just speak the word.
27. **Send the enemy's demon spirits to the waterless places in the name of Jesus.** The devil has billions of demon spirits in his evil network. The demons or evil spirits are fallen angels who rebelled in heaven with Satan.[4] Commanding them to go to the waterless places[5] and ordering them to remain there is a good strategy in deliverance. When you do this, you are making them homeless until they are judged at the end of time. It's one of the best ways to crush demons. The devil hates this, and he will hate me for letting you in on this secret! But do it anyway!
28. **Recognise that your body is the temple of the Holy Spirit and treat it as such.** "Or didn't you realize that your body is a sacred place, the place of the Holy Spirit? Don't you see that you can't live however you please, squandering what God paid such a high price for? The physical part of you is not some piece of property belonging to the spiritual part of you. God owns the whole works. So let people see God in and through your body."[6]
29. **Hate ungodliness and iniquity. Say "no" to sin.** Every time you say no to sin, you enforce Jesus's victory at Calvary and crush the devil. Saying no is not as difficult as you may think. God will never let you be tempted beyond your capacity. And with each temptation he makes a way of escape, so you don't have to give in.[7]
30. **If married, be faithful to your spouse.** Be committed to your spouse. The grass is never greener on the other side! If it appears to be greener, it is only because the parties have watered and tended it. The story is told of two teardrops who met in the journey of life. One said she was the tears of a woman who had just lost her husband to another woman. The other teardrop said she was the tears of the woman who got the man!
31. **If single, practise abstinence.** Yes, you read right! No ringing, no dinging! Sex is strictly for marriage! One of the easiest ways

to pick up demonic influences is through fornication or adultery. Keep yourself pure.

32. **Avoid idolatry**. Anything that's more important than God is an idol. Get rid of it. Make God your number one!
33. **Avoid hypocrisy**. A hypocrite is a play actor. Somebody said, "Charity begins at home but generally dies for lack of outdoor activity!"
34. **Honour your parents**. This comes with a promise. When you honour your parents, it will be well with you. And you will live long.[8] So go for it. Honour them. What are you waiting for?
35. **Look after your relatives**. If you don't, you're worse than an unbeliever, so exercising your authority as a believer will be out of the question. You need to get this part of your life aligned with God's will.
36. **Avoid gluttony**. Gluttony is derived from the Latin *gluttire*. It means overindulgence and overconsumption of food, drink, or wealth items to the point of extravagance or waste. You must *eat* to live, not *live* to eat! If you don't have control over your appetites, you will be susceptible to the devil's evil schemes.
37. **Occupy until Jesus returns**. Do business for him. Work for him. However, God is more interested in your walk *with* him than your service *to* him. Your walk with God is the key. He seeks your fellowship and communion. When you walk with him in the light of his Word, it becomes easy to work for him, because the Holy Spirit will empower you!
38. **Be the best you can be.** Arise and shine. "Arise, shine, for your light has come, and the glory of the Lord has risen upon you."[9]
39. **Preach the gospel.** When you engage in effective soul-winning, you're depopulating the kingdom of darkness. What better way to crush the devil? So preach the good news of the kingdom of God. Do it when you feel like it and when you don't.
40. **Be a witness for Jesus**. Be salt to those around you. Bring healing, deliverance, and flavour to those around you.
41. **Let your light shine**. Live for God. This will bring illumination to the dark world around you.
42. **Forgive those who wrong you**. Learn to forgive. Be kind to those who maltreat you. Pray for them. Bless them. And while you're at it, forgive yourself too.

43. **Watch and pray**. The devil always seeks an opportune time to attack. An opportune time is a time of vulnerability. He did it with Jesus: "And when the devil had ended every [the complete cycle of] temptation, he [temporarily] left Him [that is, stood off from Him] until another more opportune and favorable time."[10] The key is to watch and pray. "Keep watch and pray, so that you will not give in to temptation. For the spirit is willing, but the body is weak!"[11]
44. **Pray for those in authority**. Pray for the different levels of government in your country.
45. **Fast and pray regularly**. There are things that won't happen unless you fast and pray. Jesus told his disciples "But this kind does not go out except by prayer and fasting."[12] My definition of "this kind" would be anything that is long-standing in nature.
46. **Learn to wait on the Lord**. This is different from fasting and prayer. This is when you take time out to fast and just be alone with God. Just be still and don't do anything. You can go to a hotel or just lock yourself away in your study. This is fasting and *waiting*. Don't read your Bible. Don't pray. Just be quiet before God. Practise this in addition to your times of fasting and prayer.
47. **Pray without ceasing**. Hard as it may seem, it is actually possible to pray without ceasing. Ask the Holy Spirit to help you.
48. **Learn to prayer walk.** Prayer walking is a great way to pray without ceasing! It's simply strolling through your neighbourhood, school, or work place, praying as you go. You can do this either by yourself or in groups. You can even incorporate it into your daily exercise regime. Go for a walk and pray while you do! These prayers are intercessory rather than devotional.
49. **Pray in the Spirit**. As we saw in chapter 3, the easiest way to pray in the Spirit is by praying in tongues. However, you can also pray in the Spirit by asking the Holy Spirit to help you as you pray, and by ensuring you pray according to God's will as revealed in the Bible.
50. **Give thanks whatever happens**. As we saw in the ABCs of spiritual warfare under *A: Adoration*, this is called thanks*living*. In every situation, give thanks. And give thanks for every situation!
51. **Be humble**. God hates pride. In fact, he "resists" proud people![13]

You don't want God to resist you, because then you'll become meat for the devil!

52. **Do to others what you expect them to do to you**. The Golden Rule. Instituted by Jesus.[14] Copied by everyone, including atheists!
53. **Do not accept the counsel of the wicked**. Don't seek advice from nonbelievers!
54. **Avoid the way of sinners** and **the seat of the scornful**. Don't be unequally yoked with ungodly people.
55. **Expect temptation and resist it**. Jesus was tempted. As long as you live in this fallen world, you will be tempted. But you can say no to the devil and his suggestions!
56. **Seek the good of the city where you live**. Seek the good of your neighbourhood, the street where you live, the city, the county, the state, the country, the continent!
57. **Endure hardship as a good soldier of Christ**. Hard times will come. Don't give up. Hang in there.
58. **Be steadfast in the work of the Lord**. Be faithful to God.
59. **Be purpose driven**. What on earth are you doing here? Jesus knew his purpose. And he was purpose driven. So should you be!
60. **Don't hoard**. You can save without hoarding. The rich fool in Jesus's parable hoarded.[15] God hates hoarding.
61. **Prioritise God's kingdom**. "But seek (aim at and strive after) first of all His kingdom and His righteousness (His way of doing and being right), and then all these things taken together will be given you besides."[16]
62. **Return to your first love for God**. If you've strayed away, come back home!
63. **Practise constant self-examination**. This is self-explanatory.
64. **Be a person of your word**. Fulfil your promises even if it hurts.
65. **Redeem the time**. Avoid procrastination. God has only given you today. Make the most of it.
66. **Visit the sick**. Visit them and pray for them.
67. **Provide for the homeless**. You don't have to start a new initiative to do this if there's one already in place where you are. For instance, you can support a charity that provides for the homeless, or go help out at your local soup kitchen.
68. **Care for widows and orphans**. Just do it!

69. **Clothe the naked**. Again, you can work through reputable charities and nongovernmental organisations to accomplish this.
70. **Give consideration to the poor and needy**. When you give to the poor, you lend to the Lord. He will repay with interest!
71. **Show mercy**. Be merciful and kind. Especially to those who don't deserve it!
72. **When you give to the poor, do not let your left hand know what your right hand is doing**. If you want God to bless you, you've got to learn to give in secret without letting the whole world know!
73. **Be loyal and true to God in good and bad times**. It's easy to remember God in tough times. It's more difficult when all is well. Don't forget God when it is well with you.
74. **Demonstrate the God-kind of love**. This love takes its root from the Greek word *agape*. It is unconditional love. It is patient and kind. It isn't jealous, doesn't brag, and is not proud.[17]
75. **Live for Christ daily**. Make that your goal.
76. **Determine to die empty**. You were loaded with potential and gifts from heaven at birth. Determine not to make the cemetery a wealthy place.
77. **Commit your ways to the Lord**. Acknowledge the Lord in everything you do. Do this every day, all the time.
78. **Have a reverential fear for God**. This is the beginning of wisdom!
79. **Give generously to the work of the Lord**. As a guide, a tenth of your income is the minimum that you should aim to give. Somebody once said, "A lot of people are willing to give God the credit, but not the cash!" Don't be one of them!
80. **Give God the first-fruits of your increase**. Whenever you experience a blessing, give a special thanks offering to God. Let him know you're totally his, money and all!
81. **Sow in tears**. Give generously. Be like King David, who wouldn't give God anything that didn't cost him.[18]
82. **Lay up treasures in heaven**. This happens when you seek first and prioritise God's kingdom and do what God has called you to do.
83. **Love God with all your heart and all your might**. Love him with everything you've got.

84. **Love your neighbours as yourself.** Do for them what you'd want in return.
85. **Make a joyful noise to the Lord.** Not just on special occasions, but even when things don't look so good! Make a joyful noise. When you feel like it and when you don't!
86. **Do not fret yourself because of evildoers.** Don't compare yourself with others.
87. **Be active in a local Bible-believing church.** Avoid isolation. It's a tactic of the enemy.
88. **Bring up your children in the fear of God.** Your children are a loan from God, and one day you will give an account of what you did with them. So train your children. Teach them. Model a good example to them. And pray for them. God loves them more than you do; he will hear your prayers.
89. **Take responsibility for your actions.** Avoid the blame game!
90. **Don't be lukewarm.** Instead, be on fire for the Lord. Breathe, eat, and sleep Jesus.
91. **Depend on God.** Totally. Completely. In all things. There's a curse on those who depend on man![19]
92. **Cast all your cares upon God.** God's shoulders are broad enough to carry all your anxieties, worries, and concerns. Give them over.
93. **Don't worry about anything. Instead, pray about everything.** If you don't ask, you won't receive. Simple as that!
94. **Know God, be strong, do exploits.** The Bible says those who know their God will be strong and will do exploits.[20]
95. **Partake of Holy Communion.** On a regular basis. The early church practised it. The Bible tells us "They worshiped together at the Temple each day, met in homes for the Lord's Supper, and shared their meals with great joy and generosity."[21] The communion bread represents the body of Jesus Christ that was broken for us. The wine represents his blood, by which the new covenant is ratified. So when you partake of the Lord's Table, you're remembering the death and resurrection of Jesus. You're also renewing and reaffirming the New Covenant. So go ahead and partake of it. It will do you a world of good!
96. **Walk in the Spirit.** Walk, sleep, sit, and be totally consumed and controlled by the Holy Spirit.

97. **Be a living sacrifice**. Make your life a living sacrifice. Let God know that you're sold out to him...completely.
98. **Be a mentor.** There are people who would be blessed by your life experiences. Make yourself available to them. Be a Paul. Have a Timothy!
99. **Bless those in prison.** Join a prison ministry. Start a prison ministry. Or support a prison ministry.
100. **Support Missions**. Adopt a missionary and support them financially and through regular intercessory prayers.
101. **Stand firm and keep standing**. Having done all, stand. Remain standing on Christ the solid Rock. Remain standing for Christ. Remain standing.

END NOTES

Preface: What Happened to You?
1. It is said that it takes six months to build a Rolls Royce but thirteen hours to build a Toyota!
2. Psalm 139:14 (NLT)
3. Psalm 8:4–5 (NASB)
4. 1 John 3:9, 1 Peter 1:23
5. John 10:10
6. Deuteronomy 7:9, Proverbs 13:22
7. Lamentations 4:1–2 (GW)
8. Revelation 12:4, 9; Isaiah 14:12–20; Ezekiel 28:1–19
9. Lamentations 5:7 (NLT)
10. Proverbs 26:2
11. Hebrews 10:11–14
12. Luke 19:13 (KJV)
13. Ephesians 3:10–11

Chapter 1: Your Authority as a Believer
1. The story is told by Benny Hinn in *Power in the Blood*. Milton Keynes: Word Publishing, 1993. 111–113.
2. Ephesians 1:7 (NIV)
3. http://www.biblestudytools.com/lexicons/greek/kjv/agorazo.html
4. 1 Corinthians 6:20 (NIV)
5. http://www.biblestudytools.com/lexicons/greek/nas/exagorazo.html
6. Galatians 3:13 (NIV)
7. http://www.biblestudytools.com/lexicons/greek/nas/lutroo.html
8. Titus 2:14 (NLT)
9. Ephesians 1:20–22; Ephesians 2:6.
10. Romans 8:30–31 (NIV)
11. Matthew 22:14

12. Hebrews 4:14–16
13. Smith Wigglesworth (8 June 1859–12 March 1947) was a British evangelist who was regarded as an apostle of faith.
    For more information on Wigglesworth's life and ministry visit: http://www.smithwigglesworth.com/life.htm.
14. Andrew Strom & Larry Magnello, "Great Healing Revivalists—How God's Power Came." http://homepages.ihug.co.nz/~revival/healing.html
15. Strong's Number: 1849: *New Strong's Concise Dictionary of the Words in the Greek Testament.* Thomas Nelson Publishers, 1995.
16. *Oxford Dictionary of English.* Second Edition, Revised. eBook. Oxford University Press, 2010.
17. Acts 19:13–16 (NLT)
18. James 4:7
19. Psalm 119:89 (NASB)
20. John 10:35 (ESV)
21. Ephesians 6:12

Chapter 2: Winning the Battle in Your Mind

1. Joyce Meyer, "Where the Mind Goes, the Man Follows." http://www.jmmindia.org/jmmsite/jmm/ministries/daily_word/WhereMindGoes.pdf
2. Proverbs 4:23 (NIV)
3. http://biblehub.com/hebrew/3820.htm
4. Matthew 4:1–4
5. James 1:14 (NLT)
6. 1 Corinthians 10:13
7. 2 Samuel 11
8. 2 Samuel 11:5–21
9. Genesis 39:1–10 (NIV)
10. 2 Corinthians 10:4–5 (NIV)
11. Romans 12:2 (NIV)
12. Ephesians 6:17

Chapter 3: A Spiritual Warfare Primer

1. The story is told in Quin Sherrer and Ruthanne Garlock., *How to Pray for Your Family and Friends.* Ann Arbor, MI: Servant Publications, 1990.
2. Billy Graham, *Angels: Ringing Assurance that We are Not Alone.* Nashville, TN: Thomas Nelson, 1995. 104.
3. C.S. Lewis, Preface to *The Screwtape Letters.*
4. Job 1:6–10
5. Matthew 4:1–11

6. 1 Thessalonians 2:18 (KJV)
7. http://biblehub.com/greek/1228.htm
8. Hosea 4:6 (NIV)
9. 1 Peter 5:8 (NIV)
10. 1 Peter 5:8
11. 1 Corinthians 2:6–8, NIV
12. Ephesians 6:11, NLT
13. Ephesians 6:10–18 (NIV)
14. John 17:17
15. 2 Corinthians 5:21 (NIV)
16. 1 John 3:9
17. Hebrews 4: 12 (NLT)
18. Psalm 12:6 (NIV)
19. Psalm 119:89
20. Jeremiah 1:12; Isaiah 55:11
21. Romans 10:15 (ESV)
22. Ephesians 6:15
23. Psalm 18:34
24. For the use of the Hebrew word *yare'*, translated *fear* in the Old Testament, see https://www.blueletterbible.org/lang/lexicon/lexicon.cfm?Strongs=H3372&t=KJV. For the use of the Greek word *fob-eh'-o*, translated fear in the New Testament, see http://www.biblestudytools.com/lexicons/greek/kjv/phobeo.html.
25. Ephesians 6:3 (NIV)
26. Colossians 4:12 (NIV)
27. Nehemiah 8:10
28. Psalm 16:11
29. Matthew 6:10 (NIV)
30. Micah 6: 8 (NLT)
31. See the Old Testament book of Esther.
32. James 4:7 (NIV)
33. Isaiah 60:1
34. Romans 8:19
35. Hebrews 10:12–14
36. James 1:22
37. Luke 9:62 (NIV)
38. Matthew 27:51
39. Hebrews 4:14–16
40. John 14:30 (NASB)
41. John 10:10

42. Galatians 2:20 (NIV)
43. 1 John 3:9 (AMP)
44. Ephesians 5:18

Chapter 4: Understanding Deliverance

1. Kenneth E. Hagin, *The Believer's Authority.* Tulsa, OK: Faith Library Publications, 1996. 57, 65–66
2. Ephesians 5:18
3. Robert L. (Bob) Deffinbaugh, "The Gerasene Demoniac (Mark 5:1–20)", Bible.org. https://bible.org/seriespage/9-gerasene-demoniac-mark-51-20
4. Luke 13:10-13
5. Luke 13:16 (NLT)
6. Mark 16:17 (NIV)

Chapter 5: Like Father, Like Son?

1. John 9:2–3 (NLT)
2. Exodus 20:5–6
3. A. E. Winship, *Jukes-Edwards: A Study in Education and Heredity.* Harrisburg, PA: R.L. Myers & Co. 1900. 7–29.
4. Genesis 12:1–3 (MSG)
5. Galatians 3:13–14 (NIV)
6. Ephesians 1:3 (NIV)
7. Deuteronomy 28:13
8. 2 Samuel 12:1–25
9. Larry Huch. *Free at Last: Removing the Past from Your Future.* Expanded edition. New Kensington, PA: Whitaker House, 2010. 30–31.
10. Patrick J. Kiger. "Was Kennedy Tied to the Mob?" *NationalGeographic.com.* http://channel.nationalgeographic.com/channel/killing-kennedy/articles/jfks-secret-mafia-history/.
11. "American Mafia," *Wikipedia.com.* http://en.wikipedia.org/wiki/American_Mafia
12. Edmund J. Bourne. *The Anxiety & Phobia Workbook.* 5th ed. Oakland, CA: New Harbinger Publications, 2011. 50–51.
13. Genesis 3:17
14. "Alcohol Dependence," *Drinkaware.co.uk.* https://www.drinkaware.co.uk/check-the-facts/health-effects-of-alcohol/mental-health/alcohol-dependence
15. Ibid.
16. "Hope through knowledge," www.GeneticDiseaseFoundation.org
17. Deuteronomy 8:3
18. Galatians 5:1

Chapter 6: Family Laws and Evil Patterns

1. *Mail Online*. www.dailymail.co.uk/news/article-1375024/Voodoo-human-sacrifice-The-haunting-story-Adam-Torso-Thames-boy-finally-identified.html. Ronke Phillips is a correspondent for ITV's *London Tonight*.
2. "That old black magic," *The Telegraph*, www.telegraph.co.uk/comment/4260680/That-old-black-magic.html. See also "Spin doctor to resign," *BBC News*, http://news.bbc.co.uk/1/hi/uk_politics/248203.stm.
3. For a detailed look at altars, see chapter 7.
4. "Italian Police arrest 40 and film Mafia initiation," *BBC News*, http://www.bbc.co.uk/news/world-europe-30095254.
5. 2 Corinthians 11:14
6. Matthew 2:1–12 (MSG)
7. Matthew 2:16–18
8. Chris Rogers, "Brazil's sex tourism boom." *BBC News*. 30 July 2010. www.bbc.co.uk/news/world-10764371
9. Marlon Bishop, "Goodbye Rio, Hello Recife: A Taste of Brazil's Best Hidden Carnival." *MTV Iggy*. www.mtviggy.com/articles/goodbye-rio-hello-recife-a-taste-of-brazils-best-hidden-carnival.
10. Rick Bragg, "New Orleans Conjures Old Spirits Against Modern Woes." *New York Times*. www.nytimes.com/1995/08/18/us/new-orleans-conjures-old-spirits-against-modern-woes.html.
11. "Until the late 19th century, one of the major powers in West Africa was the kingdom of Benin in what is now southwest Nigeria. When European merchant ships began to visit West Africa from the 15th century onwards, Benin came to control the trade between the inland peoples and the Europeans on the coast. When the British tried to expand their own trade in the 19th century, the Benin people killed their envoys. So in 1897 the British sent an armed expedition which captured the king of Benin, destroyed his palace and took away large quantities of sculpture and regalia, including works in wood, ivory and especially brass. Some of these things came from royal altars for the king's ancestors, but among them were a large number of cast brass plaques made to decorate the wooden pillars of the palace. These had been left in the palace storerooms while part of the palace was being rebuilt. As it later emerged, most of them were probably made between about 1550–1650, the people and scenes that they show are so many and varied that they give a vivid picture of the court and kingdom of that time. Many of the plaques and other objects from Benin City were taken to Europe, where a large number of them were later given to or bought by The British Museum. When the son of the deposed king revived the Benin monarchy in 1914,

now under British rule, he did his best to restore the palace and continue the ancient traditions of the Benin monarchy. Because these traditions are followed in the modern city of Benin, it is still possible to recognise many of the scenes cast in brass by Benin artists about five hundred years ago." Excerpted from *Benin: an African Kingdom*. The British Museum. http://www.britishmuseum.org/PDF/british_museum_benin_art.pdf.
12. Jørgen Carling, "Trafficking in Women from Nigeria to Europe." Migration Policy Institute. www.migrationpolicy.org/article/trafficking-women-nigeria-europe.
13. "The Nigerian Connection: An investigation into the plight of African women caught in a web of organised crime, prostitution and trafficking." *Al Jazeera*. http://www.aljazeera.com/programmes/peopleandpower/2011/08/201189141348631784.htm.
14. James D. Graham, *The Slave Trade, Depopulation and Human Sacrifice in Benin History*, 317. *Persee: Scientific Journals*. www.persee.fr/web/revues/home/prescript/article/cea_0008-055_1965_num_5_18_3035.
15. Joseph Nevadomsky, "The Benin Kingdom: Rituals of Kingship And Their Social Meanings." Department of African Languages and Literature, University of Zimbabwe, 1993. African Study Monographs. 14(2): 65–77.
16. Ibid., 74.
17. James 4:7

Chapter 7: Understanding the Altar

1. See chapter 8 for a detailed look at death sentences.
2. A word of knowledge is one of the nine gifts listed in 1 Corinthians 12:8. It is supernatural insight or revelation about a person or circumstances without human assistance.
3. Genesis 8:10
4. John 14:6, NKJV
5. Hebrews 10:14
6. Hebrews 10:11–13, NKJV
7. Hebrews 13:10, NKJV
8. You need to understand that nothing goes for free with the devil. The devil gives short-term benefits in exchange for long-term problems.
9. Leviticus 17:14
10. Hebrews 12:24
11. Leviticus 16
12. Charles L. Feinberg, "The Scapegoat of Leviticus Sixteen." *Bibliotheca Sacra*, October 1958: 320-33. Dallas Theological Seminary. https://faculty.gordon.edu/hu/bi/ted_hildebrandt/otesources/03-leviticus/text/articles/feinberg-lev16scapegoat-bs.pdf.

13. Here are the seven places where Jesus shed his blood and their significance:
    i. In the Garden of Gethsemane, Jesus undid what Adam did in the Garden of Eden and won back our willpower.
    ii. By the stripes on his back he won back our health, making it possible for us to live in divine health.
    iii. When he wore the crown of thorns on his head, he broke the curse of poverty and won back our prosperity.
    iv. His pierced hands won back our authority and dominion over everything we touch.
    v. His pierced feet won back for us dominion over every place we walk.
    vi. When his heart was pierced, Jesus won back our joy.
    vii. Through the bruises he suffered, he won our deliverance from inner hurts and iniquities.
14. White-garment churches originated in Nigeria and have now spread into Europe and the United States. Examples include the Cherubim and Seraphim Movement and the Celestial Church of Christ. The members wear white garments to church as a form of uniform and don't put on shoes when they go to church. These are cults masquerading as churches.
15. Proverbs 26:2
16. You can read the story in Mark 11:1–10.

Chapter 8: The Power of the Spoken Word

1. Hebrews 11:3
2. John 6:63 (NASB)
3. Genesis 1:14–15 (MSG)
4. Proverbs 6:1–2 (NKJV)
5. Proverbs 18:21 (NKJV)
6. 1 Chronicles 4:9–10
7. You can read the amazing but true story in Joshua 9.
8. Joshua 9:23 (NLT)
9. Sport Lisboa e BenficaComC OM MHIH, commonly known as Benfica or simply as SLB, is a Portuguese multisport club based in Lisbon. The club is best known for its professional football team that plays in the Primeira Liga, Portugal's top-tier football league.
10. You can read the story in 2 Kings 5.
11. "Opportunistic Infections." *Aids.gov*. www.aids.gov/hiv-aids-basics/staying-healthy-with-hiv-aids/potential-related-health-problems/opportunistic-infections
12. Exodus 1:22 (NKJV)
13. "Lawyer crushed by falling betting shop sign was on once-in-a-lifetime trip to London with girlfriend." *London Evening Standard*.

www.standard.co.uk/news/london/lawyer-crushed-by-falling-betting-shop-sign-was-on-onceinalifetime-trip-to-london-with-girlfriend-8472400.html.

14. 1 John 3:8

Chapter 9: The Sins That Enslave Us

1. James 4:17
2. Romans 3:23
3. Exodus 10:16
4. John W. Lawrence, *The Seven Laws of the Harvest: God's Proven Plan for Abundant Life.* Grand Rapids, MI: Kegrel Publications, 1975. 51.
5. Harold E. Will, *Will's Commentary on the New Testament (Volume 2 - Mark).* O C I Missionary Publications, 1976. 211
6. Revelation 12:10
7. This list is by no means exhaustive. Feel from to make your own list through your own study of the Bible.
8. Deuteronomy 28:1, 15
9. Exodus 20:3–5
10. Proverbs 30:17, Ephesians 6:1–3
11. Ephesians 6:3 (NLT)
12. Micah 6:8 (NASB), Proverbs 28:27
13. Leviticus 20:10–16, 1 Corinthians 6:18–20
14. Genesis 12:3, Genesis 27:29
15. Zechariah 5:1–4
16. Zechariah 5:3–4
17. Jeremiah 17:5 (NIV)
18. Luke 12:16-21
19. Proverbs 11:24 (NIV)
20. The tithe is one-tenth of one's monthly or annual income or produce, and is an ancient form of worship. The first record of giving the tithes is found in Genesis 14:17–20, and was when Abram (before God changed his name to Abraham) offered a tenth of the spoils of war to Melchizedek, the priest of the Most High, on his victorious return from war. See also Malachi 3:8–11 where the Bible pronounces a blessing on those who give the tithe, and says those who withhold their tithes and offering are under a curse.
21. New Testament giving is described by the Bible in Acts 4:34-35, 2 Corinthians chapters 8 and 9, and Philippians 4:15-19, just to mention a few passages. Our heart must be in our giving, because God loves it "when the giver delights in the giving" (2 Corinthians 9:7, MSG). When

you give willingly and cheerfully in appreciation of God's goodness, as expected in the New Testament, you will find that your giving invariably exceeds a tenth of your income.
22. 2 Corinthians 8:3 (NIV)
23. 2 Corinthians 8:5 (NIV)
24. 2 Corinthians 9:6 (MSG)
25. 1 John 1:8–10
26. The story is told in Joel Osteen, *Your Best Life Now*. New York: FaithWords, 2004. 121.
27. Ben Sphigel, "BASEBALL; Lima's Shot With Mets No Laughing Matter." *The New York Times*, Friday, February 17, 2006.
28. Psalm 51:17

Chapter 10: Rolling Away the Reproach

1. Deuteronomy 8:7–10
2. You can read this incredible but true story in Joshua 5:1–12.
3. See Exodus 16:11–21
4. Deuteronomy 8:2–5
5. Timothy Edmonds, "Payday loans: regulatory reform." *Parliament.uk*. www.parliament.uk/briefing-papers/SN06676.pdf.
6. "Q&A: Payday Loans," *BBC News*. 25 November 2013. www.bbc.co.uk/news/business-16067283
7. Sean Poulter, "5,853% …the Wonga annual rate of interest: Payday firm's 1,600% rise leads to calls for tighter regulation." *Mail Online*. www.dailymail.co.uk/news/article-2347021/5-853--Wonga-annual-rate-Payday-firms-1-600-rise-leads-calls-tighter-regulation.html.
8. Nanci Hellmich, "A third of people have nothing saved for retirement." *USA Today*. www.usatoday.com/story/money/personalfinance/2014/08/18/zero-retirement-savings/14070167.
9. Belinda Robinson, "At least 9m people do not have any savings, and those who do are feeling the impact of low rates on their nest egg." *ThisIsMoney.co.uk*. www.thisismoney.co.uk/money/saving/article-2574646/At-9m-people-not-savings-feeling-impact-low-rates-nest-egg.html.
10. Judges 6:3–6
11. Lamentations 5:8 (MSG)
12. "Illegal Immigrant Population Statistics," *Statistic Brain*. www.statisticbrain.com/u-s-unauthorized-immigrant-population.
13. "Homelessness/Poverty Stats," *Statistic Brain*. www.statisticbrain.com/homelessness-stats.

14. Romans 5:18–19 (NIV)
15. Psalm 51:5 (NIV)
16. John 3:16 (NIV)
17. 2 Corinthians 5:21 (NLT)
18. John 14:6
19. Colossians 2:11
20. 2 Corinthians 5:17
21. Revelation 3:20
22. John Wesley (1703–1791), quoted in Ron Rhodes, *1001 Unforgettable Quotes about God, Faith and the Bible*, #211. Eugene, OR: Harvest House Publishers, 2011.
23. Ecclesiastes 10:8 (KJV)
24. 2 Corinthians 11:14
25. 2 Corinthians 2:11

Chapter 11: But I'm Born Again!

1. Galatians 3:13 (NIV)
2. 2 Corinthians 5:21 (NIV)
3. Romans 10:9–17 (NCV)
4. John 3:18
5. 2 Corinthians 8:9 (NIV)
6. Philippians 2:7–8 (MSG)
7. Romans 8:17
8. 1 Peter 1:4
9. Deuteronomy 8:18
10. Psalm 37:25 (NASB)
11. 1 Peter 2:24
12. See note 13 at chapter 7.
13. Luke 4:29–30. See also Luke 4:28–30.
14. Galatians 3:13 (NIV)
15. John 19:30
16. See Daniel 9.
17. Jeremiah 25:11–12 (CEV)
18. Daniel 9:15–25 (MSG)
19. Larry Huch. *Free at Last: Removing the Past from Your Future*. Expanded edition. New Kensington, PA: Whitaker House, 2010. 48.
20. Beth Moore, "Beth Moore: Is there a 'generational curse' for sin?" *Today's Christian Woman*. www.todayschristianwoman.com/articles/2004/may/beth-moore-breaking-free-generational-curse-sin.html
21. James 4:7 (NKJV)

22. Matthew 10:16 (NIV)
23. 2 Corinthians 2:11 (NLT)
24. 1 Peter 1:19

Chapter 12: Breaking the Curse and Activating the Blessing

1. Kenneth E. Hagin, *The Believer's Authority*. Tulsa, OK: Faith Library Publications, 1996. 36–37.
2. 2 Corinthians 10:4 (NIV)
3. Philippians 2:9–11 (NLT)
4. John 1:7, Hebrews 12:24, and Exodus 12: 13
5. Hebrews 12:29 and Psalm 97:3
6. Revelation 11:19
6a. Matthew 6:17 (NIV)
7. Judges 13–16
8. James 5:16 (MSG)
9. John 5:1–9
10. John 8:36
11. 2 Corinthians 5:17 (ESV)
12. Galatians 3:13–14 (NIV)
13. Daniel 9:15 (NIV)
14. "Australia apology to Aborigines." *BBC News*. http://news.bbc.co.uk/1/hi/7241965.stm
15. Matthew 6:14–15 (MSG)
16. Acts 19:19 (NLT)
17. Matthew 11:12 (ESV)
18. Luke 10:19 (NKJV)
19. 2 Corinthians 5:21
20. John 8:36
21. Isaiah 54:17 (NASB)
22. 2 Corinthians 8:9 (NKJV)
23. Proverbs 23:18 (KJV)
24. John 10:35
25. Hebrews 4:16
26. Psalm 104:4
27. Quoted in Ron Rhodes, *1001 Unforgettable Quotes about God, Faith and the Bible*, #1. Eugene, OR: Harvest House Publishers, 2011.
28. John 19:30
29. "Reward for thrifty pensioners." ThisIsMoney.co.uk. www.thisismoney.co.uk/money/news/article-1520088/Reward-for-thrifty-pensioners.html.
30. Joel Osteen. *I Declare: 31 Promises to Speak Over Your Life*. Philadelphia, PA: Running Press, 2014. 102

Chapter 13: Surely There Is an End!

1. Heraclitus of Ephesus, a pre-Socratic Greek philosopher, is credited with saying, "There is nothing permanent except change."
2. Proverbs 13:12 (ISV)
3. Psalm 102:13 (KJV)
4. Zechariah 4:6 (NKJV)
5. *New Strong's Concise Dictionary of the Words in the Hebrew Bible,* # 7307. Nashville, TN: Thomas Nelson, 1995.
6. Job 1:4–6, 9–10; Matthew 26:28; Ephesians 1:7
7. Hebrews 12:24
8. Matthew 26:28
9. Ephesians 2:11–16
10. Acts 26:18, 1 Corinthians 6:20
11. Romans 5:9
12. Ephesians 1:7, Colossians 1:14, Hebrews 9:12
13. Ephesians 1:7 (MSG)
14. Hebrews 9:14 (MSG)
15. 1 John 1:7
16. Colossians 1:20 (NLT)
17. Philippians 4:7
18. Jeanette Windle, *Fire Storm: A Novel.* Grand Rapids, MI: Kregel Publications, 2004. 80
19. Isaiah 59:1–3 (NLT)
20. Hebrews 10:19
21. Hebrews 13:20
22. Revelation 12:11
23. Exodus 12:13
24. Psalm 30:5
25. Genesis 8:22 (NKJV)
26. Proverbs 23:18 (NKJV)
27. Deuteronomy 28:12 (ESV)
28. Isaiah 54:1–4 (MSG)
29. Acts 2:1–2
30. Psalm 126:1 (MSG)
31. Isaiah 49:24–26 (KJV)
32. John 19:30, emphasis mine
33. *New Strong's Concise Dictionary of the Words in the Greek Testament,* # 5055. Nashville, TN: Thomas Nelson, 1995.
34. Isaiah 10:27 (NKJV)

Chapter 14: Maintaining Your Freedom

1. 1 Timothy 6:17 (CEV)
2. John 10:10 (AMP)
3. Galatians 5:1
4. Colossians 2:14–15 (MSG)
5. Brennan Manning, *All Is Grace: A Ragamuffin Memoir*. Colorado Springs, CO: David C Cook, 2011. 192–193.
6. John 8:31–32 (NKJV)
7. Galatians 5:1 (NLT)
8. Galatians 3:3
9. Deuteronomy 28:1–2 (NLT)
10. 1 Peter 5:8–9 (NKJV)
11. James 4:7
12. Pedro Okoro, *Crushing The Devil: Your Guide to Spiritual Warfare and Victory in Christ*. Sisters, OR: Deep River Books, 2012. 199–200.
13. See Matthew 4.
14. Ephesians 6:17
15. Ephesians 4:27 (NASB)
16. *New Strong's Concise Dictionary of the Words in the Greek Testament*, # 5117. Nashville, TN: Thomas Nelson, 1995.
17. 1 Peter 5:8
18. Ecclesiastes 10:8 (KJV)
19. Thomas Manton (1620–1667), quoted in Ron Rhodes, *1001 Unforgettable Quotes about God, Faith and the Bible*, #212. Eugene, OR: Harvest House Publishers, 2011.
20. Pedro Okoro, *Crushing The Devil: Your Guide to Spiritual Warfare and Victory in Christ*. Sisters, OR: Deep River Books, 2012. 195–196.
21. "Cristina Fernández de Kirchner's letter to David Cameron." *The Guardian*. www.theguardian.com/uk/2013/jan/02/cristina-fernandez-kirchner-letter-cameron
22. 1 John 5:4–5 (NKJV)
23. Isaiah 43:2 and Psalm 23:4
24. Daniel 3
25. Job 23:10
26. John 14:30 (NKJV). The ruler of this world or the prince of this world is the devil. See 2 Corinthians 4:4 and Ephesians 2:2.
27. Song of Solomon 2:15 (NKJV)
28. Revelation 12:10
29. John 14:30
30. 1 Corinthians 10:12 (NKJV)
31. Galatians 5:16 (ISV)
32. Galatians 5:22 (NKJV)

33. James 2:17 (NIV)
34. Matthew 26:41
35. Acts 7:60
36. Proverbs 4:23 (NLT)
37. Philippians 4:8 (MSG)
38. 2 Timothy 3:5
39. Catharina Moh, "Cerro Rico: Devil worship on the man-eating mountain." *BBC News.* 2 October 2014. www.bbc.co.uk/news/magazine-29448079

Afterword: Fight from Victory, Not for Victory

1. Galatians 2:20
2. Ephesians 6:10–20
3. http://www.biblestudytools.com/lexicons/greek/nas/histemi.html
4. Ephesians 6:10
5. http://www.biblestudytools.com/lexicons/greek/nas/endunamoo.html
6. Paul Vitello, "Taking a Break From the Lord's Work." *The New York Times,* August 1, 2010. http://www.nytimes.com/2010/08/02/nyregion/02burnout.html.

Appendix: 101 Ways to Crush the Devil

1. Psalm 1:1-3 (MSG)
2. Mark 3:27 (NKJV)
3. James 4:7 (NCV)
4. Revelation 12:4, 9; Isaiah 14:12–20; Ezekiel 28:1–19
5. Matthew 12:43
6. 1 Corinthians 6:19–20 (MSG
7. 1 Corinthians 10:13
8. Ephesians 6:1-3
9. Isaiah 60:1 (ESV)
10. Luke 4:13 (AMP)
11. Matthew 26:41 (NLT)
12. Matthew 17:21(NASB)
13. 1 Peter 5:5 (NKJV)
14. Matthew 7:12
15. Luke 12:13–21
16. Matthew 6:33 (AMP)
17. 1 Corinthians 13:4-7
18. 2 Samuel 24:19–24
19. Jeremiah 17:5
20. Daniel 11:32
21. Acts 2:46 (NLT)

ABOUT THE AUTHOR

Pedro Okoro is a Pastor, Blogger, Success Coach and Best Selling Author. He grew up in Nigeria and moved to the United Kingdom in 1996. He lives in a London suburb with his wife and their 2 gorgeous daughters.

Never Miss an Update from Pedro

The best way to connect with Pedro is through his blog:
www.pedrookoro.com

You can also connect with Pedro on social media
On Facebook: **https://www.facebook.com/pedrookoro7**
On Twitter: **https://twitter.com/Pedrookoro**

www.ingramcontent.com/pod-product-compliance
Lightning Source LLC
LaVergne TN
LVHW051550070426
835507LV00021B/2510